A GLIMPSE INTO HISTORY

*What Prominent People Have Said About
Nature in Oregon and the Need to Conserve It*

MICHAEL McCLOSKEY

INKWATER PRESS

PORTLAND • OREGON
INKWATERPRESS.COM

Scan this QR Code
for more information
on this title.

Edited by Holly Tri
Cover and interior design by Masha Shubin
Illustrations and images are copyrighted by their respective copyright owners and are used with permission.

Publisher: Inkwater Press | www.inkwaterpress.com

Paperback ISBN-13 978-1-62901-531-6 | ISBN-10 1-62901-531-8
Kindle   ISBN-13 978-1-62901-532-3 | ISBN-10 1-62901-532-6

5 7 9 10 8 6 4

Contents

Introduction • vi

Foreword • viii

Acknowledgements • ix

CHAPTER ONE • 1
Exploration and Settlement

    Captain George Vancouver | 1
    Lt. W. R. Broughton | 2
    Joel Palmer | 3
    H. L. Pittock | 5
    Abigail Scott Duniway | 6

CHAPTER TWO • 9
The Early Years

    Thomas Condon | 10
    Frances Fuller Victor | 14

Thomas Lamb Eliot | 15
Chief Joseph | 15
William Gladstone Steel | 16
Judge John B. Waldo | 20
Judge Matthew Deady | 27

CHAPTER THREE • 29
Oregon Becomes a Developing State

    Clarence E. Dutton | 29
    John Wesley Powell | 30
    John Muir | 31
    C. Hart Merriam | 33
    Gifford Pinchot | 34
    Joaquin Miller | 35
    Dr. Harry Lane | 37
    H. D. Langille | 38
    Charles Erskine Scott Wood | 39

Bill Hanley | 41
C. S. Jackson | 42
George Chamberlain | 43
John Charles Olmsted | 45
Colonel L. L. Hawkins | 45
Emanuel T. Mische | 48

CHAPTER FOUR • 50
Oregon in the Early 20th Century

Joseph N. Teal | 50
Oswald West | 53
Edwin Markham | 60
George Palmer Putnam | 60
Blaine Hallock | 61
Samuel Lancaster | 63
Jack Reed | 65
Ben W. Olcott | 66
Charles McNary | 69
Zane Grey | 71
William Finley | 73
Ben Hur Lampman | 77
David T. Mason | 78
John Charles Olmsted | 80

CHAPTER FIVE • 83
Oregon in the Midst of the 20th Century

Julius Meier | 83
H. L. Davis | 85
E. R. Jackman | 86
Herbert Hoover | 87

Samuel Boardman | 89
Thornton Munger | 92
John Yeon | 93
State Senator Byron G. Carney | 96
William L. Finley | 103
Charles Sprague | 106
Tom McAllister | 108
Ira Gabrielson | 111

CHAPTER SIX • 118
Oregon in the Latter Part of the 20th Century

Stewart Holbrook | 118
William Stafford | 123
Robert W. Sawyer | 124
Bernard DeVoto | 128
Frank Branch Riley | 129
Richard L. Neuberger | 130
Charles McKinley | 136
Robert D. Holmes | 136
Karl Onthank | 140
Wayne Morse | 141
Irving Brant | 143
Dr. David B. Charlton | 144
Marshall Dana | 145

CHAPTER SEVEN • 148
Oregon in the Environmental Era

Ken Kesey | 148
Robert Straub | 149
Tom McCall | 153

Judge Alfred T. Goodwin | 160
Ivan Doig | 171
William O. Douglas | 174
Garnett "Ding" Cannon | 181
Robert W. Packwood | 182
John Gray | 183
Howard McCord | 183
Michael McCloskey | 184
William G. Robbins | 192

CHAPTER EIGHT • 194

Oregon as Environmentalism Becomes the Norm

Gary Snyder | 194
Robin Cody | 196
George Venn | 196
Chris Maser | 199
Judge William Dwyer | 200
Jack Ward Thomas | 203
Jerry Franklin | 203

CHAPTER NINE • 213

Oregon in Contemporary Times

US Senator Mark Hatfield | 213
Dr. John Kitzhaber | 216
Jane Claire Dirks-Edmunds | 218
Ron Wyden | 221
Ted Kulongoski | 223
Mike Houck | 226
Paul Hawken | 231
David James Duncan | 233

Mary C. Wood | 235
Barry Lopez | 238
Kim Stafford | 240
Dr. Dominick DellaSala | 241
Brian Doyle | 243
Andy Kerr | 244
Cameron La Follette | 246
John Des Camp Jr. | 253
Kate Brown | 254
Senator Jeff Merkley | 256
Jack Churchill | 257
Ursula Le Guin | 260
Judges' statements in salmon cases | 261
Jane Lubchenco | 267

Sources • 271

Introduction

I had thought that history dealt with people who were dead and silent. But in doing research, I ran across quotes from historical figures that awakened me to the fact that this was not entirely true. As I read their words, I began to get a feeling for their personalities, passions, and times. To me, it was almost like listening to a recording of their voices. History began to come alive. This was a feeling that I did not get by just reading about them.

As I read their words, I began to see patterns in history and how much of their perspectives we still share. I also learned how one promoted another as the older ones helped the younger ones get ahead; their careers were often tied together. I saw their similarities and differences, and how the issues evolved.

Some were so moved by their experiences in nature that they spoke in language that was almost poetic. In the nineteenth century, it was common to link the beauties of nature with the handiwork of the Creator. Others expressed outrage and didn't shy away from strong language, for instance denouncing "greed" and those who "looted the public domain." Some hammered away at themes that gripped them, while others ranged widely. Even in tense times and moments of peril, humor could emerge in their words.

Some were almost lyrical in praising our progress, while others were fearful of sliding back. Some were driven, some were reverential, and others were angry.

As I became almost addicted to digging out the words of those who had gone before and shaped Oregon's environmental programs, I began to see that the quotes I was extracting from their works might constitute a book—one that had not been done before. This is that book.

The leaders quoted in this book all shaped our values and programs. They shaped the culture that made nature a public value and made its conservation an important concern. They all deserve our gratitude. Their words are still with us, and in one sense, so are they.

Michael McCloskey

Foreword

This book focuses on two related topics: appreciation of nature in Oregon and emerging efforts to conserve nature. The book shows how a "green" culture developed in the state that laid the groundwork for the many public policies that followed. The culture was embraced by a wide variety of public personalities, in many lines of work.

In selecting passages to quote, I looked for language with certain qualities—language that was evocative, provocative, or that introduced new concerns of conservation. I left out passages that dealt with technical matters, obscure concerns, and matters of little interest today.

I often edited wording that was unclear or awkward.

In the text that follows, I have used typography to indicate passages of different kinds. Profiles of the figures are quoted are put in boxes; the topics being addressed are in bold.

This work can be used in varied ways. It can be read straight through, it can be used as a text in environmental history courses on Oregon, or it can be used a reference work. Happy reading!

Michael McCloskey

Acknowledgements

Many people helped me dig out these quotes from figures who have shaped Oregon's environmental programs. Alice LaViolette of the Oregon State Library in Salem stands out; she helped me find writings by many people I might have missed. Dave Hegeman there was also helpful. Kylie Pine, the curator of the Willamette Heritage Center in Salem, also helped me find things that Sen. Charles McNary had written.

Various people at the reference desk of the central Multnomah County Library also helped me find documents, as did specialists in the library of the Oregon Historical Society, such as Scott Daniels, and those at the Reed College Library. Reference specialists in the law library of Lewis & Clark College also helped me pursue notions I had.

I want to thank my brother, David McCloskey, for reviewing this work in draft form and leading me to poetry suitable for inclusion. Alice LaViolette also gave the draft a careful and helpful reading. Ron Eber was also helpful in reviewing the text. As always, Chris Williams kept my computer going properly. And Jim McMullin has been instrumental in handling the process of getting the illustrations ready for publication. And I am grateful to all those who offered supporting statements: Alice LaViolette, Kim Stafford, and Ramona Rex.

In doing this research, I also learned more about the difficulties one faces in doing research of this kind. For instance, documents from the Congressional Record have only been digitized for the last twenty-five years. And the Oregon Historical Society has not had the money to prepare guides to many of the materials in its archives. And most of the documents from the career of Senator McNary are not in Oregon but are instead held in the archives of the Smithsonian Institution in Washington, DC, and are held at remote sites.

But the wonder is that so much has been digitized in just a few short years. The Oregon Encyclopedia is very helpful, as is Wikipedia. This kind of a book could not have been written a few decades ago. I am grateful to all who made it possible.

Michael McCloskey

CHAPTER ONE

Exploration and Settlement

When **Captain George Vancouver** sailed up the Oregon coast in 1792, the cliffs north of Cape Blanco made a deep impression. In his journals, he said:

> This cape … is a conspicuous one, particularly when seen from the north—being formed by a round hill on high perpendicular cliffs, some of which are white, [rising to] a considerable height from the level of the sea.

He thought it was what Captain James Cook had called Cape Gregory, but that was really much farther north. In 1605 Spanish explorer Martin d'Aguilar first sighted this point and called it Cape Blanco (which is what it is called today). Vancouver also noted that white, sandy beaches extended north of this point for eight leagues.*

---

* Vancouver, *Voyage of Discovery*

Captain George Vancouver (1757-1798), British naval officer, explorer. Starting his naval career as a young teenager, he accompanied Captain James Cook on his third voyage (1776-1780). After Britain and Spain settled their differences with the Nootka Convention, he was sent to survey the coasts of North America, along what are now Oregon, Washington, and British Columbia. In the ship *Discovery*, he began the work in the spring of 1792. This was his was most important life's work, which he recounted in his book *A Voyage of Discovery to the North Pacific Ocean, and Round the World* (1792).

In his journals of his 1778 trip along this coast, Captain Cook also noted Cape Perpetua and Cape Foulweather—but because of bad weather could not observe much.

A bit later in the same year, a British naval party, detached from the expedition of Captain George Vancouver, stood on a point near today's Troutdale (at what we now call the Sandy River Delta). Headed by **Lt. W. R. Broughton**, it reported:

> We had a beautiful view of very remarkable, high-mountain, whose summit (and a considerable extent below it) was covered with snow, and presented a very grand view.
>
> His party first spotted this mountain from Sauvie Island, at which it then noted "a very high, snowy mountain [which] appeared [and rose] … beautifully [to the east]. …"

Lt. W. R. Broughton (1762–1821), British naval officer, explorer. Broughton went to sea at an early age, rose to become a commander, and served a long time. Eventually, he was given the Order of the Bath. His explorations took him to the North Pacific, along the Asian coast of the Northwest Pacific, and to the East Indies. Many areas are named after him, such as points along the Queen Charlotte Straight in British Columbia. In Oregon, Youngs Bay near Astoria was named by him.

Broughton named this mountain Mt. Hood, after British admiral Lord Samuel Hood, who fought for the British in the Battle of the Chesapeake in our War of Independence. Native Americans had called it Wy'east.

Thirteen years later, the American expedition headed by Lewis and Clark noted a mountain here of "conical form covered with snow" (October 30, 1805). The map that Broughton prepared was used in planning the expedition of Lewis and Clark.

British botanist David Douglas was the first one to use the term "Cascade mountains" for the range of which Mt. Hood is part (1826). On the northern approaches to the mountain, Douglas was frustrated in his efforts to collect cones of the Pacific silver fir and the noble fir. But with advice from Indians, he was able to collect the cones of sugar pine in the mountains east of what is now Roseburg. And farther south, he was the first to identify the giant chinkapin tree.

When settlers started arriving via the Oregon Trail, they were also struck by the magnificence of Mt. Hood. Some tried to climb it. **Joel Palmer** was the first.

An account of Palmer's exploration of the area around Mt. Hood on October 11 and 12, 1845, and his attempt to climb it:

> I had never before looked upon a sight so nobly grand. We had previously seen only the top of it, but now we had a view of the whole mountain. No pen can give an adequate description of the scene.
>
> After taking some refreshment, we ascended the mountain, intending to head [up] the deep ravine, in order to ascertain whether there was any gap in the mountain south of us, which … [would permit us] to pass. From this peak, we overlooked the whole of the mountain. We followed up a grassy ridge for … [a] mile and a half, when it became barren. My two friends began to lag behind, and show signs of fatigue; they finally stopped, and contended that we could not get round the head of the ravine, and that it was useless to attempt the ascent.
>
> But I was of a different opinion, and wished to go on. They consented, and followed for half a mile, when they sat down, and requested me to go up to the ledge, and if we could a affect a passage and get round it, to give them a signal. I did so, and found that by climbing up a cliff of snow and ice for about forty feet (but not so steep but that by getting upon … [the] cliff and cutting holes to

JOEL PALMER

stand and hold on by [that it could not]), … be ascended. I gave the signal, and they came up.

In the meantime, I had cut and carved my way up the cliff, and when I was up to the top, was forced to admit that it was something of an undertaking; but as I had arrived safely at the top of the cliff, I doubted not but that they could accomplish the same task. …

After proceeding about one mile upon the snow, continually winding [upward] … I began to despair of seeing my companions. …

I then went round to the southeast side, continually ascending, and taking observations of the country to the south, and was fully of the opinion that we could find a passage through. … At the head of many of the ravines, are perpendicular cliffs of rocks, apparently several thousand feet high; and in some places those cliffs rise … precipitously to the summit [so] that a passage around [them] … is impracticable.

He is thought to have climbed to about 9,000 feet.

I think the southern side affords the easiest ascent. The dark strips observable from a distance, are occasioned by blackish rock so precipitous as not to … [permit] snow to [be] lying upon it. The upper strata are of gray sandstone, and seems to be the original formation. There is no doubt, but that any of the [other] snow peaks upon this range can be ascended to the summit. …

… The day was getting far advanced, and we had no provisions, save each of us [had] a small biscuit, and knowing that we had a least twenty-five miles to travel, before reaching those working on the road, I hastened down the mountain.

I had no difficulty in finding passage down; but I saw some deep ravines and crevices in the ice [that] … alarmed me, as I was compelled to travel over them. The snow and ice had melted underneath, and in many places had left but a thin shell upon the surface; some of them had fallen in and presented hideous looking caverns.

I was soon out of danger, and upon the east side of the deep ravine, I saw my two friends slowly winding their way [on] … the mountain.

Palmer later admitted that his conclusion that the peak could not be climbed was erroneous. However, his account was the first recorded effort to climb Mt. Hood. The Palmer Glacier and snowfields are named after him.

The first documented ascent was in 1857 (July 11) by **H. L. Pittock** and a few friends; Pittock later became the owner of the *Oregonian.*

Here is an account of Pittock's first ascent (finally published in the *Oregonian* on August 2, 1864):

On the 6th of August, 1857, a party of five … and the proprietor of this paper, ascended [Mt. Hood] from the south side and reached the summit …. five and half hours from the time of leaving the prairie below the snow line. The top they found to be a narrow crag in the form of a crescent, the main ridge running from west to east, and turning abruptly to the south at the east end, the inner side of which angle forms a black precipice, a thousand feet high—always noticed from this city as being never covered with snow.

Expecting to find a level spot on the top, the party was astonished to find at the point they reached it, that another step would precipitate them thousands of feet down the north side, and it was some time before they could summon [the] courage to stand erect on the dizzy[ing] height. The highest point of the mountain was a little to the east, and clambering round a huge rock, each stood upon it in turn. …

The view was indescribably grand. To the north, Mts. Rainier, Adams, St. Helens, and Olympus were plainly visible, and to the south, down the Cascades, in their order, standing boldly above the range, were Jefferson, the Three Sisters, and Mt. [McLoughlin]. The Columbia could be seen at intervals … .

After an hour spent tumbling loose rocks over the north side, and watching them bound over the ice till broken to pieces or [becoming] lost … [from] sight, they made a descent without difficulty in about two hours. The ascent was made entirely on the snow, and gradually grew steeper … [in] the last three hundred feet—which were very steep. …

The crescent spoken of forms two sides of what was once a crater, and on the south-west side only an isolated peak remains, while the south side is entirely gone. From fissures in the peak a sulfurous smoke issued, which blowing down the mountain in the faces of the party, … [produced nausea], but no other effect was felt from the great altitude.

Over the years, Pittock climbed Mt. Hood a number of times.

In the early days, Mt. Hood was thought to be America's highest mountain (in the 1860s and 1870s).

Other pioneers were moved to write about their first views of Mt. Hood, even those who mainly focused on other concerns. **Abigail Scott Duniway** was one of them.

From her book about her trip on the Oregon Trail in 1852, *From the West to West: Across the Plains to Oregon*:

After moving across the Grande Ronde valley through a veritable Eden of untamed verdure, and crossing the Grand Ronde River by ford, our travelers began the ascent of the Blue Mountains.

The air was cool and delicious. The cattle, much refreshed by their luscious feed in the bountiful and beautiful valley, moved more briskly than had been their wont, and were soon in the midst of grand old forest trees, which, at that time (untouched by the woodman's ax), stood in all their native grandeur upon the grass-strewn slopes.

In the midst of one of the groves of stately, whispering pines, the company halted for the night near a sparkling spring, with scenery all around so enticing that Jean [a younger sister] exclaimed in her journal: "Oh, this beautiful world … ."

On and on the teams kept crawling, until on the 6th of September, the summit of the Blue Mountains was passed, and the wearied travelers gazed for the first time upon the Cascade Mountains: lying to the westward in the purple distance; and in their midst arose, supported by a continuous chain of undulating tree-crowned, lesser heights, the majestic proportions of Mount Hood—the patriarch of the solitudes, his hoary head uplifted in the shimmering air, and at his feet, a drapery of mist.

ABIGAIL DUNIWAY

Abigail Scott Duniway (1834–1915), pioneer, writer, champion of suffrage for women. Abigail Scott Duniway came to Oregon on a wagon train in 1852 and settled on farms in various spots in the northern Willamette Valley and eventually in Portland. Notwithstanding a limited education, she turned herself into a prolific writer, producing twenty-two novels and turning out a weekly human rights newspaper for sixteen years. She also raised five sons and became the sole source of family support (after her husband suffered a permanent injury). In the process, she became the Northwest's most prominent champion for women's suffrage, earning recognition at the national level. When Oregon at last granted women the right to vote, Governor Oswald West asked her to write the state's official proclamation.

When pioneer George Wilkes passed through the Powder River Basin in the early 1840s, he was awed by the forests he saw on the slopes of the Blue Mountains, commenting on the "immense forests of majestic pines."[*] And a little later, Joel Palmer also noted the "beautiful groves of yellow pine" there.[**]

---

[*] Wilkes, *History of Oregon*, 86–87.

[**] Palmer, *Journal of Travels*, 110.

CHAPTER TWO

The Early Years

In his book *That Balance So Rare*, Terence O'Donnell quotes a settler from French Prairie, "From almost any point of view, the panorama of distant mountain scenery was uninterrupted." O'Donnell continues:

> What astonished the immigrants, however, was not so much the Valley ... but something above it—that great white escarpment against the eastern sky—the mountains.[*]

Some found the entire Willamette Valley to be such a paradise. Another settler exclaimed:

> The natural flowers upon this extensive plain are the most beautiful that our eyes even beheld. [The settler] found it a veritable paradise with its rich black loam, abundant water, and ample timber. Stately groves of fir and oak, or belts of deciduous timber along the water courses, broke the monotony of the grassy levels.[**]

---

[*]   O'Donnell, *Balance So Rare*, 35.

[**] Hussey, *Champoeg*, 2, 7.

Other early settlers found beauty elsewhere, as did **Thomas Condon**, who found it in fossils.

> The marine rocks form the outer rim, or shoreline, of what was in those early times, a lake, of irregular outline, extend[ed] from Kern Creek Hill on the west to Canon City on the east, and from the hills north of the John Day River to the Crooked River valley on the south. …
>
> How strangely out of place a score of palm-trees, a hundred yew-trees, or even a bank of ferns, would seem here now! And yet here these once lived, and died, and were buried; and beautiful beyond description are their fossil remains even now, as they are unburied.
>
> Seen from the summit of Kern Creek Hill (its western border), this vast amphitheater of lesser hills presents a wild, wonderful grouping of varied outlines and colors. …
>
> The varying shades of brown that characterize the older marine rocks rise in vast border masses, almost treeless and shrub-less, in an irregular circle, while the lighter shades that fill the deeper depressions of the central portion mark the later sedimentary deposits; and then, like the vast ink-blots on a painting, one sees, here and there, a protruding mass of dark-colored trap [rock trapped as molten magma beneath the surface]. Through the heart of this wild region winds the John Day River, running westward until it passes the middle ground of the picture, and then turn[s] northward to join the Columbia.
>
> This stream, so insignificant in appearance, has done wonderful work among these hills. …
>
> It has for unnumbered ages gone on excavating vast gorges and canyons, as all other streams in central Oregon have done, till lake after lake was drained off, and their beds laid dry, stripped of enduring moisture, and slowly changed to a treeless desert.
>
> The deep excavations that resulted could hardly fail to lay bare

important records of the past, cutting as they do through the whole extent of the Tertiary periods. In a deep canyon, through which runs a branch of the Kern Creek, may be found the remains of a beautiful fern—gems of their kind—which no thoughtful mind can see without wonder and admiration. …

But the great geological importance of that old lake-depression does not arise from the fossil remains of its forests—beautiful, varied, and abundant as these are—but from its finely preserved fossil bones. Two species of rhinoceros lived their quiet, indolent lives among the reeds that lined that old lake-shore. …

… The bones of the rhinoceros are [found] frequently; but the remains of an extinct animal, allied in some things to the camel, in others to the tapir family, are most abundant. Paleontologists have designated the *genus* by the name of *Oreodon*. The remains of three or four species of this animal are found in central Oregon. …

A tapir-like animal, to which the name *Lophiodon* has been given, lived here too. His remains indicate an animal of the size of the living tapir. Not far from these last were found some bones of a fossil peccary, of large size. Another of the denizens of these ancient lake-shores bore some resemblance to the horse. …

But the richest chapters in the history of the horse, in Oregon, are not from these rocks of the lower valley; for another, and a later, record in the upper valley contains these. …

Upon the hills that overlooked these lake-shores, there lived three or four different species of the horse family. Their remains are easily distinguished; for the teeth are well preserved, and the teeth of the horse are well marked. Almost all as well marked as these equine remains, were some teeth that apparently represented a member of the camel family—found

Thomas Condon (1822–1907), minister, geologist, professor. Brought as a child to the US from Ireland, Thomas Condon grew up in New York and was trained as a minister. He came to Oregon to take up service as a minister. During his early service in The Dalles, Oregon, he began to hunt for fossils along the Crooked and John Day Rivers. While later teaching at Pacific University, he was appointed as the first state geologist. Following that, he became the first professor of geology at the University of Oregon. Late in life, he was known as "Oregon's Grand Old Man of Science."

there, too, is a fine specimen of a lower jaw, silicified completely, and in solid rock. …

But the most remarkable thing about this upper lake record is that which reveals the way in which its history of this period was brought to a close. The last rock of the series fill[s] the place of a cover to this volume. Never was a cover better defined, nor more distinctly separated from the well-written and well-illustrated pages it serves to protect.

In the ravines that separate these ridges, the "gold" of this region is found; and in the diggings that result, the bones, teeth, and tusks of the elephant are often uncovered—a few of which have been preserved. In the loose materials that form these ridges, the closing annuals of that remarkable lake-period of central Oregon may be read as in a book. The last facts noted there are the records of the mammoth; the horse, the ox, and their contemporaries. …

The first one of these views is characteristic of the old marine life of the original sea-bed. It is made up of a number of patches of sea-beach, strewn with shells; a tooth or two, of some extinct reptile; a vertebra of another—and the marine record closes. The shoals on which these marine remains lived became elevated into the frame-work of the future Oregon; while in the depressions between them, her earliest historic records at once began. Oregon's Eocene, Oregon's dawn! Strange, beautiful coincidence of fact with system!

The next glimpse we get is of the Middle Tertiary period. It is distinct enough to enable us to recognize upon those lakeshores the rhinoceros, the oreodon [sic], the tapir; and then closes abruptly, to give place to a record of fire and volcano, and the violence of the earthquake—bringing upon the life of the period a blotted, illegible night-record in its history.

But another dawn came then; and we see, among the forms that move along those shores, the familiar ones of the horse and camel. Again the legible record closes, and thirty feet or more of ashes and volcanic cinders cover the land, and choke and poison the waters.

A long, dark, and nearly illegible part of the record follows, during which no life-history was written; but during which the old throes of violence seem to have passed away, and the laboratories of the earth seem to have lost the power of forcing heated vapors to the surface, capable of changing all to stone that they touched.

The mammoth, the horse, and the ox appear in the light of the dawn that follows this long geological night; and not fire, as before, but frost, seems to have closed the record marked by their fossil remains. …

… In this John Day Valley, quiet has been restored. The hills have been again clothed in verdure, and the waters had … covered … their vast strata of volcanic ashes; then animal life returned too—but not the same that had previously existed. The whole fauna … [had] changed; and even where the same type was restored, as in the case of the horse, it is in some new species; the old has passed away—and forever. …

… Indeed, one can hardly look over its historic archives of the Tertiary period without a conviction that this Columbia basin is destined yet to be the great battle-ground of conflicting theories: upon the question of the Origin of Species.[*]

Following his discovery of important fossils in the John Day region (1864), Condon sent specimens to the Smithsonian and to universities with research interests in fossils. A professor at one of these universities, John Merriam at the University of California, urged the state of Oregon to protect the area following his own field work there.

---

[*] Condon, "John Day Valley," 393–98.

In the 1930s the state began to purchase land there, eventually turning it into a state park. In the middle of the 1970s, the state cooperated with the federal government in turning the area into a national monument (1975).

Paleontologists have said, "No place in the world reveals a more complete sequence of Tertiary land populations than the John Day formations." It is the longest sequence of fossil formations anywhere, nearly fifty million years.

Frances Fuller Victor (1826-1902), writer of fiction and western history. Frances Fuller Victor was born in the East and raised and educated in the Midwest, but as an adult she lived in the West, mainly in Oregon. She is remembered for researching and ghost writing *The History of Oregon* for Hubert Howe Bancroft, as well as the histories of other western states.

Beauty was found in other places in the Cascades. **Frances Fuller Victor** exulted in what she saw at Crater Lake.

In 1875, upon visiting Crater Lake (the site of a future national park), she wrote:

A choking sensation arose in our throats and tears flowed over our cheeks … .The water of Crater Lake is of the loveliest blue imaginable in the sunlight, and a deep indigo in the shadow of the cliffs … . It impresses one as having been made for the Creator's eye only, and we cannot associate it with our human affairs. It is a font of the gods, wherein our souls are baptized anew in their primal purity and peace.

Some felt reverence for Oregon lands, particularly native peoples. Chief Joseph the Elder expressed this most memorably. The words that guided him:

Inside this boundary [demarcated by them with a series of poles], all our people were born. It circles the graves of our fathers, and we will never give up these graves to any man.

In 1871 he told his son, Young Joseph:

When I am gone, and you go into council with the white man,

always remember your … [land]. You will be the chief of these people. They will look to you to guide them. Always remember that your father never sold his … [land]. You must stop your ears whenever you are asked to sign a treaty selling your home. …

My son, never forget my dying words: this country holds your father's body. Never sell the bones of your father and mother.

He was constantly guided by his father's admonition: *do not sell the land or give it up!*

In 1877, when he refused to negotiate a treaty that required him to relinquish their land, this younger **Chief Joseph** (now the new chief) led his people out of Wallowa Valley away to the Canadian border—away from the attacking the US Army. He never would sell their land.

Later in the 1950s, other Oregon Indians agreed to the termination of their reservations—believing assurances that they could keep their forests. This did not happen, as was the case with the Grand Ronde Tribe. In the case of the Klamath Tribe, some of their forests then became national forests.

Often those who spent time in the wild lands of Oregon, as in climbing mountains, also came to revere these lands and drew inspiration from them. **Thomas Lamb Eliot**, a Unitarian minister, was one of them.

Extracts from a sermon preached in Portland in 1879:

Chief Joseph (1840–1904), leader of the Wallowa Band of the Nez Perce Tribe in northeastern Oregon. At first known as Young Joseph, in 1871 he became Chief Joseph when his father died. His tribal name was "Thunder Rolling Down the Mountain" (or Hin-mah-too-yah-lat-kekt). He refused to sign treaties that relinquished their lands in the Wallowa Valley and was one of the leaders in their long withdrawal to the Bears Paw Mountains in Montana, amid skirmishes with the US Army. He signed the final peace agreement there. Notwithstanding terms of that agreement that their band could return to lands of the tribe, they never were allowed to go back. He spent the rest of his life trying to get permission to return to his homeland. In 1858 various chiefs of the Nez Perce Tribe, including Chief Joseph the Elder, had signed a treaty establishing a reservation comprised of most the area of the tribe: 7.7 million acres. But in 1863 most of the leaders of the tribe were prevailed upon to sign a new treaty, shrinking the reservation to a mere 760,000 acres. But Chief Joseph the Elder did not sign nor agree to give up land in the Wallowa Valley; these Indians were then known as non-treaty Indians.

Let us climb its mountain side, dwelling on the lush greenness of its vegetation as we rise, and sharing the vision and immortal landscape that appear from its top.

"The spirit beareth witness with our spirit" … those words throw a great light upon the origin of religion itself, confirming to us the necessary character of religion as part of human nature and inseparable from that nature. …

In the very ground of our being lies a root whose life is answered by the dew and rain and sun—by the rain clouds of spiritual knowledge, the dew of ethical insight, and the sunlight of ineffable divinity and love. …

He quotes a passage from "Cathedral," a poem by James Russell Lowell:

Even as roots, shut in the dark earth,
Share in the tree-top's joy, and conceive
Of sunshine and wide air and winged things
By sympathy of nature, so do I
Have evidence of thee so far above,
Yet in and of me …

In 1899 Eliot played a leading role in establishing a municipal park commission for Portland that hired the Olmsted Brothers firm to prepare a beautification plan for Portland.

Those who ventured into Oregon's wild lands were sometimes so struck by them that they became passionate defenders of them. **William Gladstone Steel** was one of those people. His mountaineering led him to found two climbing clubs and then into making Crater Lake a national park.

One of his writings described his reaction to seeing Crater Lake for the first time on August 15, 1885:

> Not a foot about the lake had been touched or claimed. An overmastering conviction came to me that this wonderful spot must be saved—wild and beautiful—just as it was, for all future generations, and that it was up to me to do something.
>
> I then and there had the impression that in some way (I didn't know how) the lake ought to become a National Park.

Outcome: Indeed, Crater Lake became a national park, and he is acclaimed as its "father."

Extracts from his communications to John B. Waldo and others in 1891:

> Do you think there is any significance in the fact that the recent Congress gave the President greater powers in reference to the withdrawal of public lands from the market? If so, might it not be an opportune time to have Oregon Alpine Club [predecessor of the Mazama Club] petition for the withdrawal of the summit of the Cascade Range? If you think best, and will indicate a plan of operations … I will see that the Club takes up the matter … .

Subsequently:

> The matter was brought to the attention of the Oregon Alpine Club, and thereafter pretty much everything [that you suggested] was done through that organization … .

William Gladstone Steel (1854–1934), conservation activist. Steel was the chief activist in working with Judge John B. Waldo to get the Cascade Forest Reserve set aside and also in organizing to have Crater Lake National Park established. He founded the Mazamas and, before that, the Oregon Alpine Club. He wrote *The Mountains of Oregon*. After Crater Lake National Park was established, he became its second superintendent, shaping the park's development.

Judge Waldo volunteered his legal services for the period of conflict. He "prepared a petition, which [Steel] circulated throughout the state, getting many signatures."

In 1893, while lobbying in Washington, DC:

> After all sorts of difficulties and [obstacles] … have presented themselves, … we are at last approaching success in our efforts to reserve the Cascade Range. The subject has been neglected by [the] … authorities for months, but [I] have just received intelligence that it … [will] be taken up [soon] … and probably acted upon favorably in the very near future. Do not make the matter public, as there may even yet be a chance of delay. However, I think it is pretty safe.

Outcome: On September 28, 1893, President Grover Cleveland withdrew a large block of land from entry and claims along the spine of the Cascades, as originally requested by Waldo and Steel. This became the Cascade Forest Reserve, which evolved into the heart of national forest land there.

In 1896:

> [Senator Mitchell] finally told me … that a proclamation… [has been] prepared "to wipe the Cascade Reserve off the map," and would be signed by the President before the close of the week. [The] next morning I called upon [assistant commissioner of the GLO] Bowers, who confirmed the statement, adding that [Oregon senator] Mitchell had interceded with the President, and stated in the most positive terms, that the people of Oregon were unanimous in demanding that lands within the reserve be restored to the market …

I denied the statement and asked [for] time to prove my assertions. Bowers quickly got in touch with the White House, [and] then suggested that I call up S. W. Lamoreaux, commissioner of the General Land Office (and a bosom friend of Mitchell) and ask for 30 days delay.

The thirty-day delay was granted, and Steel immediately wrote Waldo as follows:

The life of our reservation is simply trembling in the balance. If I can get prompt and decisive support on the Oregon end of the line, I believe it can be saved. Otherwise, over half of it will be restored to the market, and it is merely a question of time when the remainder will follow suit.

The sheep men have money and are determined to wipe it off the face of the earth. Nothing under Heavens will save it now except the immediate filing of protests, as many … as possible should be directed to the Secretary of the Interior and the Commissioner of the General Land Office by telegraph. A telegram is sure to be read by them, whereas a letter may [be lodged] in the hands of a clerk. … A petition … should be circulated as quickly as possible. All of this work should be done promptly, energetically, and without loss of time.

It also should be done … as [quietly] as possible so as to not arouse the enemy. It is not wise to hunt a mouse with a brass band. The officials here [Washington, DC] seem anxious to reject the petition of our delegation, but there is practically no one objecting, and they cannot hold out much longer.

Have everybody [you can] … write personal letters. They all count. For heaven's sake, stir up somebody! See the Governor, the Superintendent of Schools, the Mayor of Salem, anybody and everybody, and especially those with "handles" to their names. It matters not if he is mayor of Skookumchuck, as long as he represents something. If doesn't represent anything, get him anyhow.

Steel would later recall:

Judge C. B. Bellinger was then on the federal bench in Portland and was working heartily with us, so Waldo conferred with him (while working on the brief); and when finished, they went over it together. Waldo suggested it would have a better effect if Bellinger would sign and forward it, which he did. It was an unusually strong document, and the President was greatly pleased with it and sent to Bellinger a long, autographed letter of commendation.

Outcome: As a result of their exertions, the Cascade Forest Reserve survived.

Judge John B. Waldo became addicted to exploring the trackless reaches of the Cascade forests. As an outgrowth of that, he became the guiding mind in getting them to set aside as federal forest reserves.

Extracts from 1887 letter on his explorations:

I write you on this beautiful September afternoon from this splendid spot—a lake whose name is like the aroma of some delightful perfume. At its sound, I see the mountain side, dark with pines, the summit crowned with snow, quaff the balmy air; and hear the notes of birds that dwell far from the habitations of men; the wash of waves against grassy solitary shores. In the week we have passed here, the days have been too short; the curtain of night closed down long before the play would be done. Such air to breathe, such scenes to see. Such a camp life … [where one can] play beneath the greenwood tree. The morning air has such a delightful exhilaration I feel as if I could climb the sky. …

The other day I was walking through the woods several miles from camp, and as the drooping, "boughy" limbs brushed against me, I seemed as if I was treading the ground of some long ago ancestor—whose lineal descendant and heir I was. Indeed in the woods, I seem at home. And what woods I have seen—the fair, unaltered wilderness where no sound is heard; where no track is seen save that made by its native inhabitants.

Extract from letter written in 1888:

Travel soon became delightful over open mossy ridges and flats, handsomely dotted with [a] scattering of hemlock and pine. Fragrant winds blew over us fresh from evergreen mountains.

Extract from a letter written in 1893 about the search for Lake Massey:

It lies in the wildest depths of the mountains among rock-crowned peaks rising above shadowy forests; and meadows, covered with mountain clover and succulent grass, stretch between the lake and the cliff-like mountain wall. It is indeed a scene of remarkable beauty and most inviting to a mountain walker.

Letter to President Grover Cleveland in the defense of the Cascade Mountain Reserve, April 28, 1896:

John B. Waldo (1844–1907), explorer, lawyer, judge. Waldo was an explorer of the Oregon Cascades, the strategist in the campaign to have the Cascade Forest Reserve set aside, and the guiding force in the reserve's defense. He is regarded as the "John Muir of Oregon." Waldo Lake and Waldo Glacier are named after him. He was a chief justice of the supreme court of Oregon and before then a state representative. As a boy, he was frequently taken to the mountains and forests, which became a lifelong passion for him.

Dear Sir:

At the request of Judge Bellinger of the United States District Court, I address this letter to you, giving the results of my acquaintance with the Cascade Mountain Reserve as bearing on the question of retaining this reservation as it now exists.

I learned, if not with astonishment, certainly with regret, that the Oregon delegation at Washington (or some of them) had applied to you to abrogate, in great part, this reservation, which was established under the Act of March 3, 1891, by your order and proclamation of September 28, 1893.

I am not alone, here, in thinking this action of our delegation to be very far astray, and it is my object, [namely] … to lay before you the general grounds for this opinion, and which, it is hoped, will help to show you that this reservation has been wisely established, and should never be disturbed. …

[Speaking of the Cascade Range.] Three fourths or more of this mountain mass lies westward of the divide which separates western from eastern Oregon. The abrupt and sterile eastern slopes overlook, usually, the high table lands on that side. The forests with which these slopes are covered have little value, and are not likely ever to be much sought after for lumber or other purposes. The only enemies that, so far, have assailed them are the herder's flocks and fires.

On the other hand, looking westward from the summit of the divide, the usual appearance is that of an almost uninterrupted, evergreen coniferous forest, stretching over a wilderness of lofty blue peaks, canyons and divides. …

There is a succession of snow peaks, situated on or near the divide, from Mt. Hood, near the Columbia, to Mt. Pitt [now Mt. McLoughlin] near the southern extremity of the reservation, beyond which the range suddenly drops away (without any prominent point, until it swells again into the magnificent peak of Mt. Shasta in California).

Mt. Hood is the greatest of these peaks, closely followed by Mt. Jefferson at the head of the tributaries of the North Santiam River on the west, and of the Deschutes tributaries on the east; the Three Sisters, at the head of McKenzie … [River and various forks] of the Willamette … and Mt. Pitt on the divide between Klamath Lake and the Rogue River. Besides these main peaks, there are several peaks which exceed, or closely approximate, nine thousand feet in height, and from which the snow never entirely melts. …

It is not necessary to show the service which forests perform in preserving the streams of a country. The policy of forest reservation (which our government has entered upon) is founded largely upon it as an admitted fact; and it has been regretted that the subject has escaped the attention of our statesmen so long. …

That forests exert an important influence upon climate has become an established principle. And, that these extensive forests exert a beneficial [influence] upon all the adjoining valleys of Oregon may be deduced by taking the climate as we find it, and considering the probable effect of forest removal according to settled principles of forest action. Both the heat of summer and the cold of winter would be increased. …

In regard to material interests which this reservation may affect, it may be said, in the first place, that there are no agricultural

JOHN B. WALDO

interests affected, for the reason that no part of the reservation is adapted to profitable agriculture—because of its volcanic origin, ruggedness, altitude, and forest growth. …

The so-called settlers on the North Fork of the Santiam River exist chiefly on paper—that is to say, they are not settlers in any proper sense of the word. Although their claims were taken up, in most cases, I believe, as homesteads, they never came, properly, within the purview of the Homestead Act; for they were taken, not for homes, but for the timber upon them. They are always called "timber claims" and are worthless for any other purpose. In fact, the whole country, with immaterial exceptions, is a dense forest full of streams. Too much, rather than too little, timber in this section has already fallen into private hands.

A petition has been circulated in this sect[or], purporting to come from the citizens of Oregon … praying for a release from the Cascade Mountain reservation of a large tract of land in this sect[or]. The sole object aimed at by this petition is timber, and the real complainants must be those who want to take up timber claims … .

It is alleged, among other things, that the Reservation … [gives rise to] … a grievance because it prevents additional settlements and the establishment of schools. But this can hardly be true— … [for these are] settlers without families and without children [to send] to schools.

The petition fails to call to attention, also, to the very extensive forests in the Cascade Range *outside* of the Reservation [italics added by author], and so far as to the needs of the Willamette Valley are concerned (taken in connection with the Coast Range) if [the need should ever arise to have to these other forests, they] … would last forever. In short, if the principle which underlies this petition were admitted, no forest reservation could ever be established. …

But the main opposition to the reservation comes from the sheep owners of Eastern Oregon. They appeal to the public in print, circulate petitions, draw up resolutions for party conventions, and load the air with denunciations of the outrage which has been done them. And yet, the most careful inquirer will fail to find that these complaints are based on any other ground other than that these sheep owners are liable to be prohibited from appropriating public property to private uses, for private profit—prohibited [them] ... from committing what is, strictly, a trespass.

The fact is that, in the consideration of this question, these interests, as such, have no standing whatsoever, and are entitled to no voice as to the disposition to be made of these lands. Both the legal and equitable title to them is in the hands of the people of the United States—not in the people of the State of Oregon ... but in the people of all the states. And the people so owning them, having made a disposition of them, (such as [by] the judgment of their lawfully constituted authorities), [as to what] is best calculated to promote the general welfare; no individual has any right to make any objection to such disposition on any ground of private interest. ...

In regard to the effect of the herders' flocks upon the reservation, it is certain that in a period of time no greater than the life of the trees now standing, these flocks could sweep the Cascade forests from the face of the earth. Less time would, in fact, be required, since these three causes—the prevention of new growth by the flocks, the work done by fire, and natural decay, would operate together. The appearance of desolation, which marks the path of these flocks, [would] extend ... from Mt. Hood in the north to Lake of the Woods in the extreme south. The completeness with which the forests and forest glades ... [can be] stripped of everything a sheep will eat, is surprising. ...

Some years ago, when the subject of the Cascade Reservation first began to be discussed, attention was called to the oblivion [supposedly faced by sheep interests.] A member of the legislature, himself from Eastern Oregon, said to me at the time, in commenting on the opposition of an Eastern Oregon sheep owner to any measure of this kind, that he could see a sheep farther than any other man in Eastern Oregon, and [I also felt] that he could see nothing else. ...

... Such is the zeal and appearance of outraged feeling with which these men assail the Reservation, that it might be supposed that there was some real, though inscrutable, ground for their complaints. ... And yet nothing can be clearer than that there is no substantial basis for their indignation and complaints—nothing more certain than that they might not have been called upon to give up anything which belongs to them in any moral or legal sense. ...

There are other reasons why this Reservation should be maintained. It serves other and additional purposes to those stated above. The civilization must be very imperfect in which the thoughts of men never rise above material interests. Man does not live by bread alone, and it should seem that a wise civilized government should make provisions for other wants than those solely of a material kind. ...

A wise government will know that to raise men is much more important than to raise sheep (or men of the nature of sheep); and that this is a question, which ultimately [and] immeasurably concerns even the purely material interests of men. ...

There are educational uses in mountains and the wilderness which might well justify a wise people in preserving and reserving [them] ... for such uses; and such a people might find this reservation not only wisely reserved, but to be none too great a tract for such a purpose. ...

Why should not Americans, with a continent in their hands to fashion as they would, have provided broadly for all the wants of men which can be supplied by human institutions. Not only fields to toil in, but mountains and wilderness to camp in, to hunt and fish in, and where, in communion with untrammeled nature and the free air, the narrowing tendencies of an artificial and petty existence might be perceived and corrected, and the spirit enlarged and strengthened.

The wisdom of such a policy, certainly, cannot be disproved by pointing to the results which we see around us.

Very truly yours,
John Breckenridge Waldo

Outcome: The defensive actions of Waldo, Steel, and others prevailed. Today's national forests grew out of the Forest Reserves.

Other judges did their work on behalf of public lands from the bench and often were called up to give orations, as was **Judge Matthew Deady**.

Extracts from Independence Day Oration of Judge Matthew Deady in 1885 (p. 9):

> Oregon! The matchless land of snow-capped mountains … valleys [clad with verdure]— of swelling rivers and placid lakes—of majestic forests and broad prairies. …

Matthew Deady (1824–1893), federal district judge. He presided at Oregon's constitutional convention, where he opposed letting corporations be organized; he thought that they tended to invite schemes to defraud farmers. Long serving as a regent of the University of Oregon, he also was a founder of the Multnomah County Library. Most of his judicial decisions were against firms whose activities he felt threatened the public interest. He also often ruled against those pursuing ill-founded claims to the public domain. His oration was typical of early leaders who waxed ecstatic about the state's natural beauties.

The first American community on the Pacific Coast: may she ever be such a [wondrous] state!

Then, quoting from a poem:

Look up, look forth, and on! There's light in the dawning sky;
The clouds are parting, the night is gone …

CHAPTER THREE

Oregon Becomes a Developing State

Among others venturing into the mountains were scientists who also were struck by the beauty they found there and moved other scientists to take notice. One was **Clarence E. Dutton**.

Extract from an article he wrote for *Science* magazine after a visit to Crater Lake in 1886:

> In the heart of the Cascade Range, there is a little sheet of water which is destined to take a high rank among the wonders of the world. It is a unique phenomenon, taken as a whole, though some of its component features, taken singly, may not be unexampled.
>
> It is deeper and richer than the blue of the sky above on the clearest day. Just at the margin of the lake, it shades into turquoise, which is, if possible, more beautiful still. Ordinarily the water surface is mirror-like, and reflects an inverted image [in detail] of the surrounding cliffs. Very majestic, too, are the great environing walls.

On the west side, they reach their greatest altitude, rising almost vertically more than 2,000 feet above the water.

It is difficult to compare this scene with any other in the world, for there is none that sufficiently resembles it; but, in a general way, it may be said that it is of the same order of impressiveness and beauty as the Yosemite Valley.

It was touching to see the worthy but untutored people, who had ridden a hundred miles in freight wagons to behold it, vainly striving to keep back tears as they poured forth their exclamations of wonder and joy (akin to pain). Nor was it less so to see so cultivated and learned a man as my companion hardly able to command himself to speak with his customary calmness.

To the geologist, this remarkable feature is not less impressive than it is to the lover of the beautiful … .

In 1887 Dutton's superior, **John Wesley Powell**, was asked by the Senate Public Lands Committee for his views on a bill by Oregon's senator, J. N. Dolph, S. 11, to make Crater Lake a national park. Drawing upon Dutton's findings, Powell wrote as follows:

The lake itself [referring to Crater Lake] is a unique object, as much so as Niagara, and the effect which it produces upon the mind of the beholder is at once powerful and enduring.

There are probably not many natural objects in the world which [will] impress the average spectator with so deep a sense of the beauty and majesty of nature. This will be better understood when the origin of the lake is considered.

The lake lies in the basin of a huge volcanic mountain, and the basin itself owes its origin to a vast system of explosions by which the heart of the mountain has been thrown into the air as ashes and cinders.

It is the deepest body of fresh water on the continent, and the clear, cold waters reflect the crags and peaks of the volcanic rim by which it is surrounded.

Crater Lake is the dominant object of interest in the proposed reservation; the whole tract is eminently fit to be "set apart forever as a public park and pleasure ground and forest reserve for the benefit of the people of the United States," and I might mention for the benefit of the people of the world.

There is not a square mile within the proposed tract which does not contain something of which would add to the attractiveness of such a park, either in the way of natural beauty or [for the] … instruction and entertainment of visitors.

However, it was not until 1902 that Congress finally approved making it a national park.

Powell is famous for making the first known passage through the Grand Canyon on the Colorado River (1869). He described "wonderful features: carved walls, royal arches, glens, alcove gulches, mounds and monuments." As the second director of the Geological Survey, he warned against trying to promote agriculture in much of the arid West.

John Wesley Powell (1834-1902), professor, army officer, explorer, and bureau director. He was born in New York State and educated in Illinois, and served in the Civil War as an officer (attaining the rank of a major). He yearned to explore rivers and canyons, mounting two path-breaking expeditions down the Colorado River and into the Grand Canyon (in 1869 and 1871); he published an account in 1875.

Becoming the second director of the U.S. Geological Survey in 1881 and serving in that capacity for over a dozen years, he challenged the prevalent idea that the West was suitable for homesteading by farmers. Arguing against the notion that "rain follows the plow," he tried to convince Congress that it had too little water for rain-fed farming.

Another was noted for his scientific discoveries, though he was not a trained scientist. Specializing in the natural history of the Sierra Nevada in California, **John Muir** became the most noted conservationist of all. He often visited Oregon and wrote about it.

When Muir was in Portland in 1888, he wrote:

The city of Portland is at our feet, covering a large area along both banks of the Willamette, and ... makes a telling picture of a busy, aspiring civilization in the midst of the green wilderness in which it is planted. The river is displayed to fine advantage in the foreground of our main view, sweeping in beautiful curves around rich, leafy islands, its banks fringed with willows. ...

There stood Mt. Hood in all the glory of the alpine glow, looming immensely high ... and so impressive that one was overawed (as if suddenly brought before some superior being newly arrived from the sky). [With] the atmosphere ... somewhat hazy, ... the mountain seemed neither near nor far. Its glaciers flashed in the divine light. The rugged, storm-worn ridges (between them and the snowfields of the summit) might have been traced as far as they were in sight, ... [with] blending zones of color about the base.

But so profound was the general impression, ... [an attempt at] analysis did not come into play. The whole mountain appeared as one glorious manifestation of divine power ... glowing like a countenance with ineffable repose and beauty, before which we could only gaze in devout and lowly admiration.

He concluded that Mt. Hood arises "at every turn, solitary, majestic, and awe inspiring—the ruling spirit of the landscape."

At an earlier time (1884) when climbing Mt. Shasta, he looked north into Oregon to see "the snowy volcanic cones of mounts Pitt (now McLoughlin), Jefferson, and the Three Sisters [as they rose] in clear relief, like majestic monuments, above the dim, dark sea of the northern woods."

On a visit by Muir in 1899, the Mazamas had a reception for him, where he chatted with William Steel and L. L. Hawkins. On his last visit in

1908, he spent time with E. H. Harriman at his Pelican Bay lodge on Upper Klamath Lake, where he wrote part of his autobiography. Later, he stopped in Salem to visit with Governor George Chamberlain and future US Senator Charles McNary.

Will Steel encouraged many scientists to come to Crater Lake to do research. One of them was **C. Hart Merriam**, a biologist.

In 1897 he wrote the following article in the *Mazama* about what he found there. He entitled it the "Mammals of Mt. Mazama, Oregon."

The mammal fauna of Mt. Mazama is one of more than ordinary interest. In addition to the fact that no list of the mammals of any part of the Cascade Range has ever been published, and that the number of species inhabiting the region is rather large, it is of geographic interest to note that [it has] several species which do not occur further west; and that certain northern and southern species found on the mountain, so far as is now known, [exist at] the extreme limit of their ranges. …

Several mountain animals of wide distribution are conspicuous by their absence. Thus, the elk … mountain sheep, mountain goat, wolverine, and fisher have not been known to inhabit the region in recent years.

Referring to the one-time Crater Lake Mountain, he said:

Its summit is a large caldron, nearly six miles in diameter … . The caldron contains the far-famed Crater Lake, one of the most attractive bits of scenery on the American continent. …

The whole mountain … is covered with dense forest, notable for the size and magnificence of its trees. …

C. Hart Merriam (1855–1942), biologist, ethnographer, public official. Growing up at the edge of the Adirondacks, he started collecting animal specimens as a boy. He was educated at Yale and became a doctor, but soon became a naturalist. He was a founding member of the American Ornithologists' Union and of the National Geographic Society. His collection of mammal specimens was the greatest known at the time. In time, he became the head of the US Biological Survey, which he ran for 25 years. He described over a hundred new species of mammals. But eventually, he moved into the field of ethnography, with particular emphasis on the Indians of California.

Crater Lake is a body of clear, indigo-blue water, about five miles in diameter, and 2,000 feet in its greatest depth.

While Crater Lake was not made a national park until 1902, during the decade before, prominent scientists came to do their research there. Their work strengthened the realization that this was a phenomenon of national import. Merriam's trip there in 1896 was at the time of a major Mazama excursion to the lake and the visit of the National Forestry Commission.

When the National Forestry Commission visited Crater Lake in 1896, **Gifford Pinchot** was among them and became a dedicated supporter of making it a national park. He also spent time there with Muir.

Quotes from an article by Stephen R. Mark describing Pinchot's visit in 1896 to Crater Lake and that region around it:

In 1896, the National Forestry Commission visited Crater Lake to inspect the forests in that area. Among those visiting were Gifford Pinchot and John Muir. Pinchot camped with Muir and wrote:

> We drove to Crater Lake [probably in a horse-drawn buggy], through the wonderful forests of the Cascade Range, while John Muir and Professor [William H.] Brewer made the journey short with talk worth crossing the continent to hear. Crater Lake seemed to me like a wonder of the world.

In response to a later question of why the area should be made a national park, Pinchot replied:

> You asked me why a national park should be established around Crater Lake. There are many reasons.
>
> In the first place, Crater Lake is one of the great natural wonders of this continent.

Secondly, it is a famous resort for the people of Oregon and other states, which can best be protected and managed in the form of a national park.

Thirdly, since its chief value is for recreation and scenery, and not for the production of timber, its use is distinctly … [to be] a national park and not a forest reserve.

Finally, in the present situation of affairs, it could be more carefully guarded and protected as a park than as a reserve."

In 1902 Pinchot was instrumental in breaking the political deadlock in the House of Representatives on park status for Crater Lake, opening the way to passage of the bill creating the national park around Crater Lake.

Curiously, Muir felt his 1896 visit did not give him enough expertise to promote that area as a national park. On his visit to the area at that time, Muir was more interested in the variety of trees in the forests, while Pinchot was more focused on the potential of the area to be a national park.

While observers have speculated about the reasons for this reversal of their roles, the reasons are far from clear. Perhaps Muir was just focusing on the job of the forestry commission and was used to doing more field work to support his conclusions.

Gifford Pinchot (1865–1946), forester, public official, politician. Educated at Yale as the first forester trained in this country, he joined the Agriculture Department's Division of Forestry and in 1896 served as a member of the National Forestry Commission. In time, he became the first chief of the Forest Service. Under his leadership, the size of the national forests grew from 51 million acres to 175 million acres. He was the principal advisor on natural resources to President Theodore Roosevelt. He later organized the National Conservation Association and wrote a book entitled *The Fight for Conservation*. He is now recognized as "the father of American forestry." In the late 1920s and early 1930s, he was elected twice as the governor of Pennsylvania.

Many other figures in Oregon history exulted in the glories of nature and lamented in what was happening to it. One of them was **Joaquin Miller**, a man of many talents.

In 1907, in visiting Canyon City where he had once lived, Joaquin Miller made the following reflections to a local reporter:

"Yes, it's all changed beyond recognition, but the contour of the hills

Joaquin Miller (1837–1913), lawyer, reporter, poet. Born in the Eugene, Oregon, area, he attended Columbia College there, studied law, and edited a Eugene newspaper. In 1864 he traveled to Canyon City in eastern Oregon, where he built a cabin and became a county judge. Later, he relocated to California, wrote poetry about the Sierras, and became a reporter: covering the Klondike gold rush and the Boxer Rebellion in China.

seem the same forever more." Pointing to his cabin, he said, "This is my work." But then pointing to the hills, he said, "This is God's," adding, "Holy, holy hills. See where the eternal forces are ceaselessly at work restoring the devastation of man."

Pointing to the tailings of a placer mine, he said:

Nature abhors a wound, and even an open scar. She slowly but surely softens and hides them by some of her magical art. The steeper edges of this cut are already smoothing out, and hardy grasses and brave blossoms are colonizing in the scant soil of the ruins.

In a poem of 1881, "Twenty Carats of Fire," he wrote of nature:

A thousand miles of mighty wood
    Where thunder-storms stride fire-shod;
    A thousand flowers every rod,
A stately tree on every rood;
    Ten thousand leaves on every tree,
    And each a miracle to me;
And yet there be men who Question God!

And in 1886 in passing through Shasta City, he wrote:

I went out on the porch of the old hotel … and the stars came out. The same splendid moon, and so close and so clear! I could almost hang my cane on the horn of it. And the wondrous stars! Large and glittering as the great glittering nuggets we used to gather from the gulches in the days of old.

And he provided this memorable characterization of Mt. Shasta (which can be seen from southern Oregon):

> Lonely as God, and white as a winter moon. Mt. Shasta starts up sudden and solitary from the heart of the great black forests of northern California.

Some who became accomplished politicians distinguished themselves as collectors in nature. One of them was **Dr. Harry Lane**, who became a US Senator but earlier wrote about mushroom collecting.

Dr. Harry Lane in 1896 and 1897 wrote this on mushroom collecting:

"No more savory or delicate morsel comes to the pan" than the yellow-gilled mushroom and purple russula. "One of the best varieties of edible fungi" is the morel, as well as the oyster mushroom—which he described as a "fairly good variety."

"Better than it seems," he thought, is the porcini.

Of others found in the woods around Portland, he said that "many more have such unsavory characters of taste and odor when cooked, that I have willingly foregone further acquaintance with them."

He said the fly agaric tastes "sweet and nutty when cooked, giving the palate no warning of its deadly qualities."

He warned:

> Those who do not care to join [mushroom collecting clubs] and will insist on eating fungi, can easily learn to distinguish between the wholesome and poisonous species by eating the species they find, … leaving it to the coroner to do the rest.

Some who explored wild country did it for federal agencies, such

Dr. Harry Lane (1855–1917), founder of the Mushroom Club of Oregon in 1899. He had written a number of articles for the *Oregonian* on mushroom collecting. While serving as president of the state Medical Society, he worked to have more clean drinking water made available. He later entered state politics, becoming mayor of Portland and a US Senator (Democrat). While in Congress, he served on committees dealing forests, game, fisheries, and Native Americans.

as the US Geological Survey. One of them was **H. D. Langille**, who set records in moving with such dispatch around the state's wild places.

This is an extract from what he wrote in 1903 about the northern portion of the Cascade Range:

The dominant topographic feature of the region is Mt. Hood. [It is] one of the grand chain of snow-clad peaks that rise from the broad crest of the Cascade Mountains and stand in a sentinel-like array along the range, marking the line of natural division between the widely different climatic and physical zones which extend east and westward from their summits.

The mean altitude of the Cascade Range is, approximately, 4,500 feet above the level of the sea, and their level is deeply broken only at the great gorge where the waters of the mighty Columbia have cut their way through … to reach the Pacific Ocean.

Southward from the great basaltic walls of the gorge, which rise perpendicularly to an altitude of over 4,000 feet, the narrow meandering crest line maintains a comparatively unbroken level until the slope of Mt. Hood is reached. South of the mountain, the range broadens, and the divide is difficult to trace from a distance.

Eastward from the crest, the slope is gradual toward the treeless plains of eastern Oregon, but toward the West extend long, rugged ridges, rising abruptly from the deep canyons to elevations which are higher than the divide.

… From the mountain [Mt. Hood] and its ridges of perpetual snow and ice flow the more important streams which drain this area.[*]

H. D. Langille (1874–1954), field inspector for the US Geological Survey and later the Bureau of Forestry. After being educated at Yale, Langille immediately went to work for the US Geological Survey, doing field work to determine boundaries for land withdrawals. In 1903 he transferred to the Bureau of Forestry to continue this work for the new Forest Reserves.

Before going to Yale, he had been a mountaineering guide on Mt. Hood. In 1896 he showed Pinchot around Mt. Hood. His father had built Cloud Cap Inn.

Langille was the principal field inspector, who checked real conditions on the ground to guide decisions about major land withdrawals for determining the boundaries of Forest Reserves in Oregon. His difficult travels through winter conditions in 1903 are legendary. Historian Lawrence Rakestraw felt "he had an ardent desire to save the woods of Oregon from eastern lumber syndicates bent on exploiting them."

---

[*] Langille, *Northern Portion*, 28.

Langille thought he saw evidence even then of the shrinkage of glaciers on Mt. Hood.

Most of the land withdrawals that determined the boundaries of the Forest Reserves were made permanent in Oregon in the period between 1903 and 1904. Langille's work stood up to criticism.

Others who celebrated Oregon's beauty in painting and poetry were also disturbed by the decimation of public lands and denounced those who were filing fraudulent claims. The most prominent was **Charles Erskine Scott Wood**, a lawyer, among other things.

Regarding the beauty of the Harney desert, where he painted with the impressionist Childe Hassam in 1904 and 1908:

> The flowers bloom in the Desert joyously— …
> They are careless whether they be seen, or praised. …
> They spread a voluptuous carpet for the feet of the
>   Wind …
> "Our day is short, but our beauty is eternal."
> Never have I found a place, or a season, without beauty.
> Neither the sea, where the white stallions
> champ their bits and rear against their bridles,
> Nor the Desert, bride of the Sun, which sits scornful,
>   apart, …
> The Sun is her servitor, the Stars are her attendants, running
>   before her. …
> Dazzling, so that the eyes must be shaded. …
> I have come to her, that I may know freedom; …
> To be melted in Creation's crucible and made clean;
> To know that the law of Nature is freedom.[*]

---

[*]   Wood, *Poet in the Desert*, prologue.

CHARLES ERSKINE SCOTT WOOD

Charles Erskine Scott Wood (1852-1944), lawyer, artist, writer. Wood spent his most influential years (about thirty) in Portland, Oregon, though he spent his formative years in the East and his final years in California. When he first arrived as a young army officer, he was engaged in the last of the Indian Wars (and wrote movingly about them). While he helped his Portland law firm sell wagon-road land grants in eastern Oregon (for a French banking firm), he did show sympathy for public lands and conservation, though he flirted with anarchism. He also often represented radicals and underdogs. Along with Thomas Lamb Eliot, Wood played a leading role in the founding of various cultural institutions in Portland. His descendants in Oregon have become prominent.

It seems to me that this great beauty and solemnity [of the virgin forests] is perhaps as valuable as the shriek and clamor of the mill. It is a pity to have all this majesty of antiquity wholly destroyed. Man cannot restore it. … There is no spot where the primeval forest is assured from the attack of the worst microbe, the dollar.*

Regarding land frauds:

Timber lands have been stolen right and left—by fraudulent entries and fictitious entry-men. The public domain has seemed a great treasure house with the doors wide open; for a generation or more, thieves have been carrying off all the valuable lands.

But [you argue] thieves cannot carry off forests and mines in Oregon in their pockets. Yes, they can. One man can carry … away half the forest lands in Oregon in an inside pocket—if he can get a patent or a deed to these lands. And even though he has got the deed by fraud, if he sells to another (who has no knowledge of the fraud), that other will hold the title.

A few plutocrats are gobbling up all the valuable lands. Future generations will be born landless.

The thievery has been going on since the first day of that law. Many eminently "respectable" citizens made their fortunes years ago [by]… the same perjuries and purchases … .**

Wood was one of the voices of prominent people in Oregon calling for prosecution of those perpetrating frauds in their public land claims. As an

---

*   Wood, "The Worst Microbe."

** Wood, "Impressions."

upshot of this clamor, President Theodore Roosevelt sent in federal prosecutors who sent a majority of Oregon officials to jail.

Some actually lived among these public lands in eastern Oregon and wanted to save them as habitat for the waterfowl that prospered there. **Bill Hanley**, in Harney County, was one such person. He was a rancher who was also a conservationist.

Extract from his memoir, *Feelin' Fine* (1930), describing an early wagon trip:

Native spring flowers [were] everywhere on … [the] old raiding ground: blue camas lilies (the Klamaths used their roots for potatoes) … the restful, quiet, peaceful sagebrush with its "forever" promise of being friend to man, … characterless rabbit brush that [doesn't] … express much—except beauty in its yellow flower in the fall when it adds to be decoration of the plains …

… Then the decorative juniper, giving a touch of bright green to the cheeks of the foothills— … [it] fills the air with fragrance.

… Tonight [I] walked around the meadows, covered with water. The moon was full, light as day, warm, still—all but the little frogs hollering everywhere. Everyone seems to be working to get frogs singing with a little more understanding—to bring out [their] … own identity.

[I] looked at the sky, so blue beyond the stars. Every little star seemed to stand out alone like the little frogs, as if we [were] … the important one. It all says there [isn't] … anything but what's

William "Bill" Hanley (1861–1935), Harney County rancher, personality. Hanley turned himself into one of the largest and most successful ranchers in the country. With five ranches near Burns, Oregon, he also propagated wildlife, particularly water fowl, on habitat that later became part of the Malheur National Wildlife Refuge. He was known as a conservationist. He was also a progressive thinker, who was allied with the Bull Moose branch of the Republican Party. He even ran for governor and the US Senate.

He was particularly celebrated as a host, who had Theodore Roosevelt as a guest, as well as William Jennings Bryan, C. E. S. Wood, painter Childe Hassam, and railroader James J. Hill. Will Rogers was also a friend who visited him.

When he visited New York City, the *New York Times* heralded him as a "pioneer, philosopher, and one the most prosperous and influential men on the Pacific Coast."

important, and that we are all part of the whole Big Thing. ... Happy is understanding. Feelin' fine.*

Other businessmen also cared about wildlife. One such person was the publisher of the *Oregon Journal*, **C. S. Jackson**. In 1907 he wrote Governor George Chamberlain to urge that a bill he felt harmed songbirds be vetoed.

February 23, 1907

My dear Governor:

... Young Mr. [William] Finley is an ardent friend of birds and is worthy of encouragement. He tells me that the law passed by the legislature means the slaughter of many harmless birds by "human heathens" and is in no way as favorable to orchardists and others (against the ravishes of birds) as the present law.

I believe that he knows what he is talking about. Every living thing in my mind is here for a purpose, and there is more "good" in its existence than "bad."

Finley knows the habits of birds, knows their value as well as their destructiveness, and is a safer pilot in this matter than those who have perpetrated this legislation against important members of the bird family, ... [which] are engaged in more good work than bad, and are performing a service for mankind: that more than offsets the destruction they may commit in instinctively following the natural law for self-preservation.

The birds, all of them, have a right to pursue "life, liberty, and happiness" in their own way and should be protected against

C. S. Jackson (1860-1924), newspaper publisher. Jackson revived the *Oregon Journal* in the early years of the twentieth century, styling it as a Democratic-leaning paper (but a fair one) and claimed it would be a "credit to" the land "where rolls the Oregon country." He ran it for twenty-two years. He exhibited sympathy for wildlife and supported conservation issues.

---

* Hanley, *Feelin' Fine!*, 38-41.

needless slaughter—rather than have their slaughtering encouraged (as the bill passed and awaiting your signature would permit).

You … should not permit … this injustice against this family of God's creatures. … If you see it in this light, … this bill will not become a law, particularly so when the present law is practically better and more fitted to the needs of those suffering from the so-called destruction of certain birds.

Sincerely yours,
C. S. Jackson

Outcome: A few days later Governor Chamberlain vetoed this bill (H.B. 367), pointing out that bird "depredations do not justify the indiscriminate destruction of [these] birds that afford protection to horticultural and agricultural interests of the state by [destroying] … insects and pests—more than compensating for the occasional injury [they do]… to crops." The bill did not become law.

GEORGE CHAMBERLAIN

The governor to whom Jackson wrote was a very successful progressive politician, who served in many positions and could even have become president. **George Chamberlain** also was one of the first Oregon politicians to champion conservation causes and public lands.

Extract from message of *Governor* George Chamberlain to the legislature (1909):

George Chamberlain (1854–1928), lawyer, politician (Democrat). Chamberlain served as a governor of Oregon and two terms as a US Senator, having also been Oregon's first attorney general (all from 1891 to 1920). He was viewed as a progressive reformer and supporter of conservation causes, promoting protection of the national forests and seeking protection also for the salmon.

He fought those trying to perpetrate fraudulent claims for public lands. As governor, it was he who appointed Oswald West to be Oregon's land agent, who was assigned to investigate fraudulent claims for Oregon school lands and who was charged with recovering them.

He took the lead in the enactment of the Chamberlain-Ferris Act, revesting Oregon's O & C lands in the federal government. At times, he was allied with the People's Power League. President Woodrow Wilson offered him the position of vice president on his ticket in 1916, but Chamberlain declined, wanting to return to Oregon.

Oregon is the richest state in the union in forest and mineral resources which have not been disposed of by the national government or wasted or destroyed to satisfy individual or corporate greed, and it behooves our people to see to it that these resources are cared for and protected.

Remarks made by *Senator* George Chamberlain on April 23, 1910, in support of the president continuing to have authority to make withdrawals from the public domain:

It seems to me that a policy which has proved salutary in the past, and resulted in the prevention of the monopolization of many of the natural resources of the country, ought not to have been lightly swept aside by this or any other administration. …

There is no question but through the instrumentality of the Timber and Stone Act, the most valuable timber in the country has gone into the hands of the timber syndicates, who are thus enabled to fix extortionate prices upon a product that enters into the everyday life of every man, woman, and child in the country. … Their looting of the public domain has been made possible by the laxity of administration.

But Congress is not less to blame, for these frauds were known by all men years ago, and nothing has been done to make them impossible by repealing the law—although repeal has been recommended as the only panacea.

Remarks regarding ending President Roosevelt's Conservation Commission:

Not only did Congress not then see fit to enact any legislation therein recommended, but unfortunately declined to print the report in sufficient numbers for adequate distribution to the people.

More disastrous than this, however, was the Congressional enactment forbidding this or other executive commissions from pursuing their important work in the service of the people. This action, … designed to wipe out the national Conservation Commission, [plainly did] accomplish … its purpose. It put an end to that commission—removing the only national organization which was dealing with the conservation question as a whole.

This presented the strange spectacle of a nationwide movement—inaugurated by the governors of the states, the presidents of great organizations of our national industries, and other distinguished citizens, and heartily endorsed by the people of the country—by legislative enactment … [was not only denied] appropriations, but even permission to continue its work.

Visitors to Oregon also fostered the culture that would promote understanding of the value of nature and the need to protect it. One of the most prominent was **John Charles Olmsted**, a landscape architect, who came here often to work on projects. One of those projects was a report on potential parks for the city of Portland.

When Olmsted came to Portland for this purpose in 1903, he was taken around Portland to look at sites that might be suitable to be parks. The person who took him was **Colonel L. L. Hawkins**, a wealthy nature lover who transported him in his carriage. As a founding member of the Portland Park Board, he and his friend Thomas Lamb Eliot had contrived to bring Olmsted to Portland.

Hawkins had been indefatigable in fending off depredations against

Macleay Park, building a trail system there to bring in more defenders. He had also proposed a trail system for the west hills.

When Olmsted issued his report that year, Hawkins signaled his support, saying that he hoped "to have a part in putting [his ideas] … into execution." He expected Olmsted's report would awaken "our people to the importance of securing more parks."

In connection with 1905 Lewis and Clark Exposition, Hawkins issued a tract on the wonders of the Wildwood Trail in Macleay Park.

In it he said:

You may find yourself seated on a moss-covered log, gazing at the lofty spruce, cedar, fir, hemlock, and the other trees which are so richly decorated with the yew, dogwood, vine maple … and numerous other small [plants] …

The stillness here is immense. The only voice is the musical murmur of Balch Creek, and the singing of birds. The carpet of the woods is unsullied … nor is the undergrowth broken … .

Here are spots as wild and unchanged as [they were] … when Lewis and Clark … first planted their feet on Oregon soil. Coming out the canyon, climbing under logs, picking [your] … way across [a] a gigantic deadfall (moldering giants fallen long ago, and now helping to enrich the earth for more of their kind to follow), you soon reach the top of the ridge.

Describing the view from there, he said the eye moves across:

The rolling Columbia, and on and on [until it] … is carried [to] … a forest-clad range of foothills and [to] the mounting hills that reach up to the snow-line of St. Helens, Mt. Rainier, Mt. Adams, [and] Mt. Hood … —jewels in an incomparable setting. It is enough to fill one with awe and admiration.

Little of Olmsted's plan was implemented at the time because of the perceived cost. The South Hillside Parkway (now known as the Terwilliger Parkway) was his most significant proposal that was built. However, if Olmsted's ideas about the value of the old forests in what later became Forest Park had been followed, a lot of money could have been saved, as well as a wonderful virgin forest.

In his 1903 report on park planning for Portland, Olmsted spoke of this area in these terms:

> No use to which this tract of land could be put would begin to be as sensible or as profitable for the city as that of making it a public park.

In making the case in detail for this park, he went on:

> From this spur northwesterly [which was identified as southwest of the northwest arm of what had been Guild's Lake], there are a succession of ravines and spurs covered with remarkably primeval woods, which have relatively little commercial value. The investment of a comparatively moderate sum in the acquisition of these romantic wooded hillsides for a park or a reservation of wild woodland character would yield ample returns in pleasure to taxpayers. …
>
> Future generations … will bless the men who were wise enough to get such woods preserved. Future generations … will be likely to appreciate the wild beauty and the grandeur of the

John Charles Olmsted (1852–1920), pioneering landscape architect. The nephew of Frederick Law Olmsted (who is regarded as the father of American landscape architecture), John Charles Olmsted continued the family business (Olmsted Brothers in Brookline, Massachusetts). He was heavily engaged in work in the Pacific Northwest, including designing the grounds of the 1906 Lewis and Clark Centennial Exposition in Portland. In 1903 he wrote a report for Portland on park planning for its future.

tall fir trees. … If these woods are preserved, they will surely come to be regarded as marvelously beautiful.[*]

While Forest Park was not established at this time, it eventually was (though, these fine virgin forests were lost, to be replaced, for the most part, by second growth).

Earlier in that report, he had observed that:

From almost all the high hills, extremely beautiful views are commanded of all the distant snow-clad mountains and especially of the five great snow-clad peaks: Mt. St. Helens, Mt. Adams, Mt. Hood, Mt. Rainier, and Mt. Jefferson.[**]

Emanuel T. Mische (1870–1934), landscape architect. Mische served as the Portland park superintendent from 1903 to 1913, after having trained under Frederick Law Olmsted. He took the lead in developing Olmsted-style parks around Portland: Peninsula (regarded as his great triumph), Laurelhurst, Mt. Tabor, Columbia, and Sellwood Parks. These were all financed from a bond measure passed in 1907. Mische also designed the rose gardens in the Ladd Addition.

A disciple of Olmsted was hired as the superintendent of Portland's parks at the time Olmsted filed his report. He was **Emanuel T. Mische**, who developed the type of naturalistic parks that Olmsted favored.

Quote in 1910 from a letter Mische wrote to the *Oregonian* in response to Mayor Simon's penury in park spending:

Portland will have parks in spite of any individual … who would dare attempt to halt her onward march on whatever pretexts.

In 1913[***] he deplored "grievous mistakes of short-sighted policies in acquiring insufficient areas" for parks. (14)

---

[*]   Olmsted, "Outlining a System of Parkways," 40–42.

[**]   Olmsted, "Outlining a System of Parkways," 34.

[***]   Mische, quoted in Willingham, "Open Space."

The greatest mistakes of short-sighted policies in acquiring insufficient areas is recognized throughout the land. (15)

Park properties, if too small at the outset, cannot usually be extended without inflicting severe damage on the ... [arboreal] growth which has developed to properties of extreme value, [and] beauty ... . (16)

In planning then for Portland's Laurelhurst Park, he urged that "... every effort must be made to preserve the undulating topography on which the firs depend for their survival." (19)

A few years later, this park was named as the most beautiful park on the West Coast by the Pacific Coast Parks Association. In recent times, it was the first urban park added to the National Register of Historic Places (2001).

CHAPTER FOUR

Oregon in the Early 20th Century

Governor Chamberlain lamented the loss of the national Conservation Commission under President Theodore Roosevelt. But Oregon had one for a while as well (from 1909 to 1917), with **Joseph N. Teal** chairing it.

Here is an address Teal made at the University of Oregon on February 13, 1909, entitled "Oregon's Heritage of Natural Resources—Shall They Be Conserved for the People?":

> This state is singularly blessed in soil, climate, and natural resources of all kinds, and, while in the past, their very abundance has made us profligate [in the use] of our patrimony, it is fortunate that we are yet in a position to conserve [what remains of] … them. ….
>
> During the past year or two, owing to the patriotic work of a few men, led by President [Theodore] Roosevelt, the attention of the country has been riveted on the fact that many of our … [natural] resources are diminishing and being destroyed so rapidly that

in some instances the time can be predicted ... when under present conditions of use (misuse and waste), some of the things we look on as necessaries of life will be gone.

It is undeniable that on every hand, there has been wanton waste in use and a steady [movement] ... toward monopolization in ownership. This tendency is as apparent in this state as in any other [region]. ... Until of late, there has been no conception either of this enormous waste or monopolization, or any heed given to the consequences. A common heritage has been dissipated with a lavish hand, and [any] ... protest ... met with but slight courtesy, let alone attention. ...

But we have now arrived at the turn of the road and the battle is on for the preservation of the rights of the public and to the public wealth. It is now recognized ... by every one that something must be done, some way found to prevent the waste of the past, to make the best use of our resources for the present and to conserve them for the future. ...

[Why do we] give to one man, and to his heirs and assigns forever, the most valuable rights and property, without the slightest thought as to our moral right to thus bind unborn generations. The saving grace in it all, however, is the fact that none of us [does this with any thought that we might be trustees] ... . Therefore, if we once can [grasp] ... the fundamental principle that in dealing with the rights and property of the public, we are handling a trust estate, many of our difficulties will disappear. ...

Our treatment of the salmon industry is [an] ... excellent illustration [of this problem] ... . This resource clearly belongs to the state. It is subject to state regulation and control—even to the extent of total prohibition of fishing. Properly conserved, it will not only be a never ending source of food supply and revenue, but an increasing one.

How have we treated this munificent endowment? We have

made a pretense of an attempt of protection and conservation. Every one knows (who has taken enough interest in the subject to keep in touch) that our legislative halls have been a place where the down-river fisherman and the upriver fisherman, where the gill netter, the seiner, [and] the wheel man, [have] met in mortal combat—to have laws framed in [their] … respective interests. And [those interests have been keen] … to devise ways and means so that the salmon could be taken more readily and for longer periods, and if possible to prevent the other fellow from getting any.

Who ever saw anyone standing up and fighting on behalf of the real party of interest—the people of the state? Most of those who had built canneries and owned other gear were interested only in securing the greatest catch in the shortest possible time. … Did anyone, not directly interested in the taking of fish, venture a suggestion, he was treated by both sides as a common enemy—as one interfering in a situation with which he had no concern.

The result was what might have been expected. A steadily diminishing supply, a magnificent fish threatened with extinction, an industry with destruction, a natural resource with exhaustion. Such a wicked policy carries with it its own condemnation.

But who is responsible for this situation. We all are. To put it mildly, it is not an edifying spectacle to see a sovereign state sub-mitting to the dictation of a few, who, for immediate gain, would destroy a patrimony belonging to all, as well as those to follow. …

It is time all these acts of colossal folly were stopped. It is time the people aroused themselves and asserted their rights. Supreme selfishness on the one hand and deadly indifference on the other, is at the root of all of it. … But if my opinion [is soundly based], that this resource is a trust,

Joseph N. Teal (1858–1929), attorney, civic leader. Teal chaired the Oregon State Conservation Commission under governors Frank Benson and Oswald West. He also spoke in 1909 at the first National Conservation Congress in Seattle.

that it is ours to use, not to destroy, ... no man would dare to thus dissipate [this] ... trust estate. ...

Is it to the interests of this state to have all her public resources absorbed by the few, or so handled that the people as a whole will receive her benefits? Shall we sit idly by and allow our magnificent water-power [sites] be monopolized and their ownership and control pass from us forever? Shall our fisheries become extinct, our forests wasted, the springs of our rivers dried up, and vast areas remain barren wastes?

We are at the parting of the ways. One road leads to prosperity and the welfare of the public as a whole, the other to private gain and in the end destruction of our resources of necessaries of life and all that implies.

The idea of state and federal conservation commissions was controversial. Oregon's did not last.

When George Chamberlain was governor, he started **Oswald West** on his way as a public official—in this case, as the state land agent pursuing those guilty of fraud in laying claim to state school lands. Following success in this role, he then was elected governor. In this role, success also crowned his efforts, with West becoming one of Oregon's most popular governors and a renowned conservation leader.

Extracts from West's inaugural message in 1911:

The state has already received a grant of four of five million acres of rich agricultural and timber land, and by mismanagement and inattention has very little to show for it. ...

During recent years, the affairs of the State Land Department have been administered in the interest of the taxpayers and school children … it has ceased to be a breeding ground for scandal and a place "of easy picking" for members of the "old-school, land ring." An effective land law has made it possible for the State Land Board to adopt many long-needed reforms … [thus it has been able to] secure a fair price for the remnants of that magnificent grant of over 4,000,000 acres … [that] was given to Oregon by the federal government to aid in the support of the common schools.

The records show that on January 1, 1903 three-fourths of all the lands and swamp[land]s … granted to the State (for schools, colleges, and universities) had been sold, and that the average price received by the State was $1.25 per acre. … Since that date [the State has] sold another one-eighth of the grant, for which it has received $2,500,000—or an average price of $5.00 per acre. This leaves about one-eighth of the original grant remaining unsold.

If the present policy of the board continues, it is safe to say that the State will have realized as much from the [sale of the] last one-fourth of its grant … as it did from the sale of the first three-fourths … (notwithstanding [the fact] that much of it is inferior land). …

Conservation, as I view it, means the development and the utilization of the natural resources, but, in such a manner and under such regulation and safeguards, as will give the people of the present day and … generations [coming in] … the future, the maximum of benefit and of utility, with a minimum of waste and destruction.

The State [that] … permits the great storehouses of its God-given wealth to be vandalized by selfish greed is indeed a very poor guardian of the rights of its children: the present-day citizens. And it is equally true that the State [that] … neglects, through delay and inaction, to provide a speedy, adequate, and effective conservation of its resources is an unfit trustee of the property and privileges of its citizens that are yet to be born. …

OSWALD WEST

Speaking of the fifth of the national timber supply then in Oregon:

> Fifty years will see every stick of this vast forest cut and sawed if the present demand keeps up. …
>
> In the past … the salmon fishing industry has been one of the greatest of the industries of the State, … [it should be] one of the greatest in the future. Once the streams of the State ran full with fish, but inadequate laws have permitted the hand of greed to dip deep into [our] … waters until the great salmon runs have begun to disappear. …
>
> There is but one way in which the fishing industry can be saved from extinction, and that is through the adoption of a definite and sensible policy of regulation. … [to that end], I would suggest:
>
> 1. The passage of laws [that] … will enable a fair proportion of the fish to reach and use their natural spawning grounds;
> 2. Liberal appropriations for hatchery purposes [now understood to be problematic]; [and]
> 3. Take the office of Master Fish Warden out of politics and keep it out.

He got approval by the legislature of the following proclamation, issued on February 13, 1913, which he intended to issue to protect Oregon's beaches:

> The shore of the Pacific Ocean, between ordinary high tide and extreme low tide, and from the Columbia River on the north and the California line on the south, is hereby declared a public highway and shall forever remain open … to the public.

He pointed out that twenty miles of beach and tidelands had already been sold and lost, saying:

> We have got to put a stop to this. Let's not sell any more tideland.

It is too valuable. No selfish interests should be permitted, through politics or otherwise, to destroy, or even impair, this great birthright of our people.

In the administration of this God-given trust, a broad protective public policy should be declared and maintained.

In response to later inquiries as to how he got the legislature to approve this proclamation, he explained:

I pointed out that thus we would come into miles and miles of highway with no cost to the taxpayer.

From a 1915 message:

A Fish and Game Commission, having control of all matters pertaining to our fish and game, was created by the legislature of 1911. The Board is supposed to be non-political and the members to fairly represent the different sections of the state. Good men have been appointed from time to time [to] ... this Board; none of whom, however, has been able to curtail the extravagances [which] cling to the department ... like barnacles to a ship. The commission should be abolished. ...

Oregon stands as the champion of a policy of conservation which, while [facilitating] ... the early development of our resources, will [now want] ... every safeguard [to protect] ... these great birthrights of [our] ... people. While we [resist] ... [thoughtless] ... red-tape entanglements ... and [want to keep] the door [open] to legitimate endeavor, we have always opposed the encroachments of ... selfish interests.

There are representatives of organized greed and monopoly who oppose every [measure of the] conservation movement; their sole desire being freedom to loot the public domain. To accomplish this end, they desire to seize every opportunity to poison the mind of the public against the policies of the federal government.

A favorite method of attack is through the charge that the [federal] government has a large acreage of agricultural land locked up in its forest reserves, and that settlers are thus deprived of an opportunity to secure homes, and [that] the development of the state [thus] is greatly retarded. …

Oregon has within her boundaries 545,800,000,000 … [board] feet of standing timber, or about one-fifth of the timber supply of the United States. Two-thirds of this timber is held in private ownership; the balance by the federal government. About 35,000,000,000 [board] feet of … [this] privately owned timber was at one time owned by the state (being part of her land grant).

A careful study of past events and the record discloses:

1. That had not the federal government—through the creation of forest reserves—withdrawn certain of its lands from entry, practically every acre of surveyed timber land in the state would by this time have passed into private ownership.
2. That the lands now in private ownership are rapidly passing from hands of the original … small holders into the hands of a few powerful timber operators whose aim is to control the timber supply of the United States.

The timber records for the Pacific Northwest show a little over 23% of privately owned timber to be in the hands of three corporations. They also show that a little over 50% of this timber is owned by a group of thirty-eight holders [i.e., individuals]. …

An appraisal in 1911 of Gov. Oswald West by Theodore Roosevelt:

In Governor West, of Oregon, I found a man more intelligently alive to the beauty of nature and of harmless wild life, more eagerly desirous to avoid the wanton and brutal defacement and destruction of wild nature, and more keenly appreciative of how much this natural beauty should mean to civilized mankind, than almost any other man I have ever met holding high political position. ... He desires to preserve for all time our natural resources: the woods, the water, the soil, which a selfish and short-sighted greed seeks to exploit in such a fashion as to ruin them ... .

In retirement, West wrote an account of early day land frauds, which was published June 20, 1945, in the *Bulletin of the Oregon Grange*.

Oregon, under the act of admission to the Union, received as a federal grant, sections 16 and 36 in each and every township, and if any such section, or part thereof, became lost to the state through a prior homestead entry, mining claim, or inclusion in a federal reservation, other vacant federal government lands, or like acreage, within the state, could be selected in lieu of such lands.

Unfortunately, for the forty years following admission to the Union, our state lands were conceded as prey to the politicians. The state land office became nothing more than an adjunct to the headquarters of the old-school land rings. The losses in school sections for which "lieu" lands might be selected were hardly ever recorded by our state land officials—the job being left to the land thieves who sold the information to those who had in mind valuable lands which they wished the state to select in lieu of such losses. Such selected lands, regardless of value, never netted the state over $2.50 per acre. ...

When the Cascade Forest Reserve was created in this state, there were within its boundaries around 50,000 acres in unsold school sections—most of them rough and un-timbered and of little value. But with the passage of the lieu land act of 1897, they became valuable as "base" or "scrip" for lieu selections. The state could have exchanged them for a like acreage of valuable timber lands, but its officials made no move in that direction.

They, on the other hand, permitted Benson and Hyde [leading land fraudsters] to purchase all such sections—through the use of forged and dummy applications and at the minimum price of $1.25 per acre.

A short time after entering upon my duties as State Land Agent, I submitted to a Marion County grand jury a list of certificates of sale, covering around one million acres of school land, which had been issued against forged and dummy applications. The grand jury notified state officials … [of] the fraudulent character of these transactions and protested the issuance of deeds … [for them] … Fearing prosecution, most holders permitted the certificates to be cancelled.

In time I discovered the fact that the Puter and McKinley gang had set up a state land office of their own somewhere in the East. It had secured zinc etchings of certificates of sale and assignment forms used by our state land office, and thus duplicated certificates covering valuable tracts of timber land. It employed a crooked expert to forge the signatures of the clerk of our land board, and used a fraudulent state seal. The gang used tramps and saloon bums to forge the names of supposed original applicants to assignments attached to the certificates of sale. We were able to run down bogus transactions covering around 50,000 acres of such land.

With the help of Governor Chamberlain and a friendly legislature, we secured the passage of a new and effective state land law

Oswald D. West (1873–1960), lawyer, office holder (Democrat). After serving as state land agent (recovering almost a million acres of fraudulently obtained state school lands), he was elected governor of Oregon (1911–1915). At this time, he was a progressive reformer. As governor, he persuaded the legislature to set aside the beaches as a state highway—to prevent their disposal but also to keep them open to the public. He also was instrumental in setting up various commissions (as done for the Fish and Game Commission) and the state forestry bureau. He became a friend of President Theodore Roosevelt and Gifford Pinchot and encouraged prosecution of those perpetrating land frauds.

which forever ended all such crooked work, and guaranteed the school fund a decent price for lands of value remaining unsold.

Many famed Oregonians moved up and down the West Coast, but were still known as people born in Oregon. They seldom forgot their roots and continued to write about places they knew. One of them was poet **Edwin Markham**.

He wrote about scenes he knew in eastern Oregon around the Malheur marshes in a 1914 book:

Now, however, the bird colonies are found only on the marshes of the Malheur, in happy reservations where the [government] … is trying to save the feathered folk from extinction. Here in the reed and tule marshes, in a thunder of flapping, clapping, of honking and croncking, the bird multitudes can hatch their young in peace and joy.

It stirs you with thrills of noble emotion to see them rising in thousands, gleaming in the sun, and arcing over their hidden homes—rising in myriads for miles and miles and miles, all the water birds of the north land … .

Some wealthy newspaper publishers were sad to see the haste to destroy Oregon's virgin forests. **George Palmer Putnam** in Bend was one of them.

In 1915 Putnam observed that most people in the West were "all for turning [trees] into dollars as fast as logging roads and band saws can contrive," but there were those, like himself, "with a secret dread of the time when the old earth will be divested totally of her timber covering."

Putnam hired Robert Sawyer as a writer for the *Bend Bulletin*. Sawyer later became its editor and publisher and a leader in putting the state park system on a professional basis.

People sought different things in nature. Some sought fish to catch and often enjoyed the quest as much as the catch. **Blaine Hallock** was one of those, a lawyer who wrote a great deal about fishing. He also worked to clean up river pollution.

Following are excerpts from an article by him published in 1916 in the *Oregon Sportsman*.

> I walked out upon a rude, log foot-bridge, the only crossing for many miles up or down the river. Above, the water threaded its crooked way across the widening prairie, which stretched to the far blue jagged summits of the Cascades. Below, the pines advanced to touch branches in some places across the placid flow, and further down, the river became more turbulent, until it finally tumbled—a mad, white cascade—into the rocky gorge which it follows for about two hundred miles.

He then recounts his futile efforts to catch a fish. After almost quitting, he moves to nearby water and writes:

> A breeze came hurrying from somewhere out of the pines away off to the east, and caused the long prairie grass to nod and sweep in graceful waves. It danced along the bosom of the shining river and whipped little choppy wavelets about the reeds against the shore. It scattered the gray mists and rolled up little puffs of white cloud. It let the sun shine through and showed great patches of blue sky.
>
> And it stirred to life hundreds of gauzy-winged May flies … .

Blaine Hallock (1889–1953), lawyer, sportsman, writer. Blaine Hallock practiced law in Baker City, Oregon, but is now remembered as a person devoted to fly fishing and writing about it. As a member of the Baker County Rod and Gun Club, he was appointed as an early member of the state Fish and Game Commission, and then later as a member of the State Sanitary Authority.

They had been clinging to the shore grasses, but the lapping wavelets, the breeze and the sunshine, put them in the air. Already the water, well out from the shore, showed signs of life. It lumped and twisted, here and there, in a most surprising manner, and I knew what it meant. I knew the time had come.

Two number 10 blue Uprights went whisking out on the next favorable breeze, but they were caught by a cross gust, and doubled back, falling into the water twenty feet short. I would try again. Hauling in the line, in big swinging loops, I was on the point of retrieving the flies when a mighty tug—accompanied by a swirl of the surface—quite upset my plan.

Here I would pause.

I want to feel it all over again; I want you to feel it. That inexplicable thrill. That intense excitement—that quickening of the muscles; of the eye; of the senses. After hours of sickening disappointment—after so long and patient an effort— … when even hope seemed to be gone, this big fish, taking the fly almost at my feet, and the dozens of others rolling and leaping out there where the water flashed, told me that the crucial moment was at hand.

I could have waved my arms and yelled with sheer joy, but for the delicate business at hand. As it was, I struck firm and hard. The little bamboo curved to the work, and quivered, as the hook went home. A splash, a spurt and a lordly leap; a gleam of red and silver against the blue. I can see him now in the sun. I have seen him a hundred times since that epoch-making day on the prairie. And, as often, have I seen the many others which followed him out of the cold sparkling water onto the green prairie grass at my feet.

Your true fisherman is an optimist indeed. He is a splendid example of the time-honored proposition that there is greater pleasure in anticipation than in realization. He goes a-fishing with high hopes. He conjures up scenes of magnificent pools of great fish eager to take his lure. And he honestly thinks that some day, in some land, he will somehow find that really ideal angling.

So he plans another trip, and another, always confident that the next will work a full realization of his highest hopes. If he be a fisherman born, he is never disappointed—even when he has to admit that the fishing wasn't all he expected, because, behind it all, away back in his innermost being, there lurks still the hope, nay, the conviction that some day he will actually find the fishing of his dreams.

And so it was with me that day on Crane Prairie. I was realizing the fishing of my dreams. …

Others made their reputations beyond the parameters of their profession. One was **Samuel Lancaster**, the engineer who designed the original Columbia River Highway—which was renowned for the sensitive way it was integrated into the environment.

Quotes from comments Lancaster made in 1916:

I studied the landscape with much care and became acquainted with its formation and geology. I was profoundly impressed by its majestic beauty and marveled at the creative power of God, who made it all. … [I] want [visitors] to enjoy the highway, which men built as a frame to the beautiful picture which God created.

When I made the preliminary survey here and found myself standing waist deep in the ferns, I remembered my mother's long-ago warning: "Oh, Samuel, do be careful of my Boston fern."

And then I pledged myself that none of this wild beauty should be marred where it could be prevented. The highway was so built that not one tree was felled, not one fern was crushed, unnecessarily.

SAMUEL LANCASTER

Earlier he said, "If the road is completed according to plans, it will rival, if not surpass, anything to be found in the civilized world." He also said he was "engaged in preserving for all ages, some of the most beautiful spots in the world."

Today the National Park Service has designated the Columbia River Highway as a National Historic Landmark (2000); it is also National Historic Civil Engineering Landmark (1984). It has provided the basis for much of the National Park Service's design philosophy for park roads.

He was also entranced by Multnomah Falls, saying, "It is pleasing to look upon in every mood; ... it charms like magic; it woos like an ardent lover; it refreshes the soul; and invites loftier, purer things."

Speaking of Shepperd's Dell in the gorge, Lancaster observed:

> The tract of eleven acres ... given by George Shepperd for a public park, is unexcelled. God made this beauty spot and gave it a man with a great heart. Men of wealth and position have done big things for the Columbia River Highway [that] ... will live in history, but George Shepperd, a man of small means, did his part as well.

In 1915 (August 29), the *Oregonian* also praised Shepperd:

> One of the wonder spots on the Columbia Highway, in ... daintiness and sublimity combined with scenery, is Shepperd's Dell, which was donated to the highway as a public park by George

Shepperd—because he loved the spot and because he wanted it preserved forever for the enjoyment of people who come along the highway.

Mr. Shepperd is not a rich man and his donation is one of the most noteworthy in the history of the highway. At Shepperd's Dell is one of the finest bridges on the highway and a trail has been built leading down from the highway to the Dell and back to the beautiful little waterfall and springs in the gorge. The view back from the trail, looking through the arch made by the concrete span, is one of the most beautiful on the highway.

Samuel Lancaster (1864–1941), engineer. Lancaster was the engineer who designed the Columbia River Highway (built in 1915). He showed unusual sensitivity to the landscape and its plants and wove the highway into the environment there.

And even those who turned to radical politics and left Oregon at an early age never forgot the scenes of nature in the state that so impressed them in their youth. One such person was **Jack Reed**.

He wrote various poems about Oregon, including these:

America (1918)

By my free boyhood in the wide West
The powerful sweet river, fish wheels, log rafts
Ships from behind the sunset …
The blue thunderous Pacific, blaring sunsets,
Black smoking forests on surf-beaten headlands
Lost beaches, camp fires, [the] wail of hunting cougars …
Fishermen putting out from Astoria in the foggy dawn in
    their double-bowed boats …
Hunters coming out of the brush at night-fall on the brink of
    the Lewis and Clark Canyon …

Jack Reed (1887–1920), writer and radical. Raised in Portland by a well-to-do family, at the age of seventeen he was sent to boarding school in the East and then to Harvard. He turned himself into a writer, poet, and radical. He was buried in the Kremlin. But he never forgot Oregon.

> Forest rangers standing on a bald peak and sweeping the wilderness
>> for smoke …
> Lumbermen with spiked boots and [a] timber hook, riding the
>> broken jam in white water …

A few years earlier, he'd written another:

Twilight (1905)

> The wind has stirred the mighty pines
> That cling along Mt. Shasta's side,
> Has hurled the broad Pacific surf
> Against the rocks of Tillamook;
> And o'er the snowfields of Mt. Hood
> Has caught the bitter cold and roared.

In 1914, in the *Oregon Journal*, he wrote:

> Portlanders understand how differently beautiful is this part of the
> world—the white city against the deep evergreen of the hills, the
> snow mountains in the east, the ever-changing river and boat life,
> and the grays, blues and greens, the smoked dimmed sunsets, and
> pearly hazes of August, so characteristic of the Pacific Northwest.

Some became champions of nature notwithstanding their backgrounds. One such was **Ben W. Olcott**, who had started out as a gold miner and then became a bank officer and Republican state official. However, he first served in the state land office under Oswald West, eventually becoming governor. By the time he was done he had founded the state's movement to save natural beauty.

Message from Governor Ben Olcott to the legislature on timber, 1921:

Timber is one of our greatest resources and assets, and we should look ahead to its conservation … to the best of our ability. To denude our forests, without looking ahead to their replacement, would be a calamity to our commonwealth. (p. 21)

On fish and wildlife:

Our wildlife is the property of all the people of the state, and it is fair, equitable, and just that those who consume that life, in the name of sport, should bear a reasonable share of the burden in the cost of its propagation and preservation. (p. 36)

From his message on scenic beauty:

No other state in the Union has been blessed with so many natural glories as is the State of Oregon. Crowning all of these glories are our forest growths.

Without them, our mountains would be rocky, forbidding eminences; our streams would dwindle into rivulets; our lakes be shorn of the sylvan fringes which make them entrancing to the nature lover, and our valleys [would] be monotonous stretches.

This heritage has been too long neglected. So prodigal has nature been with us; so lavishly has she spread her feasts at our banquet table [that] we have been apt to feel that these glories would be never ending. We have become satisfied, and it has required the thousands from the outside to come and express their wonderment—before we actually have awakened to the fact that Oregon is blessed among the states.

The public realizes the importance of these things now, and is fully awake to the fact that, while have lost many things, there are many things we [want to] … cling to and preserve for all posterity. This legislative assembly may make itself remembered in the history of our state by prompt action to assist in the preservation of what should never be lost.

All of the things we have been striving for:

- the development of the tourist travel;
- the urge to make and keep our state the most livable in the Union;
- the desire to keep our children in God's own environment, surrounded by the beauties to which they are true heirs; all of these will be surrendered and lost, unless we act promptly.

… This matter should not be cast lightly aside. While the hand of man has done much … to make Oregon a great state, the hand of God fashioned here … the primeval wilderness—an ideal earthly paradise which we must preserve as nearly intact as possible (without impeding the ordinary progress of civilization).

To properly investigate the question now before us, last summer I named a committee … and this committee went into the matter intelligently and disinterestedly. One large company, the Crown Willamette Paper Company, immediately ceased cutting of timber along the Seaside-Cannon Beach Highway in Clatsop County, and I understand is marking time pending action of your honorable body.

That road probably accommodates more tourists than any other single road in the state during the summer season, and on that road is demonstrated very forcibly the difference between natural timber beauties and the naked stretches left after logging operations with modern machinery that [has] … denuded the hillsides. So marked is the difference, I venture to say no

Ben W. Olcott (1872–1952), gold miner, bank officer, public official (progressive Republican). Olcott was a protégé of Oswald West, who first hired him in the land office and then appointed him as secretary of state (filling a vacancy). Olcott was then elected as governor of Oregon twice. From his actions, it is clear that he absorbed some of West's concerns for nature.

person passes over the road but comments upon it. That is a single instance. Hundreds of others present themselves.

He thereupon recommended enactment of bills, which he had had drafted, that would make it unlawful to cut down trees along public roads without the permission of the state highway department, and for that department (which then administered state parks) to acquire forest land along those roads and to create parks along them.

Outcome: The legislature approved these bills.

Olcott is now regarded as the founder of the movement in Oregon to preserve natural scenery. He played a role in the formation of the state's Scenic Preservation Society.

Oswald West's influence was not limited to the time he was state land agent and governor. Not only did he make an indelible impact on Olcott, he also sent **Charles McNary** on his way as a public official, appointing him to the Oregon Supreme Court—from which he later went to the US Senate, becoming one of Oregon's longest serving senators. McNary was also known as a lover of trees.

In his work on the Clarke-McNary Act of 1924, Sen. Charles McNary chaired a select committee on reforestation, which, in 1923, found that of the original 800 million acres of virgin forestland in the US, only 183 million acres then remained—with 81 million acres in immediate need of reforestation.

He proclaimed:

> [The timber supply] has already become too small to support the present
> [level of] consumption, and the depletion is steadily continuing.

He wrote his brother saying:

> If there is one thing that the whole country is interested in, it is the protection of our forests, and I have an opportunity to do a grand piece of constructive work, and I am going to do it. I shall introduce a bill and put it through the Senate, and I think the Congress will know it as the McNary Reforestation Bill. It will provide the first great plan to protect and conserve forests.

Outcome: Under that law (which was passed), 18 million acres were reforested. He also took the lead in the passage of the Cooperative Sustained Yield Act (1944).

Whenever he could, McNary hurried to his home in Salem, Oregon—Fircone. His ranch there was covered with fir trees, and he knew the history of each of them. Whenever he lost one to weather conditions, he grieved for years over its loss. He constructed a spiral staircase up a giant fir tree to provide a lookout. He even planted slips of trees (from the botanical garden in the nation's capital) on his grounds at Fircone.

Extracts from a letter he wrote to a rural relative in the area of Salem on February 7, 1935, about his effort to help him set up a new wildlife refuge:

To Ben Claggett:

> Dear Ben:
>
> You don't know how much pleasure you gave me when you sent the four snow pictures of Fircone. …
>
> I am very anxious to get the blue print of Clear Lake [just over the California line]. I want to show it to our committee and Mr. Darling, the Chief of the Biological Survey. I talked the matter over

with several members of the Senate, and they think we have a real project.

I wonder if you are keeping in touch with our friend, [Ira] Gabrielson of the Biological Survey [then in charge of the Portland regional office]. I thought long before this he would be making use of your services. …

I shall write you again soon and hope that I may hear from you in connection with Clear Lake at an early date.

Very sincerely yours,
Chas

The Clear Lake National Wildlife Refuge now exists in the eastern Klamath Basin, just over the Oregon line near Tulelake, California. It has important colonies of white pelicans. During the 1930s, President Franklin Roosevelt vastly expanded the refuges in this region. He was undoubtedly encouraged by Senator Charles McNary.

Charles McNary (1874–1944), orchardist, lawyer, office holder (progressive Republican). Charles McNary was an early dean of the Willamette University law school, and then Oswald West appointed him to the Oregon Supreme Court. Later, McNary was appointed to a vacant US Senate seat—to which he was then reelected for many terms. He became a leader in the senate and prominent nationally. He was a leader of the progressive forces on the West Coast. But he was always known for his love of trees. He chaired the committee dealing with forestry and was the architect of laws for reforestation.

Some famous writers came to Oregon to fish. One of them was **Zane Grey**, who was an enthusiastic conservationist. He not only fished on the Umpqua and Rogue Rivers, but maintained a cabin on the Rogue.

Passages from a 1922 editorial in the *Izaak Walton League Monthly* entitled "Vanishing America":

I want to save something of vanishing America. For its own sake! So that our children's children will know what a fish looks like, and will hear the sweet call of a "Bob White" and see all the living and nesting inhabitants of our beautiful land. We must stand powerfully and unalterably for the future sons of America. Otherwise we will fall [short] of [seizing this] … opportunity. …

My one hope for the conservation of American forests and waters is to plant into every American father these queries. Do you want him to inherit something of the love of the outdoors that made our pioneers such great men? … Do you want him to be healthy? Do you want him, when he grows to manhood, to scorn his father and the nation for permitting the wanton destruction of our forests and the depletion of our waters?

In this materialistic day, it is almost impossible to get the ear of any man. With all men, it is the selfish zest of the battle of life. But men do love their sons, and, through them, perhaps can be reached before it is too late. The mighty and unquenchable spirit of a million fathers could accomplish much.

From *Tales of Freshwater Fishing* (1928):

But all the wilderness dwellers, hunters, and fishermen, and lovers of the forest, hate automobile roads, and know they are the one great cause, probably the greatest, of vanishing America.

In an interview in the *Oregonian* (July 28, 1935) on fishing in the North Umpqua River, referring to the North Umpqua River as "the finest trout stream on the Western continent," Zane Grey said:

[The] big problem is to give this stream … proper protection. … A mile above my camp is the natural spawning ground for the steelhead.

By all means, it should be closed permanently to fishing. … I have seen other splendid trout streams ruined for

Zane Grey (1872–1939), avid fisherman, author. Grey was a best-selling author of westerns, and actually spent much of his time angling. He grew up in the East, but made his long-time home in Southern California. However, he had cabins in various western locales, including one on the Rogue River, in Oregon, at Winkle Bar. One of his stories deals with conflict over fishing on the Rogue (i.e., *Rogue River Feud*). He was devoted to conservation.

all time because sportsmen did not demand proper protection, and history will repeat itself here on the Umpqua. Proper protection will make this steelhead stream the envy of the entire world.

Outcome: At the request of sportsmen from Roseburg, the state Fish and Game Commission thereafter closed that reach of the river, as Zane Grey had recommended.

Others observed Oregon wildlife, such as birds, wrote about them, and became deeply embedded in the Oregon Department of Fish and Wildlife. **William Finley** was such a person.

Extracts from an article by Finley and his wife, Irene, in the *Oregon Sportsman* in September 1925 entitled "The Destruction of Lower Klamath," referring to Lower Klamath Marsh:

Today Lower Klamath is but a memory. It is a great desert waste of dry peat and alkali. Over large stretches, fire has burned the peat to a depth of from one to three feet, leaving a layer of white, loose ashes into which one sinks above his knees.

One of the most unique features in North America is gone. It is a crime against our children. Their birthright has been sold "for a mess of pottage."

Among the birds that formerly lived on Lower Klamath Lake were both migratory game and insectivorous birds. A great variety of ducks, mallards, redheads, pintails, gadwalls, cinnamon teal and "ruddies" lived here. There were also large numbers of Canada geese, or "honkers."

This, therefore, was a great nursery for game birds. It was the home of bitterns, rails, avocets, stilts, phalaropes, snipe, killdeers and other waders. In the tules nested yellow-throated warblers, song sparrows, yellow-headed and red-winged blackbirds and tule wrens and others. On the wide stretches of the Lower Klamath were great colonies of California and ring-billed gulls, night herons, and great blue herons [and] Farralone cormorants, grebes, terns, and white pelicans. The marsh was white with the nesting multitudes. …

The tules, or club-rushes, had covered the waters of this lower alkaline lake as the firs cover the Oregon mountains. For miles and miles around [its edge] … and reaching far out toward the middle, the floating tule roots had spread out, and from time immemorial, each year had sent up a growth from eight to ten feet high. Dying down in the fall, the decayed vegetation of decades had formed a vast peat bed in the Lower Klamath to a depth of from six to eight feet in many places. On the floating tule islands of this vast marsh, the bird multitudes lived.

From about 1900 to 1917, events gradually focused toward building up and making what would perhaps have been the greatest wild fowl reservation on the Pacific Coast. In an early day, when market hunting was permitted, the records show that a vast amount of food was taken from the region of the Lower Klamath. One hundred and twenty tons of wild ducks were killed during the winter season of 1903 and 1904, and shipped into the San Francisco markets.

During the earlier years, when it was the style [for women] … to wear the plumes of wild birds, thousands of grebes, terns, herons, and other were killed annually and the plumage shipped to the wholesale milliners of San Francisco and New York. As the public came to recognize the value of wild birds … and as bird numbers were decreasing, state laws were passed to protect these natural resources for future generations.

When Theodore Roosevelt was President, he issued a special executive proclamation on August 8, 1908 (at the suggestion of the National Association of Audubon Societies) creating [the] Klamath Lake Reservation in order to protect the varied bird life on Lower Klamath Lake.

It happened that previously this lake had been set aside as a reclamation project. So it is important to note that this federal wild bird reservation was subject to the earlier order that placed it in the hands of the Reclamation Service.

Theodore Roosevelt was a great believer in reclamation, yet he also believed in saving the natural resources of America for the benefit of her people. His reasons for setting aside the Lower Klamath Lake as a bird reservation were:

First, because with the rapid settlement of the country and the drainage of marshes and lakes, vast nesting places of wild flocks were destroyed. Second, the wild birds belonged to the people as a whole. They are an economic necessity to the nation as insect destroyers. They are protected by state and federal laws. They cannot live without homes. Third, the Lower Klamath Lake was one of the greatest wild fowl nurseries in the United States. To preserve it is like preserving an outdoor museum which will prove of great educational value. …

Promoters are always ready to step in where experts fear to tread. Here is where the land exploiters stepped in. If they could get 85,000 acres at a cheap rate, they could surely sell off enough to make some money. These people organized the Klamath Drainage District, and

WILLIAM L. FINLEY

William L. Finley (1876–1953), birder, author, state wildlife official. Finley moved to Oregon as a youth in 1886 and began to collect birds' eggs and skins. Following college, he specialized in photographing birds in their habitats. He founded what is now the Portland Audubon Society, successfully lobbied the state legislature to make taking non-game birds a crime, and then published his first book (which was entitled *American Birds*). He was instrumental in persuading President Theodore Roosevelt to set aside Three Arch Rocks on the coast as a national wildlife refuge (the first in the West) and then the Klamath Marshes (the first large refuge). On and off, he served in a variety of roles for the Oregon Fish and Game Commission (he was appointed to it in 1911 by Gov. Oswald West) and its Department of Fish and Wildlife (e.g., its first game warden, its first state biologist).

the Reclamation Service of the Department of the Interior should answer the question as to why they turned over these vast resources of wild life to promoters. If the drying up of the Lower Klamath was needed from an agricultural standpoint, why did the Reclamation Service not handle it themselves, as they have handled the great irrigation project tributary to the Upper Klamath Lake?

Under the direction of the Reclamation Service, a dyke was built across the channel where the water flowed in and out of the Klamath River. In this dyke were gates that could be opened or closed. When the officers of the Klamath Drainage District took charge in 1917, the gates of that dyke were closed and the wide waters of the Lower Klamath [Lake] dried up by evaporation. …

… In exchange for thousands of game birds and insect-eating birds that might have been raised in this reservation, the public got nothing in return.

It will be conceded that the promoters have shown their faith in the new project by expending a considerable amount of money in trying to develop it. The question is, who is ultimately to pay the bill? …

In the destruction of the Lower Klamath Lake, the sportsmen of the country are deprived of great numbers of game birds that formerly nested and spread out to other sections. Even though state and federal laws protect these birds, a man may [even] be fined for killing one; yet promoters under the guise of making agricultural land can destroy untold thousands by doing away with their breeding grounds. …

In the annihilation of the great marsh of the Klamath country, the balance of nature has undoubtedly been overthrown to a considerable extent. … When our wild birds are driven out, the natural check upon insects is gone, and the farmer has to battle these pests alone. The value of bird life is perhaps greatest in checking a plague in its incipient stage.

The drying up of Lower Klamath Lake was a serious setback to wild life protection on the Pacific Coast—because it destroyed the ancestral home of myriads of wild fowl.

[My] investigation of the [the productivity] of the lake before … [it] was dried up, and the results since, show that the use of this 85,000 acres for agriculture was [just] not justified. …

Today, about half of these marshes have been restored and are protected in the Klamath National Wildlife Refuge. The struggle continues over water to support these marshes.

Some who wrote about unusual types of fishing were poets, as well as nature writers. One such person was **Ben Hur Lampman**, who wrote the following about those who sought smelt on the Sandy River:

The gulls are yonder, screaming, dipping, and whirling. And a breathless boy racing up from the stream … Launch and raft are heaped with silver ore. Men and women, burdened with dripping sacks, struggle and pant up the steep trail to the highway. A sprinkle of rain patters on the rock and river. They are thigh-deep in the cold water, they are balanced on perilous ledges, they are teetering cheerfully on wet gray rock. They are sharing the bounty of the sea. A splash. A welter of form and flailing arms, and up from the river rises one who has leaned too far. No matter. He has re-gained the driftwood, dripping but undiscouraged, to resume his fishing …[*]

Ben Hur Lampman (1886–1954), newspaper writer and editor, poet. After beginning at the *Gold Hill News*, he was soon hired by the *Oregonian*, where he was a reporter, nature writer, and later editorial writer. On his own time, he wrote books, articles, and poems. In 1951 he was named the poet laureate of Oregon.

---

[*]   Lampman, "Euchelon."

Many wrote about Oregon's forests and forestry. Few were as well-qualified to do this as **David T. Mason**, who had an urgent message. For most of his years in Oregon, he ran the most highly regarded firm of consulting foresters.

Below are extracts from a speech Mason made to the Oregon Bankers Association on June 12, 1928. This speech alienated many of his industry clients and was long remembered. It caused his income to drop by half.

On the depletion of forests and the need for sustained yield:

> It is … well to examine … the more important circumstances related to Oregon's forest situation. In the nation as a whole, we have approximately 1,800 billion [board] feet of softwood. Of this, about 400 billion [board] feet, or nearly one-third, is in Oregon.
>
> Each year in the United States, we are cutting and destroying approximately 43 billion [board] feet of softwood timber; at the same time, growth is restoring about 6 billion [board] feet of softwood timber; thus, our national timber budget fails to balance by about 37 billion [board] feet.
>
> If we continue as at present, with the timber budget so badly out of balance, we may expect to use up our timber in about 35 years. …

Finding "we cannot expect to increase greatly our net imports," he then said, "We shall have to grow on our own soil nearly all of the timber which in the future we may require. And unquestionably future requirements for softwood timber will be great."

> Today the total cut of softwood lumber in the United States is slightly more than about 30 billion [board] feet yearly, just as it was ten years ago; but during these ten years, the cut has been shifting from the eastern United States to the West at an average rate of 700 billion [board] feet yearly. Nearly all of this increased western

production has to come [from] … the Pacific Coast states. During these ten years, Oregon has doubled its production. …

The annual cut is poorly distributed with reference to forest capacity. In northwestern Washington, the cut is much heavier annually than the forest capacity. In southwestern Washington and northwestern Oregon [one operating district], the annual cut also exceeds the forest capacity, but not so greatly as in northwestern Washington. In southwestern Oregon, the annual cut is much below the forest capacity.

If we are to have a balanced timber budget in the United States, we must reduce somewhat present consumption of forest products; we must utilize more closely in the forests in which we cut; and especially we must secure reforestation on a vast scale. At present, both public and private forest owners are conducting some work along the lines of reforestation, but as yet the magnitude of this work is far below the requirements of the situation. …

The longer we cut without adequate forestry measures, the more serious and prolonged the timber shortage will be when it does reach us. …

The solution of this industrial prosperity problem lies mainly in restraining cut to something less than market … [demand]. We have already seen that in this country … we are drawing on our forests beyond their capacity … to supply continuously the present volume of products; this is indicated by the serious failure to balance the timber budget. …

To deal with these problems, he declared:

We shall need to practice what is called sustained yield. Sustained yield forest management is the business of managing land for the regulated production of tree crops; it is fully developed forestry.

Sustained yield forest management consists, for a given forest, in limiting the average annual cut to the continuous production capacity. …

We have seen that for Oregon of 40 to 100 years in the future, it is imperative that we [now] adopt … the business of growing crops of timber to replace what we cut.

Mason's ultimate solution for the over-cutting consisted of cooperative sustained yield units (authorized under the Sustained Yield Act of 1944). Mason and Sen. Charles McNary crafted this legislation.

These were sustained yield units comprised of a blending of private and public forest holdings in local sustained-yield working circles. They balanced the depletion of stands in private holdings with standing timber on federal forests.

However, this solution was never implemented on a widespread basis. Small operators resisted the idea, and some sportsmen feared that multiple-use constraints would be slighted. No one had much enthusiasm for them.

The basic policy of sustained yield was later established for the national forests by the Sustained Yield-Multiple Use Act of 1960. It did not involve these complicated blended units.

Landscape architect **John Charles Olmsted** (see page 47 for his profile) not only often came to the Northwest to design projects and consult on planning for city park systems, he also was called upon to make far-reaching recommendations for managing federal lands of outstanding character (see page 47 for his profile). A report prepared in 1930 for Senator Charles McNary on the best management of the Mt. Hood area using observations prepared by John Charles Olmsted and presented by McNary to the secretary of agriculture describes the significance of the scenery at Mt. Hood:

> Taken as a unit, the Mt. Hood region seems to present one of exceptional opportunities for developments of charm and beauty [in the midst] of mountain scenery. … [Its] inspirational appeal may be of enormous significance. The element of beauty may be developed [there] as is rarely possible.

> 1. First of all, Mt. Hood, as seen from a distance, is an outstandingly and notably beautiful feature of the landscape. It is greatly beloved and admired by those who live in the great region from which it can be seen. It is also greatly admired and enjoyed by strangers from every part of the world. …
> 2. The near views of Mt. Hood, particularly from about the timber line, and more especially from the northern, northeastern, and northwestern shoulders of the mountain, are very striking and beautiful—certainly quite unusual, if not altogether unique.
> 3. In general, considered as a topographic or geological feature, Mt. Hood expresses the element of magnitude … more than is the case with Mt. Shasta or Rainier.

> The more narrowly compressed or acute form of the mountain … [provides a] relatively strong expression of height and magnitude which comes out with unusual clearness by reason of the fact that the absence of bulk permits a closer approach and a more intimate view of the mountain as a whole.
> The spire or pinnacle aspect of Mt. Hood, varying as it does according to its sculpture, as seen in different views, reproduces [from] … the sheer faces of the mountain an exceptionally beautiful type of reflection … such [as] can rarely be seen in the more massive

mountains. … There is extraordinary charm in reflections from the sides of the mountains and in more intimate views from the timber-line on the north and west.

There are elements of beauty [here] scarcely excelled by any mountain in the world as seen from the valley of the Deschutes on clear or on faintly misty evenings. …

The whole mountain is approachable, accessible, and friendly in a way and to a degree differentiating it from comparable peaks in the Northwest.

[All of these qualities of Mt. Hood are] … characteristic and precious.

This study was precipitated by an application, in 1926, to construct a tramway to the top of Mt. Hood. This study recommended against it, as well as limiting the number of roads that could be built in the vicinity of Mt. Hood. Earlier studies had been inconclusive.

The tramway was never authorized, with the Forest Service Chief opposed to it. Probably the Forest Service took a more protective stand because Sen. George Chamberlain had introduced legislation in 1916 to make the area a national park, which would have removed the area from Forest Service management.

CHAPTER FIVE

Oregon in the Midst of the 20ᵗʰ Century

As the 1930s began, **Julius Meier** was elected as Oregon's governor, running as an Independent. He proved to be a dedicated supporter of conservation policies as they were understood at the time.

Passages from the first message of Governor Julius L. Meier to the legislature (1931):

> Our commercial fisheries constitute the state's third greatest industry, and our fish and game resources together with Oregon's scenic wealth, constitute one of the strongest attractions to visitors.
>
> These fish and game resources are the common property of the people, and their protection and propagation are of the utmost importance.
>
> This great heritage can only suffer if permitted to become [an object of] … the spoils of politics.

A careful, scientific field survey of our game life is needed, as we know so little of the habits of game birds, animals and fish.

With the building of mills, factories, manufacturing plants, and the growth of towns and cities along our waterways, a number of Oregon streams are facing ruin and others are threatened.

The wastes of industries, [combined with] the filth of municipal corporations, are dumped into public waters to such an extent that some streams are like open sewers, spreading disease to people and destroying fish-life.

It is a subject deserving of your serious consideration and appropriate remedial legislation. …

Unrivalled in mountain and forest scenery, picturesque rivers and angling streams, Oregon is destined to become one of the great playgrounds of America.

Much of this marvelous scenery is already accessible through the state's … highway system and more of it is being made so each year.

Since this scenic wealth constitutes one of the state's greatest assets, it is essential that we fully preserve and protect it. We should save [the] forests … [that remain] along our highways, protect our sea beaches, add to our roadside parks, and finally maintain our highways: free from commercial ugliness, and beautify them by planting trees and shrubbery. …

In conclusion, I want to make the observation that a state should be as great as its natural resources. Measured by this standard, Oregon should be one of the greatest and most prosperous states in the union—for Oregon has tremendous resources.

It is rich in agriculture, timber, minerals, fish, game, scenery, and water power. But with the exception of water

Julius L. Meier (1874-1937), lawyer, businessman, governor (progressive). He spent most of his career managing his family's Portland department store but ran for governor of Oregon when the leading Republican candidate for governor (a progressive) suddenly died and was replaced as that party's candidate by a conservative. Running as an independent, Meier was elected overwhelmingly but then chose not to run for reelection for reasons of his health.

He defended public beaches and state forests, and worked for the beautification of highways. He strongly supported conservation programs. In 1933 he appointed a group of engineers to do a study of the polluted condition of the Willamette River.

power, all these resources are exhaustible and must be protected and fostered.

H. L. Davis, the only Oregon author to win a Pulitzer Prize for one of his novels, featured a conservation theme at one point in his winning novel, *Honey in the Horn* (1935). He wrote about speculative land development in eastern Oregon, where he spent some of this youth.

> Outside [of the saloon] things were different. White survey-stakes were specked out fifty feet apart across the sunflower, … sagebrush and lupine, and at more economical intervals were neat, white posts flaunting such names as Pringle Avenue, … Railroad Street, and Orchard Boulevard.
>
> A billboard, which had been faced the wrong way to the wind (and was threatening to blow down), announced the development to be Pringleville: the Gateway to Eastern Oregon, Home Sites on Easy Terms, Industrial Locations Free. Parties interested were invited to lay their cases before the J. B. Pringle Real Estate Company, whose offices adjoined the hotel dining-room. …
>
> With little encouragement and no reason that anybody could see, he [i.e., Pringle] was spreading a new Pringleville around over enough country to accommodate a population of around thirty thousand people. Where they were to come from, or why, he hadn't bothered to figure out … .
>
> A patch of blue lobelia in a dried-up mudflat was only a temporary drapery which veiled a municipal auditorium; a big sweep of blue lupine and white everlasting strained back and forth, not with the wind, but with the exertion of holding down the subterranean

H. L. DAVIS

birth-pangs of a four-caisson grain elevator, and eight or nine warehouses for the packing and storage of fruit and vegetables—yet to be planted.

The lupine and everlasting lots were priced (in consideration of their commercial importance) at two hundred dollars for a fifty-foot front. Several were marked as sold. People in Portland and Seattle and such places, had bought them for investment … .

"It'll be built," Mr. Pringle averred, calmly. "I ain't a man to go off half-cocked on a deal the size of this one, and I got the word of somebody that ought to know something about it. There ain't no secret to it; the man that said so was nobody but old E. H. Harriman hisself. Or as good as. He stopped here and et dinner, and my wife heard him say [so] … .

One burden was that a railroad actually was being projected to hit the country somewhere, and that if he didn't cobble up some kind of town site on his holdings, somebody with more faith and enterprise was liable to start one close to him and draw a lot of settlers' money out of his lap. The other was that cobbling one ran into a lot of cash, and nobody knew for certain if he would ever get it back."*

Many of these projected towns in the sagebrush never materialized. Some quickly withered; Oregon has more ghost towns than anywhere else.

Others who spent years in eastern Oregon deserts wrote movingly about them. **E. R. Jackman** was one of those people, and his book *The Oregon Desert* has never been out of print.

---

* Davis, *Honey in the Horn*, 257–65.

Extract from *The Oregon Desert*:

> The desert in spring is something very special. Most beautiful things are short-lived. … So it is with spring in [this] … harsh and forbidding setting. The air is not yet filled with the summer dust; it is sweet, clean, and bracing; distant hills [seem to be] … magnificently close at hand … ; desert flowers tentatively offer [a] … gentle and beguiling paradise to passing insects; all of nature [there] is tasting life to the full. …
>
> Every living thing there will soon find its existence threatened, but for the time being, it is a joy to be alive … .
>
> … Out here, the world is more like it was at first. First things come first, such as thirst, hunger, and cold. Nature may be tough, but she is honest.
>
> … God made the desert. Man, as yet, hasn't made it. Meditation, the profoundest way to worship, is easier there, undisturbed by the many symbols of civilization.[*]

E. R. Jackman (1894–1967), extension agent for ranchers. Graduating from Oregon State in agronomy, he soon became an extension agent for the US Department of Agriculture, beginning in Wasco County, Oregon. He came to specialize in range crops. He won an award from the USDA for superior service. In retirement, he wrote four books. *The Oregon Desert* was his most popular one, which he wrote with Reuben Long (who had a ranch in Fort Rock Valley in Oregon).

One person who grew up in Oregon and became president was **Herbert Hoover.** In Oregon he learned the satisfactions of fishing and never forgot how much he enjoyed seeking trout in Oregon's prime rivers, such as the McKenzie.

His recollections of fishing in Oregon, as quoted by Senator Mark Hatfield:

> "Oregon lives in my mind for its gleaming wheat fields, its abundant fruit, its luxuriant forest vegetation, and the fish in its mountain streams. To step into its forests, with their tangle of berry bushes, their ferns, their masses of wild flowers, stirs up odors peculiar to

---

[*]   Jackman and Long, *Oregon Desert*, 10–11, 15

Herbert Hoover (1874-1964), mining engineer, businessman, public official. At the age of eleven, Herbert Hoover was brought to Newberg, Oregon, from Iowa (where he was born). He lived there with his uncle, Dr. John Minthorn. For a few years, he attended the Friends Pacific Academy there (during his high school years), which is related to what is now the George Fox University.

After graduating as a geologist from Stanford, he became an industrious mining engineer, working at sites around the world and becoming wealthy in the process. He wrote a textbook on mining engineering.

While he began as a progressive Bull Moose Republican, as his wealth accumulated, he became more conservative and skeptical of regulating business.

Oregon. Within these woods are never ending journeys of discovery, of the hunt for grouse and expeditions for trout."[*]

Hoover's last fishing trip to Oregon was probably in July of 1953 when he sought trout on the McKenzie River (see Donald J. Sterling, *Oregon Journal*, July 9, 1953).

During World War I, Hoover was put in charge of administering famine relief programs in Belgium and, following the war, in charge of administering the wider relief programs in Europe. As his efforts enjoyed success, his work was widely heralded. By 1920 even the Democrats tried to enlist him as their presidential candidate.

But Hoover felt more comfortable with the Republicans and became secretary of commerce under Coolidge. In 1928 he became the Republican presidential candidate and was elected. Unfortunately, it was during his term that the economy collapsed in the Great Depression. He tried various modest relief programs, but they made little difference, which led to his decisive defeat in 1932. However, during his presidency, three million acres of new national parklands were set aside, and over two million acres of new national forest lands.

Throughout his adult life, he always found solace in recreational fishing. He even wrote a book about this, entitled *Fishing for Fun: And to Wash Your Soul*. He also washed his soul through some of his work for conservation.

[*]   Hatfield, *Hoover*, xiii.

Some did a lot for conservation in Oregon, despite unassuming beginnings, such as **Samuel Boardman**, who started as a highway engineer in the state highway department. He capped off his career as director of the state parks department, where he turned into a champion for nature.

Extracts from various recorded remarks by him:

In the 1930s to his superior:

> We should [steadfastly] stand [for] the retention of the nativeness of our State Parks. Development should be held to the very minimum. There is nothing more beautiful in all the world than the verdure of our State Parks … . When man's hand at its best touches them, desecration takes place.

Speaking of acquisitions he made for the Silver Falls State Park in 1932:

> The Frank Chella property containing 120 acres, and adjoining the South Falls property, was one of the chief buys of 1932. The property, for which we paid $6,000, took in the Lower South Falls and takes in eighty acres of old growth fir, one of the only remaining stands in this section of the country.
>
> It is like walking into a cathedral: the firs towering 200 feet in the air. A hushed song is always noticeable in the tree tops. What a place for an open-air amphitheater in this setting of the sentinels. A spring on the hillside with storage will provide sufficient water for a spray-water curtain.

Speaking of the significance of the Silver Falls area:

> One thing should be noted that is outstanding (and I doubt that it can be duplicated in the United States): … you have fifteen water falls in an area of a mile and quarter by three miles and a quarter.

SAMUEL H. BOARDMAN

The composition of the park is mainly of water falls. The life of the park is dependent on water. [But] the state does not own the watershed upon which the park is dependent. This watershed must be protected if you would keep the scenic values of the waterfalls.

Also in the 1930s, regarding mistakes he made in developing the Talbot State Park:

It was fortunate this lesson came early in my park career, for it taught me that man's hand in the alteration of the Design of the Great Architect is egotistic, tragic, ignorant. I received caustic criticism for my disfigurement, but it was unnecessary. From then on, I became the protector of the blade of grass, the flower on the sward, the fern, the shrub, the tree, the forest.

Speaking of the planning in the 1930s for management of a new state park on Cape Lookout:

A primitive recreational domain [is] awaiting a directive for its preservation: … A plan for this preservation should be made and followed through all future development. There is little left today that may be called primitive.

Strange as it may seem, the more the world civilizes the primitive, the more barbaric we become. Here is still a haven of primitiveness that may be preserved in all its naturalness.

Comments made in the 1950s on the likely fate of the Cove Palisades:

While this "Grand Canyon of Oregon" is not a competitor in depth of the Grand Canyon of the Colorado, it is distinctive in its three rivers—the Crooked, the Deschutes and the Metolius. Twenty-two miles of white waters [are] within this canyon park. Waters so clear: the Deschutes, sky blue; the Crooked River, emerald green—[so clear] that the rainbow trout do not have to wear goggles to see through the silt to strike a fly.

There is a uniqueness in the sources of the three rivers; while the Crooked River watershed is in the foothills of the Ochocos, its main ... flow [which is constant] comes from Opal Springs, about four miles above the park, delivering one thousand second-feet of water. During the summer months above the spring, the river is [a] turbulent, rushing, white-water cascade of beauty. The Metolius River, which borders the park on the north, has its source in a spring at the base of Black Butte—a going river at its very inception.

[Within the park], the Deschutes River has several large springs feeding into it. The uniform flow of the Deschutes River is not excelled by any river in the United States of equal size; its yearly rise and fall being less than one foot. ...

A specter of uncertainty hangs over these park white-water rivers through the proposed construction of two power dams lower down on the river. The construction of the Round Butte storage dam would blanket the white waters with a coverlet of placid storage waters. The brown hackle would be exchanged for the night crawler. It would necessitate the Parks Division taking up all the picnic facilities and moving them to the new shoreline.

Samuel H. Boardman (1874-1953), highway engineer, director of state parks. Boardman spent most of his career as a staff person for the Oregon State Parks Department (which was then an appendage of the state highway department). He was its first superintendent and is celebrated as the father of the state parks system. Having come up through the ranks, he served for over thirty years. He vastly expanded the size of the system, adding over 60,000 acres—especially along the coast and the Columbia Gorge. He was skilled in persuading landowners to donate land for state parks. Along the shoreline in Curry County, Oregon, a scenic corridor is now named after him.

His was the loudest voice in resisting the construction of the Round Butte Dam and the Pelton Dam, though a few others did speak out.

While other public officials in the business of managing public lands were consumed with finding ways to exploit their resources, that was not true of all of them. **Thornton Munger**, a US Forest Service researcher, resisted cutting too quickly, failing to leave seed trees, and was instrumental in setting aside Research Natural Areas. He also got better protection for the Oregon Caves National Monument.

In an interview following retirement, Munger described his activities in the period when he was active: 1920 to 1950. The following was taken from the transcript of an oral interview in 1965 and '66 by Amelia R. Fry.

In a passage describing the early abusive practices common in the lumber industry, regarding the treatment of tracts of Douglas fir, Munger said:

There was a feeling that Douglas fir was just bound to come back regardless of what you did to the ground—in the way of [failing to] provide seed trees or [to dispose] … of slash. They thought it was a self-perpetuating type that would stand all kinds of abuse, which wasn't true. (p. 177)

Another passage from the 1930s described practices of industry in cutting Ponderosa pine when they were too young. In describing a study by Axel Brandstrom on the best age at which to cut Ponderosa pine (his maturity silviculture system), Munger observed:

[The Brandstrom study] marked notable progress in the more intelligent selection cutting of Ponderosa pine. … It was quite an eye opener to people to discover that many lumbermen were cutting trees … that would have brought them much more return if they had waited another twenty to thirty years before harvesting them. (p. 122)

The following passage describes his role in having Research Natural Areas set aside. He explained that he sent a letter to the Washington, DC, office of the Forest Service seeking approval to set aside the first one in the Pacific Northwest. He said:

> My letter got the approval of the Washington office for setting aside this area for that purpose.
>
> From that small beginning, we developed quite a series of Natural Areas typical of major [forest] types. Most of these areas are a thousand acres or so.
>
> While I was director of the [Pacific Northwest] Experiment Station (some years later), we had about 15 Natural Areas, and that isn't half enough—really for this region, but it assures preservation of some of the primeval forest in its natural condition.
>
> [In them] there are supposed to be no roads, no camping, and theoretically, no grazing of livestock. They are to be left, so far as possible, in their virgin condition. (p. 92)

With Research Natural Areas, the Forest Service can compare managed areas with untouched areas and find key genetic material when mistakes are made.

Some were hard to categorize but had a profound effect. **John Yeon** was such a person. Above all else, he was an early conservation activist. He was also a celebrated designer of homes and gardens, but had little formal training.

Early on he chaired the State Park Commission and then, during the 1930s, the federal commission on the Columbia Gorge. Later, he catalyzed the

JOHN YEON

process that culminated in the establishment of the Columbia Gorge National Scenic Area. Extracts from his report for the Columbia Gorge Committee, entitled *Report on the Problem of Conservation and Development of the Scenic and Recreational Resources of the Columbia Gorge in Washington and Oregon to the Pacific Northwest Planning Commission of the National Resources Board* (January 1937), follow.

On acquiring public holdings in the Columbia Gorge:

The lands they included embraced a variable territory for which many unexpected uses have subsequently developed. The most notable of these considerations is the modern recreational use of the forests and the value of these areas for purposes of scenic conservation—uses which were not given a statutory place among the basic provisions for national forest management. These uses have risen in importance beyond a secondary or incidental position, until for many areas they are now a major use. ... (p. 39)

Lands arguably set aside for timber production ... and grazing have in many instances become valued above all else for the great natural landscapes they embrace, and in perpetuation of these scenic resources lies their maximum public value. (p. 41)

This saw-tooth boundary [of public holdings then in the gorge] has no relation to geographic contours or natural features. It does not, for the most part, embrace the base areas of the high cliffs, from which their towering escarpments are most readily visible.

There is an obvious need for the expansion of the national

forest lands in the Gorge, both to protect the value of established holdings and to accomplish an important public service through a more effective conservation of this outstanding area. There is a need for readjustment of boundaries upon the basis of scientific land classification to correct the illogical pattern of ownership established largely by expediency at the beginning of the forest program. (p. 45)

Across the river on the Oregon side exist the highest mountains in the Gorge, as well as a waterfall area: second only in importance to the region in the vicinity of Multnomah Falls.

Through the consolidation of public ownership, on both sides of the river in this vicinity, the national aspect of a choice portion of the Gorge could be preserved perpetually. Private exploitation detrimental to public use would be prevented and the fullest value from established public resources would be realized.

The Gorge itself … [pays a] substantial dividend as an exhibit of surpassing natural scenery … as long as its wild and magnificent scenery survives. (p. 45)

On the Larch Mountain area:

The Larch Mountain basin is one of the oldest uncompleted conservation projects in the Northwest. The magnificence of the project is beyond the scope of state or county action. Every method by which national forest lands are acquired should be exercised to the end that the Larch Mountain basin becomes part of the surrounding Mt. Hood National Forest. … [If necessary] special departmental authority or legislative action should be sought to overcome existing obstacles. (p. 48)

John Yeon (1910–1994), designer of homes and groomed landscapes, conservation activist. As a young man, Yeon bought an endangered property south of Ecola State Park (viz., Chapman Point) and then got it added to that park. In the early 1930s, Gov. Julius Meier appointed him to chair the state park commission and later to chair Columbia Gorge Commission of the National Resources Board. He took a special interest in the welfare of Multnomah Falls, which Simon Benson bought and donated to the city of Portland in 1915. Yeon helped preserve scenic vistas of the Falls and at various key places in Oregon. He shaped early standards for Oregon highways. Over time, his design work drew national acclaim. In the 1980s, he took the lead in stimulating the organization of the Friends of the Columbia Gorge and in providing the beginning impetus that led to the establishment of the Columbia Gorge National Scenic Area.

In a letter to Sen. Mark Hatfield in mid-1980s (undated):

> I cannot possibly express my endless pleasure in the magnificence of the Gorge, nor my sense of its uniqueness. … Its serried crags and collection of waterfalls exist between rain forests and semi-deserts, combining a contrast of landscapes usually separated by great distances, if not by oceans.
>
> No other city has such a rare resource as close as a suburban park. And if it had, no other city would tolerate its imminent degradation.

In 1986 a Columbia Gorge National Scenic Area was established along 85 miles of the Gorge, totaling 292,000 acres. Over a third of it is given special management to protect its scenery. Subdivisions there have come to an end.

In the mid-1930s, the state Izaak Walton League campaigned to clean up the Willamette River. Their chief spokesman was **State Senator Byron G. Carney**, who also chaired the senate's committee on fish and fisheries. He was their spokesman on a series of radio broadcasts explaining the need for action.

Following are extracts from broadcasts he made in 1937 on the Izaak Walton League radio program to rally opinion for an initiative to clean up the Willamette River.

The Oregon Chapter of the Izaak Walton League and the Oregon Wildlife Federation were the most substantial groups in the Stream Purification League, which led the campaign. Gov. Charles Martin had vetoed the remedial legislation on this matter that the legislature had passed.

> Our own state planning board has made recommendations to the National Resources Committee, estimating amounts needed by

various cities for sewage disposal plants. The Planning Board has also made several reports dealing with sewage legislation and making recommendations as to what principles should be followed in legislation necessary for correction of pollution.

In Portland, the condition becomes very marked during low-water periods. In addition to the 45 sewers emptying directly into the Willamette, there are eleven sewers that empty into the Columbia Slough. Because of low water, there is practically no current in the slough during the summer and fall. The harmful and unsanitary condition of this slough was pointed out in a meeting of the North Portland Chamber of Commerce on October 28 by Mr. H. M. Seivert who called the Columbia Slough "an open sewer. There is practically no flow of water there," he said, "and unless something is done, the industrial plants on its banks are going to close or move out." …

In order to take steps to ameliorate this situation, a meeting of citizens of the state was called in May by the state treasurer, Mr. Holmes. As a result, the Oregon Stream Purification League was formed.

A subcommittee was appointed to consider the best method of proceeding, and it was decided that new legislation was needed. The committee followed, in general, the principles laid down in a report of the State Planning Board on stream purification legislation. A bill will be submitted to the people in the form of an initiative measure. …

All the friends of wild life conservation are asked to help by making their friends acquainted with the conditions of pollution that exist in many places.

Many people do not know that when industrial wastes or sewage from cities [are] … poured into a stream, the oxygen content of the water is destroyed in proportion to the amount of sewage. In low water, the condition becomes so aggravated in the Willamette that there is literally no usable oxygen left in the water in that part of the river below Ross Island Bridge for several miles. Fish cannot live without oxygen in the water any more than human beings can live without oxygen in the air. …

A few weeks ago, when the high tides came up the Columbia Slough during the low water and forced slow-moving sewage back up the river, thousands of crawfish came crawling out of the water and many perished from lack of oxygen. …

There is not much chance for fish life under conditions such as these. …

It is quite likely that some large chemical and other manufacturing plants will locate at Bonneville or along the lower Columbia. Some of them will undoubtedly have industrial wastes that will be detrimental to fish life if allowed to go into the Columbia. The way to prevent this is to see that plans are made to properly treat this waste before any concern is allowed to build. The proposed initiative measure (spoken of before) provides that all proposed new industrial plants shall submit their plans … [to the Sanitary Authority of the state for approval as to how they plan on] … taking care of industrial wastes and sewage approval before construction begins.

In addition, … the proposed initiative measure … sets forth that the general policy of the state of Oregon is to preserve the natural purity of all our streams, lakes, and watersheds, [and is to provide] for the setting up of a Sanitary Authority to take charge of stream purification.

Not only pollution but our other uses of water and our reckless deforestation are already having great effects upon the supply of fish. Many of our smaller streams which used to have a good run of water in the summer, and which were literally crowded with salmon going up as far as they could get to spawn, are now practically dry in the summer, and hardly a fish in them.

This is because the forest cover has gone, floods and silt from the erosion have destroyed their spawning grounds and the plants which furnish food for the animal life upon which fish live. In many places, dams have been put in and too much water diverted for irrigation. These uses of water must be further studied and means found [to reserve the water needed for fish] …

From another broadcast:

The pollution of our streams in Oregon is far more serious than some would have us believe. Along the coast, sewage and industrial waste is creating a serious condition in some of the tidal waters. In the Willamette River, the situation is the most serious of all because the large portion of the state's population lives in its watershed. The river carries the pollution of all the rivers and towns on the watershed, such as Eugene, Corvallis, Albany, Salem, Oregon City, and Portland.

The outlets of 48 sewers in Portland dump all the city's sewage into a front yard that could be used for boating, swimming, and other attractive recreational features. This [sewage from] … Portland—together with the valley cities—largely destroys this [possible use of] public property. The Portland Board of Health forbids people [from attempting] to swim in the river because of this menace to public health. …

That this menace to the health is real is evidence by the fact that Baker and La Grande installed sewage disposal plants because of a typhoid epidemic they experienced a few years ago. Ashland, Medford, and Grants Pass all installed modern systems of sewage disposal so as to guarantee a clean Rogue River. All other cities should follow before epidemics come and force them to act.

The effects of pollution upon the natural life of a stream

Byron G. Carney (1875–1971), state senator, water purification activist. In the 1930s he chaired the committee on fish and fisheries in the state senate.

are not always noticeable at first. The first indication a river [is being ruined] … is the exhaustion of oxygen. … [The] first effects are in the destruction of insect life: such as of the stoneflies, the caddis flies, and others, which are the food of game fish. Next, certain species of plants life in the water disappear. When mills, factories, and cities dump their wastes into the rivers, our game fish cannot live, not only because of the absence of oxygen (which they breathe from the water), but also from the lack of food, which has been destroyed by this pollution. …

Pollution is exceedingly destructive to fish life, and subversive to the use of our waters for recreational enjoyment; [it also is] … dangerous from a health standpoint. The streams in this state must be cleaned up, and cities, towns, factories and industries must be required to take care of their wastes.

A decade before, the City Club of Portland issued a report titled "Stream Pollution in Oregon" (1927), which raised similar alarms. Here are some extracts from it:

Every one should understand that the possible purification of drinking water by chlorination and filtering solves only one of the problems which arises from the use of rivers and streams into which domestic waste is discharged. Bathing in polluted water is hardly less dangerous than drinking it, and gross nuisances must always exist at points where large quantities of untreated sewage are discharged. …

The danger to public health from the use of streams or lakes as depositories for untreated sewage lies in the fact that typhoid fever is never contracted except as the result of allowing germs [in rivers] which come from the excreta of a previous case. …

Through the sewers, millions of the deadly organisms are poured into streams from which water is taken for domestic use, and in which hundreds of people may bathe. The danger of bathing in polluted streams requires special emphasis because it is not generally appreciated. [The higher rate of typhoid fever in Lane County in 1926 is ascribed by health officers there] … to infections received while swimming in the Mill Race. …

The presence of *Bacillus coli* in water is positive evidence of pollution, and all water containing these organisms is dangerous—a potential source of typhoid infection. …

The experience of Eugene shows clearly that swimming in water containing 10 *Bacillus coli* per cc is a dangerous sport.

Because of its larger size, Portland is by far the worst offender among the cities of the state in this matter of stream pollution. …

During the summer months and with a rising tide, there is little current, and with these conditions, sewage gathers at the outlets with results which must be left to the imagination. …

1. Seventeen cities outside of Portland are creating serious nuisances, and twenty-two are creating minor nuisances as a result of their present methods of sewage disposal.
2. Approximately 75,000 people, living in eleven different cities, draw their water from sources which are either seriously polluted or are likely to become so in the near future. …

Conclusions and Recommendations:

1. There is evidence that a number of cases of typhoid fever have been directly due to sewage pollution in the Willamette River, and this is a matter of vital interest to all parts of the state.
2. One of the most serious problems of stream pollution in Oregon is caused by Portland's use of the Willamette River as its main

trunk sewer. This use of the river has already seriously lessened its recreational values. The completion and use of the intercepting sewer along the west side waterfront threatens to create an intolerable nuisance at the point of discharge, which is in the very heart of the city.

The report then called for "reasonable legislation" to address these statewide problems.

As early as 1905, the state Board of Health began to issue warnings about the pollution in the Willamette River and repeated these warnings periodically. The state Fish and Game Commission joined in as well, saying in 1914 that "many of the most beautiful streams are being transformed in to public sewers." And in 1894 an official of that agency in speaking of the salmon said, "By … wastefulness and lack of intelligent provision for the future, the source of [Oregon's] wealth [in the salmon] is disappearing and is threatened with annihilation … ."[*]

In the 1920s an Anti-Stream Pollution Committee was formed, triggering a series of reports. One done by Oregon Agricultural College in 1929–1930 found the Willamette "to be polluted and grossly polluted in the lower reaches."

Outcome: In 1938, by a three-to-one margin, the voters of Oregon at last decided to do something about this pollution: establish the State Sanitary Authority. The initiative proposed by the Stream Purification League became law.

---

[*] "Report of the Fish and Game Protector," 1894.

William L. Finley (see page 76 for his profile) kept pushing for more attention to the needs of a wide variety of wildlife—from salmon, to water-fowl, to pronghorn antelope. In the mid-1930s, he was invited to make a presentation at the national level to the North American Wildlife Conference (February 3–7, 1936), at which he showed slides of his and spoke of the problems that such wildlife faced in Oregon.

On the impact of Bonneville Dam on salmon passage, he said:

> The question is why in the world, one industry—for the production of power—is allowed to destroy another industry [i.e., the fishing industry]? That shows the necessity for an organization to bring [about] a study of these things … .
>
> … [Fifty] million dollars are being spent in building this dam on the Columbia River at Bonneville. They are digging into the very heart of the earth to make the foundations. There are two channels: a south channel and a north channel. Fortunately, that dam is not to be more than 51 feet in high water, and about 71 feet in low water.
>
> We have had a great deal of difficulty in getting enough money to … have four different fish ways [installed]. We must have these gravity fish ways, or fish ladders, in order to permit these salmon to go on upstream to the headwaters, where they have a chance to spawn. [Their challenge] … is very simple: [as they swim into] one pool after another, [making] just a jump of two or three feet. Any salmon can leap that, and up to the next and the next. …
>
> Now listen: if you destroy this gift of nature … it seems to me [you will be making] a great mistake. … The Indians have tribal fishing rights at Celilo on the Columbia. When the salmon come in, … the Indians of eastern Oregon and Washington come to fish. …
>
> When Lewis and Clark came down this river, they sat here on [these] rocks [showing a photo of it] and ate salmon with the Indians.

And as you know, they fish today very much as they fished a long, long time ago. … Sometimes they use little dip nets. They have to literally catch the salmon on the fly, as they leap to get above the rapids. … The Indians fish here during certain seasons, and they use these fish almost entirely [by drying them] … for winter food supplies.

Here is the question: you might not think the salmon can find their way up over a great swift current and a lot of water … but they do. They fight, and finally get on up and go on to the headwaters.

It costs $50 million to put in the dam, and it will take 50 years to pay this back. At the same time, you [will be destroying] … this valuable gift of nature, which is not encumbered with debt [at all].

Note: Finley was one of the few people to raise questions about the wisdom of beginning the process of putting dams on the Columbia River. While the fish ladders were installed, it was not then known that small fish would have trouble finding their way downstream through the reservoirs and the dams.

Comments on the destruction of the Klamath Marshes:

You know [that in] … 1905, we considered [the] Lower Klamath Lake [to be] one of the greatest wildfowl refuges in the country—greatest because of the actual number of birds it produced all around the … [area]. …

This is what happened. The channel was dammed from the river to the lake, and the lake was dried up. …

And what have you got? You had a great reservation, with untold numbers of birds. Now you have, not agricultural land, but a lot of alkali soil—a desert. …

I was talking with "Ding" Darling [the director of the Biological Survey]. [From discussing this problem with him], I don't know whether the Lower Klamath will ever be restored. Maybe it will, and maybe it won't. That is what it looks like today—good for nothing.

Note: Currently, about half of the Klamath Marshes have been restored.

Speaking of the pronghorn antelope in the Hart Mountain area:

One difficulty is that antelope are crowded out by sheep or cattle. Domestic stock graze over this whole area, and naturally around the water holes. The antelope had to go back 12 miles, sometimes 15 miles, to get food.

I was very much surprised to see a bunch of 16 or 17 antelopes come into water, with perhaps only three or four fawns—a great reduction of fawns for some reason. It seemed to me that they were not protected as they should be around this area, because there has been no protection of the public domain from overgrazing by sheep. …

You have heard that the government has established the Hart Mountain Antelope Range. One serious mistake in this is that the antelope are limited to a [maximum] … of 4,000. There are [likely to be] … more than 4,000. Why should these be killed off?

Outcome: There are still less than half that number of antelope there, but the numbers of grazing sheep and cattle have been cut sharply, and the habitat has begun to heal. But it is still not clear for how long.

Charles Sprague (1887-1969), educator, editor, governor (progressive Republican). For most of his career, Sprague was an editor and publisher of newspapers in medium-sized towns in the Northwest. For many years, he was the owner and editor of the *Oregon Statesman* in Salem. As the most respected editor in Oregon, his editorials were often reprinted nationally. While most of his editorials dealt with civic matters, some of them dealt with conservation. He was a regular hiker who had a cabin on the North Fork of the Santiam. For instance, he supported preservation of the Mt. Jefferson Wilderness and the Wilderness Act. In 1938 he chose to run for governor of Oregon and got elected when the vote was split among competing Democrats. He served only one term, from 1939 to 1943. Under his leadership, Oregon became the first state to regulate forest practices: requiring that some mature trees be saved for seeding purposes (about 5 percent, but, as it turned out, not always the best) and that standing trees be protected from slash fires. He initiated a forestry research program and obtained authority to acquire abandoned, cut-over lands so that they could be planted again and stocked with timber.

Sometimes, the unexpected occurs. For instance, in 1938 **Charles Sprague** was elected governor of Oregon. He was a career newspaper editor, for most of his years as editor of the *Oregon Statesman*. A progressive Republican, he was elected when the Democratic vote was split. He was also a hiker who had a real concern with conservation, and periodically wrote about it.

Extracts from his inaugural message (1939) on forestry:

From the time when Rev. Jason Lee set up a sawmill at the mouth of North Mill Creek in what is now Salem, Oregon has been converting its great forests into lumber. This harvest has advanced so far that now there are vast areas of logged-off lands, which are virtually a desert.

Many of these tracts have reverted to counties for non-payment of taxes. Divisions of government face hard times as the timber wealth is removed, and the whole economy of the state is endangered unless the timber industry of the state is conserved and tree growth renewed for the future.

This subject is one of pressing importance and under general discussion among public officials, [among] persons interested in logging and lumbering, and [among] leaders in public life. Some progress toward a solution of the problem has been made, but much more needs to be done and needs to be done speedily.

… I am convinced that the wise handling of natural, forest lands calls for their consolidation under public ownership (except for those lands in the hands of strong private interests capable of carrying them through long-growing periods). The public forests should remain public, and only the timber crop sold as it matures.

… I contemplate the creation of a strong forestry department for reforestation of these lands, for proper protection against fire and pests, for orderly marketing of mature timber, and maintenance of forests on the basis of sustained yield. The state must be prepared to expend money for this purpose, but this expenditure is an investment in future prosperity.

New legislation is needed to enable the state to acquire lands from counties or private owners, or to enter into arrangements with counties for management of reverted lands. The state should qualify under the federal Fulmer Act, under which the federal government is [supposed] to supply funds for acquiring and reforesting lands.

On gold dredging:

The practice [of those] … dredging [for gold,] of sluicing away fertile topsoil and leaving in [its] wake … piles of gravel is a fit subject for legislative inquiry. The destruction of rich alluvial lands will be an enduring loss to the state (regardless of the compensation to the present landowner).

The assembly may very properly study [this] question and ascertain what regulation, if any, is practiced in other states or is needed here. I have no desire to cripple the mining industry, but the state must protect its interest in the land, which must support future generations.

CHARLES SPRAGUE

Note: This problem continues to this day.

In 1941 at the organizational meeting of Keep Oregon Green, referring to the "rich beauty of our state," Sprague said:

> We have the green floor of the valleys with dooryard flowers, shrubs, groves, and orchards. And rising on the hills and [on] the flanks of the mountains are the forests—our "evergreen" forests—which magnificently frame the beauty of lowland and valleys. How jealous we are of this natural beauty; how eager we must be to preserve it.

In 1961, as editor of the *Oregon Statesman*, he endorsed the federal wilderness bill and urged permanent protection for both the Three Sisters Wilderness and Mt. Jefferson area, saying they "ought not to be defiled by the accouterments of civilization."

Note: The Wilderness Act was passed in 1964, and both of these wilderness areas were established and are protected today.

One of those involved with wildlife wrote outdoor columns for newspapers such as the *Oregon Journal* and the *Oregonian*. **Tom McAllister** wrote from a base of expertise as trained biologist. But first and foremost, he was a birder.

McAllister began his birding around Portland in the 1930s. He remembers some of his early times out birding with David Marshall, who later become a noted professional with the Fish and Wildlife Service.

> The places that I particularly enjoyed … [were places at Mt. Tabor where] David showed me new birds like the Lazuli Bunting, … Mac-Gillivray's Warbler, and the Hutton's Vireo. … It was a particularly

great place … to see those beautiful Lazuli Buntings, especially on the southwest and west slopes [before the parks department made a clean sweep of everything in the shrub understory].

The other place that we had some of our highlight birding was from Kelly Point and back to the old stockyards and the dike (which the railroad put in to protect the rail line through there). … The whole peninsula [including Smith, Ramsey, and Bybee Lakes—all that country] was a completely wild natural area, and what was especially nice about it [was that] it flooded every spring. … It was an annual spring event, … [flooding] all the lowlands and then, as it receded, you had all the depressions that … [supported] natural aquatics—lots of bur-reed … and the Wapato. And there was no reed canary grass. There was no Himalayan blackberry.

It was all natural: sedges, ash and … the red osier, and willow, and then the big cottonwoods along the borders of the sloughs—that was where we got the last records of the Yellow-billed Cuckoo. … There were heron rookeries out there and lots of Wood Ducks nesting in the area, [and] the Western Painted Turtles. There'd be lines of them [out sunning themselves] … on the logs in the water; … the place was just a natural paradise. It was [just] as described in the journals of David Douglas and Dr. Townsend, who were the two naturalists that stayed at Fort Vancouver.

In retirement, he wrote a paper on the history of the Portland Audubon Society entitled *Our First 50 Years—1902–1952*. These are extracts from it:

In the beginning, Portland birders formed a John Burroughs Club in 1898 under the leadership of Reverend William Rogers Lord. …
Lord authored the first book of the "Birds of Oregon and

Tom McAllister (1926-), wildlife biologist, outdoor writer. McAllister was born in Portland and active as a birder in the 1930s. In 1953 he began writing an outdoor column for the *Oregon Journal* and wrote for it (and later the *Oregonian*) for forty years. Trained as a wildlife biologist, he began surveying streams and stocking streams with trout. In retirement, he has served as a naturalist/historian on Lindblad tours and has aided the Portland Audubon Society.

Washington" (1902) and was a lecturer of national prominence. He illustrated his programs with stereopticon slides of paintings by his artist friend Louis Agassiz Fuertes. ...

Astoria birders organized as the Oregon Audubon Society (OAS) in 1901, and in 1902 the John Burroughs Club of Portland merged with them under that name. ...

Over the years OAS reached out to establish other chapters, but changed its name to the Audubon Society of Portland in 1966 when [those other] ... members [i.e., clubs] voted to affiliate with the National Audubon Society. This was a good will gesture to recognize the independence of those other Audubon societies within Oregon. ...

Speaking of the society's most influential early members, William Finley and Herman Bohlman, he said:

[They] spent weeks, even months, on location once their camp and blind were established. They followed the development of Red-tailed Hawk, Golden Eagle, and Great Blue Heron nests from egg to fledgling. They spent a full four months by a cliff-side nest of a California condor. Finley and Bohlman were the key personalities of the early OAS. ...

They rowed a 14-foot dory through the breakers with all their gear and used block and tackle to raise their equipment onto the ledges of offshore sea stacks.

Foremost, among these wild settings that teamed ... with colonial nesting birds, were Three Arch Rocks, Lower Klamath Lake, and Malheur Lake. ....

Their derring-do ... captivated audiences and readers nationwide. Finley packed the lecture halls.

When [President] Roosevelt saw their work, he must have bellowed his "Bully! Bully!"—for he made all three Oregon sites federal refuges by executive order. Three Arch Rocks in 1907 became the first bird refuge in the West. Lower Klamath and Malheur Lakes were designated refuges in 1908, but that was only the beginning in the Society's long struggle to secure these refuges from drainage and water diversion. …

Because there were no federal or state regulations in 1902 that protected wildlife (other than game species), the first major OAS undertaking was passage of an Oregon model Bird Protection Act in the 1903 Oregon legislature. It was essentially [a measure] to protect non-game birds and to strike [at] the trade in bird feathers and plumes.

The eventual head of the US Biological Survey and the Fish and Wildlife Service spent career time in Oregon, where he wrote the *Birds of Oregon* and was instrumental in the establishment of the Hart Mountain Antelope Range. This was **Ira Gabrielson**, who subsequently became the first head of the Wildlife Management Institute.

In 1941 he wrote an influential textbook entitled *Wildlife Conservation*, which included the following characterization of conservation:

> The conservation battle cannot be a short, sharp engagement, but must be grim, tenacious warfare—the sort that makes single gains until renewed strength and good opportunity make another advance possible.

He wrote *Birds of Oregon* the year before. In an early chapter on the economic impact of birds, he wrote:

> The greatest value of birds as insect destroyers lies in the steady toll they exact when insects are present in normal or less than normal numbers. Such repressive effects may go far toward preventing the building up of great surpluses … . (p. 17)

Ira N. Gabrielson (1889–1977), teacher, wildlife biologist, conservationist. After being educated in biology in Iowa, Gabrielson went to work for the Biological Survey, beginning in rodent and predator control. From 1918 to 1930, he had responsibilities for this in Oregon and thereafter in various West Coast states. In 1935 he was made the director of the Survey, which in 1940 became the Fish and Wildlife Service (as the Bureau of Fisheries was then added to it). He continued to direct it until 1946. Thereafter, he became the head of the Wildlife Management Institute, where he was a national leader of the conservation movement. During his years in Oregon, he wrote the *Birds of Oregon* with Stanley Jewett (1940). He was also instrumental in having the Hart Mountain Antelope Range set aside.

Mt. Hood by Alfred Bierstadt (1909)
Provided courtesy of the Portland Art Museum

Mt. Hood by Thomas Hill (ca. 1870)
Provided courtesy of the Pittock Mansion

Mt. Hood from Fisher's Landing on the Columbia by Cleveland Rockwell (1891)
Provided courtesy of the Oregon Historical Society

Rooster Rock on the Columbia by Cleveland Rockwell (1891)
Provided courtesy of the Oregon Historical Society

Crater Lake by Marius Hubert-Robert 1932
Provided courtesy of the owner: Coburn Grabenhorst
Image photography courtesy of Mark Humpal Galleries

Klamath Lake with Pelicans and Mount McLaughlin by William Keith (ca. 1908)
Provided courtesy of the Hearst Art Gallery, St. Mary's College

Mt. Shasta Sunset by Dolores Manning (2002)
From the author's collection, photograph by Jim McMullen

CHAPTER SIX

Oregon in the Latter Part of the 20th Century

Stewart Holbrook was a curious figure. On one hand he celebrated the life of the logger and became the principal historian of the lumber industry. On the other hand, he was concerned about the industry's "cut and get out" tendencies. He was regarded as a "low-brow historian" who was not that happy with the way the industry behaved and became a spokesman for discouraging migration into Oregon.

In his book *Tall Timber* (1941), Holbrook tells the story of the migration of the lumber industry across the country to the Pacific Northwest. Here are some passages from that book expressing his concern with its "cut and get out" mentality:

> And, in 1845, Isaac Stephenson (soon to be one of the greatest timber kings) came from New Brunswick, by way of Maine, to start an

immense lumber business in northern Wisconsin and Michigan. They thought the timber in these states would last forever. But it actually lasted little more than fifty years. (p. 38)

The first migration was completed just before 1872. In that year, the State of Michigan cut more logs and made more lumber than did the states of Maine and Pennsylvania combined. (p. 43)

No one knew how many million [board] feet of lumber went out Wisconsin and Michigan woods … but the figure must … [have been] stupendous. It was all done in such a hurry, such a frenzy of speed, that no one seemed to have time to judge what was going on and what the result would be. The America of that age, sure its natural resources would last forever, was [just] interested in how fast a thing could be done. (p. 55)

But, by 1920, the South's old-growth timber was getting pretty thin, so it was high time for many of the restless lumber jacks to move again. One of the biggest migrations westward began in 1923, when the Long-Bell interests … bought timber near the Columbia River in far-off Washington, erected a bigger sawmill than man had ever seen before, and founded the city of Longview.

A bit later, other old-time Southern pine companies followed in Long-Bell's tracks. Some of them went to western Oregon, while one large firm acquired government timber in central Oregon and built a new city around its large mill. By 1930, the migration from the South had mainly been completed. (p. 95)

STEWART HOLBROOK

Stewart Holbrook (1893–1964), logger, writer, "low-brow" historian. While he had a limited education, Holbrook wrote with great facility. Prior to writing three dozen books, as well as for the *Oregonian* for over three decades, he began as a logger in the Northwest. Over the years, he became the principal historian of the lumber industry. At the time, he made himself into the best-known personality in the Northwest and into a real character. He was the first to advocate limiting the numbers of those who move to Oregon, founding something he called the James G. Blaine Society to further that end.

After a separation of some thirty years, the two divisions of lumber jacks, which had split when the industry was leaving the Lake states, were to meet again in the tallest, the biggest, and the thickest timber of all. (p. 97)

And near the end of his book *Holy Old Mackinaw* he wrote:

And now, though probably not one of them realized it, the loggers were in their last stronghold [the Northwest], their backs to the sea. There was no hump to go over from here. Civilization had caught up with them at last, and civilization would lay them lower than any stump they ever cut.

In writing *Tall Timber* in 1941, Holbrook looked hopefully to the future in the industry. He felt their best men would want to "mend [their] past [i.e., the rapacious record of stripping the land]."

They would talk no more about timber that would "last forever." Their talk [would turn] … to actual conservation measures.

Selective logging … [was coming] into practice—not on a large enough scale as yet, but indicative of a trend. Selective logging means that only the mature timber is cut and that in a manner to leave seed trees on every acre of land. The idea behind it is that timber is a crop … and that a new crop should be raised while mature timber is being cut. (p. 163)

Note: Holbrook's hopes were premature; little selective cutting was ever done; even the Forest Service lost interest by the end of the New Deal.

Holbrook also was gripped by fear that Oregon would be overrun by too many people coming to the state. In a 1962 article for *Look* magazine, he described his concerns, saying that he:

> Had been urging prospective migrants to God's country not to be in haste, but first to wander a couple of hundred miles south and to consider lovely California. In glowing terms, I have called their attention to the fact that in California, it never rains, seldom freezes, and all hands live gloriously in perpetual sunshine …
>
> For a long time, mine was a lonely avocation, unsuspected by chambers of commerce, and various Boost the Northwest groups and by the press. Even when my efforts came to be noised about, the very idea seemed so incredibly wicked as to warrant belief that I was either of unsound mind or a smart-aleck eccentric, who would bear watching.
>
> Gradually, however, over the years, I discovered that I was not alone. By word of mouth and by friendly letters now and then, other far-seeing and dedicated citizens of Oregon … let me know that they were on my side. Although we have never formally organized, I was wonderfully cheered to have company and, in a wild moment of enthusiasm, suggested that we call ourselves the James G. Blaine Association.
>
> This name for our group was adopted by acclamation. It has no connection whatsoever with the man who was once a senator from Maine. It merely struck me as having the right antique flavor to confuse a public into thinking us a crowd of old-time fuddy-duddies, still living in the past, devoted to some obscure cause, but harmless.
>
> Harmless? Harmless, that is, as a cobra. We believe that the Pacific Northwest is the Promised Land, and we mean to protect it from the steadily mounting danger of overcrowding by the hordes of Goths and Vandals who have been touring our blessed region in increasing numbers.

In our area ... there is almost everything from stark desolation to lush green jungles of nigh-tropical aspect. ... And there remain vast sections of wilderness where no people live, and where only the owl and the cry of the coyote break the immense hush of solitude. I can think of no overall conditions so comforting as our own, and if only the majority of my neighbors will awaken to the facts in time, we shall all be saved. ...

I had got the point of wondering whether I could make my neighbors realize that they must help stem the tide of tourists who had been infesting the area. ...

The 1960 [census] figures were a real shock [showing less growth than anticipated] to many of our chambers of commerce, but I contemplate their disappointment with understandable satisfaction. Our James G. Blaine Association, it would seem, has not labored in vain. ...

When once softened by doubt, the prospective settler is more likely to listen to other and more general reasons why that area, which unfriendly critics call "The Remote and Forgotten Land of the Northwest Corner," might not be for him.

We helpful members of the James G. Blaine Association know how to handle the Remote-and-Forgotten-Corner business. Instead of losing our temper, we admit graciously that we *are* somewhat remote and forgotten. For example, we point out, that the Pacific Northwest had to wait for many years for a branch railroad line from San Francisco, and it not have a direct road to Chicago until late in 1883. The more than a decade of waiting saddled us with a branch-line mentality. ...

In addition, so far as Oregon and Washington are concerned, I naturally bear down hard on the old, time-tested and reliable fact of everlasting RAIN. Here is something a dedicated protector of the Northwest can work with. ...

Let us hold fast to our first line of defense—that of RAIN. Let us brag about our remarkable climate. What, for example, is the popular and self-chosen nickname of Oregonians? Stranger, we proudly call ourselves "Webfeet."

Holbrook's cry was later picked up by Governor Tom McCall and others, but to little effect.

Other writers were connected to academia, but also wrote mainly about nature. **William Stafford**, a prolific poet, served as the poet laureate of Oregon for a long spell and even advised the Library of Congress.

Two of his poems:

Malheur Before Dawn[*]

An owl sound wandered along the road with me.
I didn't hear it—I breathed it into my ears.
Little ones at first, the stars retired, leaving
polished little circles on the sky for awhile.
Then the sun began to shout from below the horizon.
Throngs of birds campaigned, their music a tent of sound.
From across a pond, out of the mist,
one drake made a V and said its name.
Some vast animal of air began to rouse
from the reeds and lean outward.
Frogs discovered their national anthem again.
I didn't know a ditch could hold so much joy.
So magic a time it was that I was still both brave and afraid.
Some day like this might save the world.

---

[*] Stafford, "Malheur Before Dawn."

The Tillamook Burn[*]

These mountains have heard God;
they burned for weeks. He spoke
in a tongue of flame from sawmill trash
and you can read His word down to the rock.
In milky rivers the steelhead
butt upstream to spawn
and find a world with depth again,
starting from stillness and water across gray stone.
Inland along the canyons
all night weather smokes
past the deer and the widow makers—
trees too dead to fall again He speaks
Moving the criss-cross trees and the listening peaks.

Another writer and publisher contributed to conservation. He was **Robert W. Sawyer**, who for many years edited the *Bend Bulletin*. When he was a member of the State Highway Commission, he got Samuel Boardman elevated to be in charge of the state parks system. Many of his editorials campaigned for better protection of the state's forests.

From the article Sawyer wrote for *American Forests*, entitled "The Whole Story" (March 1953):

> For some months, federal ownership has been under attack by the Chamber of Commerce of the United States. [They are saying]: "federal bureaus now own 24% of all land in the United States. … [They] pay no state taxes. Private landowners do. This means that you pay

---

[*]   Stafford, "The Tillamook Burn."

not only your own share of state taxes, but you must pay more to make up for what the bureaus don't pay."

One who has read the rest of the article was left with the impression that this extensive federal ownership brings only burdens—no benefits—to the states and their citizens. …

[Their remarks] … [but thinly] conceal an attack on federal forest ownership—[viz.], the national forests. [The Chamber president] … raises the same cry, as does the Chamber article, about tax losses resulting from government ownership.

Let all the facts be put on the record, and of these the first and most important (as an answer to the Chamber attack) is that there are millions of acres in that 24 percent that no one would ever want, or be willing, to own or pay taxes on. There is no tax loss on these lands.

Another is that thousands, if not millions, of acres went into the hands of citizens and, after being raped of their timber, went back to the "federal empire" on the solicitation—not of a federal bureau—but [of] that of their private owners.

Many other thousands of acres [that] left government ownership, went first on the tax rolls, and then [became] tax delinquent. Now they are owned by the counties where they are a headache for the assessors and a sorrow to the conservationists. They ought to be returned to the federal domain.

A final fact is that though taxes are not paid on any of these

ROBERT W. SAWYER

federal lands, numerous financial benefits, in lieu of taxes (and otherwise), do come to the states where they lie. ...

[While federal lands fall in many categories,] ... by far the largest acreages are those in the national forests and in the (once) so-called unreserved public domain.

Mention has been made of the lands that have been turned back to the government and of those that went into private ownership and then [became] tax delinquent. The latter [includes] ... lands that were homesteaded.

The category just named, the unreserved public domain, is made up of the acres left over after the western homesteaders had had their pick. It is nontax paying because no one ever wanted to own it. [But they bring] ... benefits in highway construction, and here is the story.

Since 1921, there have been federal appropriations for state highways. The general rule is for the states and the federal government to share costs on a 50-50 basis. In the public land states, however, on a federal aid highway contract, the rule is varied in recognition of the federal acreage; and in Oregon, for example, the state's share is 37.5 percent [in comparison] to the federal 62.5 percent. ...

Of less importance, but yet [yielding] a return (because of the existence of the public domain) are the payments made to many counties under the provisions of the Taylor Grazing Act.

So much for the public domain income. Of greater importance are the returns to counties and states and property owners in general by reason of the existence of the national forests. ...

Federal law requires the payment to each state of 25

percent of the annual gross income of each national forest. The money must be used for the benefit of roads and schools. …

That 25 percent is in lieu of taxes.

In addition, the states benefit road-wise from the existence of the national forests for there are regular federal appropriations for forest highways. …

In Oregon, in addition there are two special situations in the field of forestry and government landownership. These are the Oregon and California re-vested lands and the Coos Bay Wagon Road lands. …

[Seventy-five percent of the timber sale receipts from them] … bring substantial annual receipts to the counties in which they lie. …

In the light of all these facts … it is difficult to find justification for the charge that federal landownership deprives the states of taxes. …

There is another fact to be added to the list already given. This relates to the national forests. As to them, let it not be assumed that they consist entirely of timber-bearing acres. [Some of them are non-commercial lands; nonetheless] … all acres bring a return in lieu of taxes to the counties in which they lie, and they bring to the state annually millions of dollars that have no recognition on the part of the Chamber of Commerce. …

National forest timberland is not sold. If it were, there would be an end to the uses and services that the public enjoys as a result of government management. Water supply protection would cease, recreation would suffer, consistent and long-term forest and range planning, study, and control and direction would stop, and in the end a great share of the nation's timber supply would be exhausted.

It is unlikely that the attack will succeed. Certainly it cannot do so on the strength of the arguments so far presented. If the proponents undertake to carry their case further, let them tell the whole story.

Note: More laws have since been enacted to keep public lands from being disposed of, but attacks on them continue.

Bernard DeVoto was a fierce defender of the West's public lands and deeply enmeshed in conservation politics. Having been born in Ogden, Utah, he wrote a series of books on the history of western exploration and settlement. He wrote a popular column in *Harper's Magazine*, in which he reported on events in Oregon.

Extracts from his column in *Harper's* in January of 1955, "The Easy Chair," regarding the politics of conservation in Oregon in 1954:

Bernard DeVoto (1897-1955), historian, author, columnist. DeVoto was born in the West (in Ogden, Utah) and taught briefly at the university level. He spent most of his adult life writing the history of the West and columns for magazines such as *Harper's* (for 20 years). Among the books he wrote was a popular version of the journals of Lewis and Clark. For his books, he won a Pulitzer Prize and a National Book Award. He was known for his fierce defense of public lands and of the importance of conservation.

Though Oregon elected a Democratic congressman as an advocate of public power, Congressman Ellsworth, who spends his time assisting attacks on public power, survived the campaign. Mr. Ellsworth, however, will occupy the same hot spot as [Interior] Secretary McKay who—with Senator Morse on one side of him and Mr. Neuberger on the other—now becomes the most uncomfortable member of the [Eisenhower] Administration.

A very tall pine, indeed, toppled when Senator Cordon was defeated. Mr. McKay—the giveaway emcee—is understood to have been his appointee and certainly has been his footman.

The progressive curtailment of the public power program has been carried on under his direction. In his quiet backstairs way, he has led or helped most other giveaways! And no one with his skill at the job is left in either house of Congress. …

The meaning of Mr. Neuberger's victory is incalculable, and it is national. Oregon has had enough of the principal architect of the Administration's resources policy. He has spent two years utilizing the golden opportunity, which the Republican victory of 1952 provided, to destroy our historic and once bipartisan policy of federal conservation. Mr. Neuberger stood squarely on that policy.

Note: Senator Richard Neuberger was probably the first senator to make his reputation as an advocate of conservation, but he died before the era began of popular enthusiasm for the broader goals of environmentalism. But in some of his writings, he foresaw the need to combat pollution.

Another mountain climber made his reputation writing and giving speeches about the quality of the scenery in Oregon and the Northwest. He was **Frank Branch Riley**, who was a well-known member of the Mazamas.

Extract from his *Ambassador of the Pacific Northwest* (1956):

From Part II, "Autumn":

The cottonwoods along the river were attired in pale gold, the ravines lined with vine maple were pools of crimson, and all these well-loved foothills were warm with color, and I overheard the bugles of the wild geese winging witchlike to the South … .

Close by are the … rapids and deep blue pools of singing mountain streams, refreshing all summer long with the chill of newly-melted snow. … We enter into the shadowy aisles and under the green canopies of ancient cathedral forests—sanctuaries of wild life, wild beauty, wild flowers and wild waters. …

We lie there, without even a shelter tent to shut out the mystery of the night, [and] under the low-hanging stars, breathe deep the healing incense of the cedar and the fir—and save our souls!

Richard L. Neuberger, who was elected to the US Senate from Oregon in 1954, was an established journalist who was the Northwest correspondent for the *New York Times.* In the senate, he championed such causes as establishing a national seashore at the Oregon Dunes and putting restrictions on billboards. His career there was brief (he died at an early age of cancer), but his enthusiasm for conservation foreshadowed the emergence of the environmental movement fifteen years later.

Extracts from *Our Natural Resources and Their Conservation* by Richard L. Neuberger (a public affairs pamphlet, No. 230, 1956):

Many elements united to make conservation a reality in the United States. The gifted naturalist, John Muir, had been trying to educate people to the protection of the Grand Canyon of the Colorado and of the Yosemite's plumed waterfalls before it was too late. E. H. Harriman, the railroad magnate, had given financial backing to some of Muir's ideas. Gifford Pinchot, a graduate of Yale, had become America's first professional forester. He was arguing that forestry could not be separated from soil erosion and flood control—because a permanent cover of trees was the most effective way to retard water coursing off the mountains. This seems commonplace today, but at the start of Pinchot's career, it was highly controversial.

Such men as Pinchot found their leader in Theodore Roosevelt, twenty-sixth President of the United States. The President was fascinated by the outdoors. He had hunted and tramped through the states of the West, and for a time had been a cattle rancher. He listened carefully when Pinchot told him that the continued survival of America's wildlife, forests, and rivers involved one central problem—conservation. …

President Roosevelt sponsored the White House [Conservation] Conference of 1907 which resulted in the establishment of departments of conservation within many state administrations. More important, the President put his prestige and popularity behind Pinchot's recommendations that most of the remaining forested uplands, belonging to the United States government, be reserved for all time. Under federal supervision, they then might be … [managed] for what Pinchot called "multiple use." He emphasized such uses as grazing of domestic cattle and sheep, selective … [logging], watershed control, preservation of wildlife, and wilderness recreation like fishing, camping, and hiking. If the forests were managed properly, they might provide all these benefits and still endure permanently. Logging operations, for example, would be patrolled by Forest Rangers. Only mature trees could be cut, and the total volume of … [timber] felled would have to be kept approximately in balance with the new growth. …

… Because they blanket a least a dozen times as much land as the national parks, the [national] forests undoubtedly are more significant to conservation generally. People in such busy western cities as Denver, Portland, and Seattle, for example, depend upon national forest watersheds for pure and ample drinking water … . In addition, the establishment of the national forests provoked one of the bitterest controversies of American political history. Many timber operators regarded these public reserves as a peril to employment and free enterprise. They wanted the western solitudes left wide open to the ax

Richard L. Neuberger (1912–1960), journalist, politician (liberal Democrat). Neuberger was an established journalist for nearly three decades before he became a well-recognized politician. Between 1936 and 1954, he served as the correspondent in the Northwest for the *New York Times*—building a national reputation in the process. He also wrote a number of books, beginning in 1933. After serving as an army officer in World War II, he then won seats in the Oregon legislature. In 1954 he pried a US Senate seat from the incumbent, who had focused on protecting the interests of the lumber industry. Building a reputation as an enthusiast of conservation, Neuberger supported the Wilderness Act, putting restrictions on billboards along federal freeways and trying to get legislation enacted to authorize a unit of the National Park System along the Oregon Dunes (a National Seashore). The impetus he provided for that proposal helped pave the way for the eventual designation of the dunes as a National Recreation Area (under the Forest Service). He did take the lead in rescuing virgin forests from the unfortunate termination of the Klamath Indian Reservation—turning these forests instead into holdings of the new Winema National Forest. However, he did not do much for anadromous salmon. Opinion had not yet turned against the dams that blocked the way of these fish. He died prematurely at the end of his first term, with his wife soon succeeding him.

and the saw. Western politicians were induced to denounce Theodore Roosevelt and Pinchot as reckless theorists, who were catering to birdwatchers, dreamers, and poets. …

Out of this beginning have come not only government efforts in the realm of conservation, but also many of the national citizens' organizations concerned with the problem. The Izaak Walton League, the National Wildlife Federation, the Wilderness Society, the Sierra Club, the Wildlife Management Institute, the Audubon Societies, the Roadside Councils—these are a few of the groups which try to mobilize Americans to prevent raids on the resources still remaining in public custody.

Practically everybody has followed some of the controversies in this field. Conservationists protested the plan of commercial lumber operators to open 225,000 acres of the famous "rain forests" in the Olympic National Park to logging. They fought off the proposal that a reservoir flood out some of the most picturesque gorges of the Dinosaur National Monument. They demanded that the Three Sisters Wilderness Area be kept to its present boundaries—and not be reduced for tree-cutting purposes. …

A number of these controversies have reached the floor of Congress and made spectacular headlines. In 1954, a bill was introduced to allow large lumber companies to exchange some of their land (under certain conditions) for choice acreage inside the national forests. Virtually all conservation organizations were against the bill, which was defeated in the House of Representatives (after a tense debate) by a vote of 226 to 161. That same year a bill to grant increased national forest grazing privileges to private stockmen was tabled in the House, after adoption by the Senate. In this instance, too, emphatic opposition by conservation groups was undoubtedly the decisive factor. They insisted that 18,000 ranchers did not deserve rights superior to those of millions of recreationists. …

Our national forests were set aside behind protective boundaries, before the ax and chain-saw could repeat in the West the bleak ruin of broken stumps that had been left in the once-proud forests of the Lake States. Yet the trees have been removed from enough American mountainsides to demonstrate the direct relationship between forests, and not only an adequate layer of topsoil, but also the existence of a stable water supply. …

In the United States today there are more than 22,000 sources of stream pollution, fouling our water supplies with sludge, offal, and chemical wastes. The nation needs at least 6,000 more municipal sewage plants … and 3,500 more plants to treat and eliminate industrial wastes. In the Willamette River in Oregon, I have seen baby salmon die from lack of oxygen in the water—suffocated by refuse from paper mills. …

But there may be no rivers to pollute unless we guard our trees. Flash floods, following by crippling drought, form the inevitable cycle when the ground-cover is gone. The U.S. Forest Service points out that "the paramount service of a very large part of our forest land is as a source of water, an erosion preventive, and a regulator of stream flows." …

RICHARD L. NEUBERGER

In most areas of production in the United States, total output has consistently expanded. Yet this is not true of lumber. The record year for American lumber production was 1906, at about the time when the national forests were being withdrawn from unrestricted entry and cutting. In 1906, lumber production totaled 46 billion board feet.

In 1954, although the population of the nation was 80 percent greater than in 1906, the total lumber cut amounted to 37 billion board feet. A whole lot of the old virgin growth had been felled, forever.

Trees, after all, are different from virtually any other natural resource. They are not merely important for lumber alone—far from it. They not only safeguard wildlife, anchor watersheds, and provide recreation. They are also part of the majesty and glory of America. Few other raw materials, important though they may be, quite fit this same category. …

Waterfowl refuges have been an important factor in the continued existence of Canadian geese, ducks, and teal—as the birds migrate in massed flights from the Arctic to the islands off South America. With marshlands drained or filled up, these travelers of the sky had no place to breed or nest.

The dwindling away of marshes and swamps forced the birds into smaller areas and onto exposed ponds, where they could be slaughtered by ruthless hunters who were out for record "bags." Without migratory bird refuges managed by the U.S. Fish and Wildlife Service, many important species of waterfowl might have been virtually exterminated. …

Americans, even those in crowded cities, feel deeply about "the wide open spaces." It gives assurance to a man in a New York City apartment house to know there is a Bryce National Park or an Eagle Cap Wilderness Area, although he himself may never visit these places of grandeur and beauty. …

Wilderness Areas represent a prized goal of conservationists everywhere in the land. They are genuine sanctuaries from the pressures and tensions of the 20th century society.

Commercial encroachment upon recreational areas is a continuing threat. Although visitors to the national parks spent approximately $240 million in those localities in 1954, some interests want the Olympic National Park opened up to lumbering, Yellowstone Park to water diversions, and Glacier Park to a reservoir.

When … [these] national park[s were] established, Congress ordered "the preservation from injury or spoliation, of all timber, mineral deposits, natural curiosities or wonders within … [them] and their retention in their natural condition … ."

Eternal vigilance is required to defend this rigid code. Yet, with 2.5 million future campers and skiers being added by the birth rate to our population every year, we must assure the next generation of some of the outdoor zest and thrills which we ourselves have enjoyed.

This, then, is the condition of some of the principal natural resources belonging to the American people. We possess far fewer of most of these resources than our forefathers found on this continent.

Yet we probably have sufficient to last us for many generations if we are prudent and can control our own greed and carelessness. We must remember that these resources are not ours alone. They also belong to the men, women, and children who will come after us.

Note: This was the first modern primer on the status of conservation in our society.

A more conventional Democrat was **Robert D. Holmes**, who was elected governor of Oregon in 1956 and served for a couple of years. But he also was part of a new turn toward conservation, even on hard issues.

Soon after being elected governor, he spoke out against the Pelton Dam in the following statement to the press (after speaking at the Izaak Walton League convention):

> I argued that too much harm—irreparable harm—would result to our great fisheries resource for the limited kilowatts involved. Pelton Dam was, and is, in my opinion, the wrong dam, in the wrong place, at the wrong time.

On conservation in general, Holmes said:

> We must think into the future. We can't work a piece of land just for this year's crop. We can't go on a binge and shoot every buck and doe in Oregon this fall, we can't put dams across every stream big enough to turn a generator. We dare not spend everything we have by right at this minute, even if spending would make us incredibly rich in money or incredibly happy just this year.[*]

Charles McKinley was a political science professor at Reed College who was regarded as an expert on the management of natural resources in the Pacific Northwest, often writing reports and books on the subject.

From a report he wrote in 1939 on the decline of lumber towns:

> We have still the chance to save many of the menaced [lumber]

---

[*]   Holmes, *Oregonian*, 4.

communities from wreckage—if we act in time. But time is of the essence. Nor will half-way measures, half-way financed, avail us.

Here is one of the greatest challenges to the people of our region: a challenge which the planning agencies have done much to make clear, a challenge which must be met soon. The last five years of work [have] … brought the problem out into the open as never before.

Signs multiply that people are generally awakening to the issue. When county officials … demand … to know what can be done to stabilize their communities by obtaining sustained yield management, it is most heartening.[*]

Passages from *Uncle Sam in the Pacific Northwest* (1952):

Good management of their forests is fundamental to the continued economic well-being of the people of the North-west. … It is also of great national moment because these forests constitute the largest reservoir of standing saw timber in the United States—amounting to nearly half of the remaining total.

The magnitude of this timber industry represents a terrific drain on the timber supply. The trend, punctuated by cyclical recessions, was steadily upward from a little less than four billion [board feet] in 1904 … to over 15 billion in 1926 and 1929. … The industry was hard hit by the end of construction in 1932, [and then reduced its] cut [to] only slightly above that of 1904, [and the cut] then began to climb again.

With the coming of the Second World War, the felling of trees resumed its tempo of the … twenties, and [the felling has] further

CHARLES McKINLEY

---

* McKinley, *Five Years of Planning*, 10–11.

Charles McKinley (1889–1970), political science professor. After receiving degrees from the Universities of Washington and Wisconsin, he taught political science at Reed College from 1918 to 1960. He also taught intermittently at various other universities: the University of Oregon, the University of Washington, and Portland State. In the 1930s, he was vice chairman of the Northwest Regional Planning Council. He wrote reports for Resources for the Future, as well as a number of books. At various times, he served as president of the American Political Science Association and the City Club of Portland. He was regarded as an expert on the overall view of the management of natural resources in the Pacific Northwest.

accelerated since the end of the war. The demand [then] blew the ceiling off man-power and prices. The mad scramble for stumpage, spurred by unprecedented war and postwar profits, produced much over-cutting in private timber management … .

In addition to the reduction of the timber supply by cutting, there are the losses from fire, insects, fungus, and other diseases—which brought the total drain from all sources in 1944 to an estimated 16.3 billion board feet. The significance of this to the perpetuation of the timber industries and their dependent communities is clear when that drain is compared with annual timber growth, now calculated at 5.5 billion [board feet].

Briefly put, the timber is being used and destroyed three-times as rapidly as it is being produced.

Even before the war boom, some of the most productive sub-areas in the region were facing the permanent stagnation of their timber economies, and [were facing] the repetition of difficulties akin to those which have cursed the cut-over regions of the Great Lakes states.

In 1937, the staff of the Pacific Northwest Regional Planning Commission compiled a list of 76 towns where severe loss of population had followed the abandonment of lumber mills. In western Washington and along the lower Columbia River, community after community had already seen its mills close or [had to] reduce their cut because the available good stumpage was exhausted.

When this last spasm of timber activity is over, … the dependent communities will face a wait of two generations or longer before the forests will be ready for a resumption of the kind of timber industries the communities have lived upon in the past.

In a recent summation of … the outlook for wood-using

industries in the Pacific Northwest, the Forest Service points out that the lumber industry … is greatly over-developed in relation to the available supply of logs.

Some timber towns will never revive.

We must face the fact … that no matter what may be done to spin out the utilization process, the elimination of waste alone (important as it is) will not prevent the ultimate reduction in the annual timber cut.

The Pacific Northwest and the nation may choose between two alternatives:

(1) high industrial activity merrily pursued for a few decades, then suddenly dropping to the stillness of dead communities falling one by one into decay; and

(2) a planned program of reduced annual harvest adjusted to a total perpetual yield from forests set aside for the economic support of specified timber-producing communities.

This is the stark reality.[*]

Note: Notwithstanding the fact that the Forest Service pursued a policy of applying the "even-flow" version of sustained yield, the timber industry appears to have chosen to pursue the first of McKinley's options, with most of the timber towns dying.

A guiding figure for many later conservation activists was the dean of men at

---

[*] McKinley, *Uncle Sam*, 38–44

Karl Onthank (1890–1967), university official, conservation activist. After graduating from the University of Oregon in 1913, in 1915 he earned a master's from the same university. He also completed graduate studies at Stanford and Columbia. After completing his master's in Oregon, he began a long train of service to that university as an administrator, in such roles as dean of men. Upon retiring in 1957, he won its Distinguished Service Award, with a statue being erected there to honor him.

He was recognized as a determined champion of conservation, serving as president of Friends of the Three Sisters Wilderness, the McKenzie River Guides Association, the committee to Save Waldo Lake, and the Federation of Western Outdoor Clubs. He chaired the conservation committee of the Obsidians and was active in the state Sierra Club. He also served on various public bodies, such as the state Water Resources Board. For many summers, he and his wife worked for the Forest Service at a guard station at Scott Lake, not far from McKenzie Pass.

the University of Oregon, **Karl Onthank**. From the 1930s and into the 1960s, he was an admired activist himself.

Here is an extract from a letter he wrote in 1966 to Stewart Brandborg (of the Wilderness Society) on the situation then at Waldo Lake:

The Waldo Lake Limited Area was originally adjacent to the Three Sisters Wilderness Area, and the portion around the lake itself is still one of the choicest portions of the de facto Three Sisters Wilderness (as described in the ORRRC [Outdoor Recreational Resources Review Commission] report). It should be preserved as an unmatched and unique natural scene—both scenically and biologically (not to mention its fascinating display of alternating volcanism and glaciation). For a time, it was scheduled by the Forest Service for Wild Area status; they even made maps showing it so.

But a change of Regional Foresters stopped that, and after a long and bitter controversy [of which the author, Michael McCloskey, was part], it was cut down to a mere recreation area … around the lake—of which the west shore of the lake is "planned" to be left more or less in its natural state …

It is the largest mountain lake in the Northwest—[and] resembles Tahoe more than any other. It is glacial in origin, 540 feet … [deep], crystal clear, has a drainage basin scarcely larger than the lake itself, and the whole scene is extremely fragile.

The Forest Service is now building a fast road to it, [and] expects … that there will be a thousand people or so a day [coming there] during the season. As soon as the road is finished next year, the place will soon be another Tahoe in terms of wear on the area [and] pollution of the lake … .

He said they would do what they could to head this off, but in any event it would be important to carefully measure and record its decline.

In May of 1963, the Senate Interior Committee held field hearings in Eugene on Senator Maurine Neuberger's bill to establish an Oregon Dunes National Seashore (as the Park Service had recommended).

Here is an extract from Onthank's testimony at that hearing:

> [I want to emphasize] that generally speaking the whole of the dunes area should be included [in the national seashore boundaries]; that is, not only the sandy shore and the more or less treeless and moving recent dunes, but also the *ancient* dunes, among which lie the dunes lakes—large and small. This is all one intimately interrelated and inter-dependent complex of sand, water, and associated plant and animal life.
>
> Access to the lakes is needed for boating and fishing but not *just* for that. The lakes are part of the dunes area just as much as the dunes that created them. Furthermore, they are an essential and out-standing part of the beauty of the scene.
>
> The designated boundaries should, in my opinion, be so drawn as to permit ultimately the acquisition, by *gift* or *voluntary* sale, of the area *around* the lakes—not necessarily all [of it] (but certainly enough) to include comprehensively a unified whole in the dedicated area.
>
> The [area of the] Oregon Dunes … together with their associated natural surroundings, should be protected and kept for the enjoy-ment, and for the study of the mysterious processes of nature—of our generation and all of the generations to come. Future generations will think the better of us if we do. After all, we are essentially trustees for the future—certainly not the final owners. …

A one-time colleague of Onthank on the University of Oregon faculty was **Wayne Morse**, who was a law professor and dean of the law school. In 1944

Wayne L. Morse (1900–1974), law professor, arbitrator, US Senator. Morse was raised in Wisconsin in the progressive tradition of Robert La Follette. Soon after earning his degrees, he came to Oregon to teach at the University of Oregon law school and, before long, became dean of it. In the late 1930s and in the 1940s, he became an indispensable government arbitrator of disputes along the Pacific Coast docks. Elected as a senator in 1944, he then served from 1945 to 1968. Defiantly independent, he adopted and shed various political labels: Republican, Independent, and Democrat. Morse did not think of himself as a conservationist, but he did support the Wilderness Act, resist shrinking of the Three Sisters Wilderness, and help save the Minam River Valley from roads and logging, as well as work for an end to logging in high-country forests. He also called for steps to stop nuclear testing. But he regularly promoted federal dams (blocking salmon runs) and massive timber sales in most national forests. He also blocked establishment of an Oregon Dunes National Seashore and complicated designating the Rogue River as a wild river.

Morse was elected as a US Senator and served in that capacity for four terms.

He was a defiant progressive, though nominally a Republican. By the end, he had become a Democrat. However, his positions on conservation reflected the tensions surrounding changing outlooks on logging and salmon. He rarely championed conservation the way Senator Neuberger did, but sometimes he went along with him.

Statement of Wayne Morse in the debate over the Forest Service's decision to shrink the size of the Three Sisters Wilderness:

> I would make the same fight for the preservation of a wilderness in any other state if the facts existed in support of its preservation, as they do exist in the case of the Three Sisters Area.[*]

Note: Once when the author was in Morse's office to discuss a wilderness designation, Morse showed him how he was responding to protests from mill workers opposing the designation—he summarily dumped a stack of their cards, with identical printed protests, into a waste can.

Statement on nuclear weapons testing:

> I agree that the United States, in the interests of peace and human survival, should take the lead in arranging an end

---

[*] 103 Cong. Rec. 1909 (1957).

to the H-bomb testing. … Hundreds of nuclear scientists, plus other national leaders, also agree. Increased radioactivity caused by H-bomb fallout could easily become disastrous to life on earth. It would be a great boost to our world prestige … if we proposed and obtained a worldwide ban on H-bomb testing.

One nationally important writer and conservation activist spent his last years in Eugene, Oregon, where he had relatives. He was **Irving Brant**, who advised President Franklin Roosevelt and Interior Secretary Harold Ickes. He told the author of his advice to Roosevelt on how to protect what became Olympic National Park.

During his time in Eugene, Brant visited scenes of contention in the Willamette National Forest, and in the early 1960s wrote Agriculture Secretary Orville Freeman on what he saw.

In due course, he characterized his letter in these terms:

> I was hardly surprised to find the Forest Service fighting against its own system of wilderness protection. The supervisor [David Gibney] of the Willamette National Forest … was addressing a public meeting, telling people that the pending wilderness bill (which became law in 1964) was a scheme to lock up timber resources and prepare the way for conversion of the entire wilderness system into national parks. The same forest supervisor, I reported, was working for a recreation plan that would open the beautiful Waldo Lake area to logging. Also, the Forest Service had in 1957 taken a large area out of the Three Sisters Wilderness and had begun bulldozing roads into the eliminated areas to frustrate any movement to restore their

Irving Brant (1885–1976), journalist, historian, biographer. Educated at the University of Iowa, Brant spent much of his career working for Midwestern newspapers as a reporter, editorial writer, and managing editor. But he often took time off to write books, the most important being a series on President James Madison. These are now recognized as the standard biographical resource on Madison.

He also had an intense interest in conservation and was part of the group that guided the influential Emergency Conservation Committee, and he wrote about conservation for *Forest and Stream*. During the 1930s, he was a key conservation advisor (behind the scenes) to Interior Secretary Harold Ickes and President Franklin D. Roosevelt. He wrote an account of Roosevelt's personal interest in the establishment of Olympic National Park, on which Brant advised him. This is embodied in *Adventures in Conservation With Franklin D. Roosevelt*, published in 1988, after Brant's death.

protection. I concluded with the hope that Freeman would tackle the difficult job of making national forests serve the national benefit.[*]

The most distinguished activist who pushed for cleaning up the Willamette River was **Dr. David B. Charlton**, a Portland chemist. In the 1950s he headed the tenacious efforts of the Oregon Izaak Walton League to curb polluting activities, particularly by pulp and paper plants.

At a hearing held in Portland in 1965 by the federal Department of Health, Education, and Welfare on pollution in the Lower Columbia River and its tributaries, on behalf of the Oregon Izaak Walton League, Dr. Charlton characterized the situation as follows:

The low dissolved oxygen condition [of the Willamette River] during the summer and early fall exists only in the Willamette River. It has been destructive to summer and fall runs of salmon and steelhead, at least since 1926. [Since then,] improvement has been slight.

Why does the [Willamette] River continue to be in a critically polluted condition? The answer is simply that steps taken to reduce the industrial waste-load have been inadequate. A recent report states that the untreated organic waste-load amounts to 6 million population equivalents, with over 90% [of it] being contributed by industrial activity.

It should be noted that there has been only one pollution abatement measure affecting the wastes of the pulp and paper industry on the Willamette River. This came about after much prodding by the [Oregon] Sanitary Authority. That was back in 1952, and it

Dr. David B. Charlton (1904–), chemist, water-pollution activist. Born in Vancouver, British Columbia, he earned degrees from the University of British Columbia and a PhD in chemistry from Iowa State University. He founded Charlton Laboratories in Portland, serving as director of research. That laboratory did consulting work on varied topics: water pollution, food chemistry, and sanitary bacteriology. He was most well-known for his role in the Izaak Walton League of Oregon in working to clean up pollution in the Willamette River. At one time, he was president of the state Izaak Walton League and served as one of the national vice presidents of the League.

---

[*]   Brant, *Administrative History*.

consisted of lagooning the strong sulfite digester liquors during the low water period, for [later] release during the high-water flows.

At last action is being taken by the Sanitary Authority that should result in a significant reduction of this huge industrial waste-load. The pulp mills on the Willamette River have received orders to achieve an overall reduction of not less than 85% in biochemical oxygen demand loading of the effluents from [each mill] … and [orders to] install primary treatment [equipment for] … the removal of settleable solids. …

Progress in the abatement of pollution in Oregon has been slow but significant. Recently orders have [also] been issued by the Authority [to] … cities on Willamette River [requiring them] to install secondary sewage treatment facilities.

Eventually, compliance with these orders was achieved. But the pulp mills avoided doing much from 1951 to 1965, and some of the cities also delayed in meeting their obligations.

Note: Charlton's dry recital of the facts fails to reveal how hard the Oregon Izaak Walton League had to work to obtain these improvements.

Marshall Dana was a respected editorial writer who often served in various public capacities. For many years, he wrote for the *Oregon Journal* with a strong interest in natural resource policy. His years chairing the Oregon Fish and Game Commission left a deep impact. In 1951 he was chosen as the "man of the year" in Oregon.

In 1962 he wrote the following proposed editorial about the Forest Service's new high mountain policy in the Pacific Northwest:

> Beyond the roofs of the mountains lies a far blue line under the warming sun of spring.
>
> There grow the tall trees only to be seen from Portland's heights as … [a] forest mass. There are the high rock cliffs, and down in canyon depths are streams that laugh because winter's bolts are loosened.
>
> Imagination raises a tent near an upland trail—although the … reality [underneath] consists of crowded buildings and traffic jams.
>
> So there is a rare charm in reading that "the high mountain area includes all of the Alpine Resource Association and all of the Landscape Management Areas of the Upper Forest Association."
>
> In other words, it is the announcement from the U.S. Forest Service that a new value in terms of recreation and pleasure is being given to more than four million acres in the Pacific Northwest (Region 6) that can be reached only by climbing, there to find meadows, rock slides, and placid mountain lakes.
>
> The high mountain areas thus described are outside the areas classified as primitive, wild, and wilderness. They are above close-growth forests. They're the birth places of rivers.
>
> There are trails that reach into the high mountain areas and … roads [reach there too]. And under the National Forests policy now … [being applied]: "specialized recreation facilities will be developed to give a greater number of people an opportunity to enjoy high mountain scenery and activities."
>
> To the development will be added "roads, trails, campgrounds, picnic areas, scenic vistas, winter recreation sites, mountain resorts and shelters." There will be protection of

Marshall N. Dana (1885–1966), writer, editor. Dana joined the staff of the *Oregon Journal* in 1908, advancing to the editorial staff and finally serving as editor in chief between 1938 and 1951. He had a particular interest in natural resource policy. Early on, he served on the committee of the Portland mayor to promote Edward Bennett's City Beautiful park plan of 1912 (modifying Olmsted's). He served as chair of the Oregon Fish and Game Commission in the early 1930s, later advised the National Park Service, and won a service award for conservation from the Interior Department. He was urged to run for governor of Oregon in 1948 but declined (he was a Democrat).

beauty and inspiration. "These facilities will be designed to retain scenic qualities, recognizing the needs for both concentrated family recreation and primitive-type recreation use."

Now this high mountain development will not violate the law which requires multiple use of the national forest. Sources of domestic and municipal water supply will be given "high priority." To meet downstream water needs, "structural measures such as dams or other devices will be permitted." But such structures must, with studied care, be "designed to blend with the natural setting."

Note: The Forest Service established the High Mountain Policy in 1962, but it is not clear how long it lasted. It applied to the high country along the Cascades in Oregon and Washington. One of the controversies the policy was designed to quell concerned proposals to log around Waldo Lake.

CHAPTER SEVEN

Oregon in the Environmental Era

An Oregon writer who enjoyed commercial success for a while was **Ken Kesey**, who grew up in Pleasant Hill. While not viewed as a conservationist, this point of view, nonetheless, is implicit in passages found in such popular works of his, such as his *Sometimes a Great Notion* (1964).

Most of this novel focuses on the rigors of logging in the coastal forests near the mouth of the Umpqua River. Near the end of the logging job, the crew depicted:

> Fell quiet, looking out across the hacked landscape. "Always puts me in mind of a graveyard," one logger observes. "You know, tombstones? Here lies so an' so, here lies Douglas Fir, Born the Year One, Chopped down the Year Nineteen Sixty-One." … "How's that? Turning forests into cemeteries? No, Seein' How Them Mighty Are Fallen." (1964, 457)

And later, the text includes this passage:

> The forest fought against the attack on its age-old domain with all the age-old weapons nature could muster: … the wind shook widow-makers [which came] crashing down … boulders reared silently from the ground … streams turned solid trails into creeping ruts of icy brown lava … . (1964, 497)

Richard Hill, a literature specialist at Concordia College discussed Kesey's comparison of pictures depicting nature.

> We look at the pictures of Sierra Club photographer Eliot Porter and those used in Weyerhaeuser Company advertising and contemplate the difference.
>
> Kesey writes: "Now since … [both are] pictures of the same thing, what really is the difference in the two pictures? … Eliot Porter [depicts scenes] in relation to the world [of nature] … whereas poor old Weyerhaeuser [sees itself] … in possession of the forest [it] … pictures."
>
> Kesey's ecological perceptions finally recognize both the strength and weakness of human beings, relying neither on exclusively subjective nor objective views of reality, nor exhibiting the possessiveness of a Weyerhauser, nor what Leo Marx calls the simple pastoral view of those who think nature is merely beneficent.
>
> He also demonstrates a better relationship with our natural environment, one which encompasses the needs of both civilization and nature.[*]

Ken Kesey (1935–2001), Oregon author, counter-culture figure. Kesey grew up in the Springfield, Oregon, area and graduated from the University of Oregon. He did some graduate studies in the creative writing program at Stanford University and then began writing novels. His first two novels garnered good critical receptions, with both being made into popular films. But then he got caught up in the counter-culture movement of the times. After that led to problems, he retired to the family farm at Pleasant Hill in Oregon.

---

[*] Hill, "Ken Kesey," 6–12.

ROBERT STRAUB

In the 1960s and '70s, Oregon had two governors who forthrightly embraced the environmental cause, though both were less willing to speak out on timber issues. **Robert Straub** was one of them, the other was Tom McCall. Unfortunately, they had to run against each other, and Straub's beliefs were not always accepted by the media as bona fide (the media often saw him just as another ambitious politician using the issue).

McCall won in their encounters, but afterwards, Straub became governor, being elected by one of the largest margins in decades. At the time, he was a long-serving state treasurer. As state treasurer, he championed the defense of a contested piece of Oregon coastland—Nestucca Spit. Following are Straub's remarks (as state treasurer) at a hearing on the coast on November 29, 1967, against building a major state highway along Nestucca Spit:

I think the people … all over Oregon have just as much interest, and just as much right and as much authority, to determine whether the magnificent beach resources of Oregon shall be used for highway construction, as do the businessmen who are located on the Oregon Coast.

I want to make emphatically clear my strong, determined opposition to the destruction of the priceless natural heritage we have in Oregon—our magnificent beaches—by building on them a high speed, interstate highway, such as Highway 101. I am opposed to building a highway on either the beach or a sand spit on the Oregon Coast—here or elsewhere on the Oregon Coast, when an alternative is available

It is unthinkable that we should even have to be debating … the issue of whether part of that beach resource should be destroyed by building a main highway on it. And, yet [with]… this proposed beach highway that's been outlined this morning, the right-of-way itself would consume 109 acres across beach and high-value recreation areas. At least an additional 100-foot strip on each side would be made useless for recreation. This makes a total loss of a minimum of 320 acres of the finest sections of beach and ocean view property that is left on the Oregon Coast today.

Supporters of this highway say the highway is an access road that is needed to serve the "recreation area." They even go so far as to say it is the only way to get access to this park. We all know … the facts, and that this is not true.

What kind of highway then are we talking about that's being considered for rerouting and building on our Oregon beach area? U.S. Highway 101 is an interstate highway designed to carry heavy commercial traffic. It is sure sometime in the future to become a four-lane highway … . It is hardly a mere access road.

Who can even deny that [sometime] in the future … this highway will be enlarged to a four-lane highway? Let's not kid ourselves. Once that asphalt is poured on the sand in the Pacific City area, nothing will be changed in the future except to make that asphalt wider and thicker.

Why don't we learn in Oregon? We should be planning for the future—the long-range future, not just for today and tomorrow. The … best hope for Oregon's future economic development and well-being lies in our ability today to clearly foresee, plan for, and protect long-range needs. Our beach resource is a limited resource. The demand for it, the need for it, the value of its beauty, is stronger every day.

What I would hope would be the precedent that should be [set here is that]… the beaches and coastal areas will be saved for

Robert W. Straub (1920-2002), businessman, politician (Democrat). After earning degrees at Dartmouth College, Straub moved to the Eugene, Oregon, area and built a career in business and politics. He established a construction firm and prospered with good investments. Following service on the Lane County Board of Commissioners, he was elected to the state senate and was then elected to two terms as state treasurer. After the frustration of losing twice to Tom McCall, Straub eventually succeeded in getting himself elected as governor of Oregon (1975-1979)—winning election to the office of governor by the largest margin in decades.

In various state offices, he led the campaign against a proposed state freeway along the Nestucca Spit, originated the idea of the Willamette Greenway, defended Oregon's land-use laws, and strengthened its energy laws. He was a staunch believer in wilderness but took a cautious position on many timber issues.

recreation, for scenic beauty, as places where the awe and the majesty of nature, the force and the reach of the ocean can be observed and contemplated—without the distraction and danger from vehicles zooming past, ... without the distraction and the fumes of log trucks or lumber trucks, [and] commercial trucks passing you as you try to absorb the peacefulness of the ocean—one every 45 seconds.

... [This is the policy that]... the vast majority of Oregonians hold and ... want followed. Every measure of public opinion that has been taken on this issue shows overwhelming support for a policy of keeping [this] highway off our beaches. ... Inexperienced volunteers, during a four-week period, easily obtained over 12,500 signatures on petitions opposing this highway being located on the beach. 12,500 signatures is a lot of signatures ... reproduced on a continuous sheet of paper. That paper rolls out for one quarter of a mile—that's a lot of people in Oregon who have expressed themselves in four weeks' time as being opposed to the destruction of our beach resource.

Gentlemen, you have no right to ignore this clear evidence of public opposition. Now ... the recreation and the conservation aspects [certainly] ... are valid and strong enough reasons ... to relocate this highway and keep it off the beach area.

[But]... from an economic ... point of view—if we're thinking long range (rather than just a [for] a quick dollar today), we'll recognize the importance of preserving this asset—the resource—that is the most valuable resource for future economic development that we have in Tillamook County and probably in all of Oregon. That's our beach resource.

In summary then, let me say that this beach route ... is not needed either as an access road or as a scenic drive. … Let's close the door in Oregon to building highways on beaches or through parks and choose, rather, one of the numerous alternate routes that are available—which will better serve the scenic needs, the access needs, and the future needs of the people of Oregon.

Outcome: Because of these protests, the road was not built on Nestucca Spit.

Tom McCall spoke like a New Englander (where he was taken as a youngster to visit with relatives), but he was born and raised in eastern Oregon. Trained as a journalist, he worked as a newsman and broadcaster, until he discovered environmental issues.

His coverage of those issues paved the way for him to become a state officer, first, secretary of state and then governor of Oregon. He ran as a nominal Republican, but he was quite independent and definitely a progressive. His speeches always reflected his way with words and his enthusiasm for environmental concerns.

By the time he was done, he was credited with being instrumental in the enactment of over one hundred environmental measures in the state and making it a "green" state.

Statements made by Tom McCall in a documentary he produced and narrated in 1962, *Pollution in Paradise*:

America was wild and clean and beautiful. But there is also a [bad] dream of a dying America where the waters are poisoned by the

TOM McCALL

wastes of man, and the breeze is strangled by the fires and fumes of civilization.

No part of America still retains more of nature's original works than the state of Oregon, a paradise for those who treasure the unspoiled in sight, in smell, in sound.

But who are these foul strangers in Oregon's paradise? …

Insecticides, that sometimes upset nature's balance, and the less well-known threat of chemical pesticides, are poisoning man's environment. Many man-made chemicals, acting in the same way as radiation, live in the soil and enter into living organisms, or travel in subterranean waters and emerge to plague vegetation and livestock and trigger strange human maladies. Insecticides, indiscriminately applied, are massacring birds, mammals, fishes, and indeed every form of wildlife. …

On some mornings, when the city should sparkle in the sun, guarded by the clean, silver cone of Mt. Hood, Portland is shrouded—as if by the murk of some filthy twilight in a shadow world. …

Motorists on Highway 99 often are assailed by billows of offensive smoke from the pulp plant of the Western Kraft Company. … The process here is another that puts unrecovered waste either in the water or in the air. This plant is a little of one and obviously a whole lot of the other. …

Speaking of the air, then of the town of Toledo:

The bad air in this long-suffering little town … [has been labeled by health officials as] "… a veritable time bomb." …

The pulp and paper industry [is] the largest contributor of organic wastes to the waters of Oregon. Where these wastes are not treated in a safe manner, the effluent becomes an oxygen-gulping, slime-making scourge. It destroys fish life, fouls fishing gear and fishing boats. Sometimes it churns at river's bottom, forming into rafts that rise to the surface in sluggish, foul-smelling masses of filth.

Test nettings in the Willamette show that only carp and other warm water trash fish can survive. And at times, even these scavengers perish for lack of oxygen. There is scarcely a season when fishermen's nets do not become weighted with the thick, foul slime created by bacterial action in wasted, bloated waters.

He then asked "why more hasn't been done [to combat this] by more people?"

He then concluded, "There can be no compromise with this invader. And it could be only the beginning. For how far pollution marches in Oregon is a matter in the final analysis of [how citizens respond] …"

Extracts from his 1970 remarks to the bottlers association:

The environmental crisis towers over us like a massive cresting wave. If we establish standards and hold to them, we [can] resist engulfment and save ourselves and business from inundation—by bottles and containers.

Just listen to a few incredible statistics:

The annual estimate of production by 1975 is: 5 billion soft drink containers. These 5 billion containers (10 oz. size) would cover all of downtown Portland—from the new Ramada Inn to Burnside, and from the Multnomah Athletic Club to the river, to a depth of 82 feet. And that depth is two-thirds the height of this building [the Benson Hotel], where we are gathered now. …

And may I remind you that in all these discussions, we seem to forget: what are we ultimately going to do with them? How do we dispose of them? ... The avalanche tumbles about us, ever-threatening, ever-swelling. ...

While the over-all thrust in this issue will have to be national, the national attack will start at the state level and move outward. ...

Oregon again is in a bellwether position. What happens to Oregon is going to set a precedent for the rest of the nation. We are the key state in what ... will be a domino reaction—and as the key domino, the way we move will set off a chain reaction.

It is a fitting and a traditional role for Oregon. We have exerted over a century of leadership with our long and continuing list of innovations in the area of public service. ...

Oregon has been a leader in pollution control and in all forms of environmental control legislation.

Back in 1950, I was secretary of a committee that drew up the first statewide air pollution law in the United States.

We have passed more environmental quality regulations in 30 months in Oregon than most states pass in 30 years.

We are setting the pace in nuclear plant controls, in billboard controls, in beach preservation (as public property), in fish and game laws of all kind (as for steelhead). ...

That is the kind of confrontation the one-way container faces in the state of Oregon:

- that is our climate of firm resolve in the protection of livability;
- that is the kind of determination Oregonians have shown time and time again; We are dogged in our dedication to the preservation of our environment!

The phrase "industrial growth" is anathema to hundreds and

thousands of Oregonians. In that phrase, they see acres of smoke-stacks, miles of felled trees, blackened skies, and dirtied waters. All of Oregon comes to the alert when the beauty of Oregon is threatened.

We measure success or progress in Oregon by quality, not quantity. The number of heads we count measures nothing: the income per capita does; the distribution of people and land do; the degree of health and beauty in Oregon living is a [proper] measure. We are not racing the calendar for the top headcount.

If we matched and competed with California for population quantity, and if we came anywhere near their rate of growth, in five short years Oregon would be a disaster area.

Of course, we seek new industry in Oregon, and new business, and new jobs. And we are growing: happily. But we want a control on what kind of business it is that comes in, and we exert definite controls over what business can do to Oregon's environment.

Our message is clear and direct when speaking to industrialists: "come, bring your business to Oregon." You will find superior employees, and a superlative livability. But come to Oregon only if you come to it on our terms—and that means restrictions on anything that might insult [its] environmental quality, the livability of Oregon. …

Against this new threat (and all others to the environment), we have a strengthening force: the awakening citizen, including the dedicated youth who are appalled at the menaces to our livability, and who are willing to spend time and energy … to defy [all these menaces] …

We have an exquisite jewel to protect, and we are devoted to that cause, no matter what the odds.

Please believe me, however, when I say that it is your faith in the jewel and desire to defend it (as much as my faith and desire) on which the fate of this issue rests.

I am confident that together we will find the wise way: find it through reason, goodwill, and [our] common love for nature. …

Extracts from 1973 legislative message:

Oregon is an inspiration. Whether you come to it or are born to it, you become entranced by our state's beauty, the opportunities she affords, and the independent spirit of her citizens.

Oregon is an inspiration even to those who [did] not come here to live. The story of the Willamette River (our ecological Easter) has evoked cries of—Hurrah!—across the nation and in distant parts of the world. And we have heard (along with applause for Oregon) lamentations for other states where progress has fallen prey to expediency.

Oregon's story is an inspiration to all Americans who believe they should be able to influence their government and the lawmaking process. The most intensive special interest pressure ever brought to bear on this legislature was by a lobbyist who declared that the bottle bill should not pass. But it did pass—because you and your constituents were inspired by a love for the traditions and beauty of our home.

You and I should not claim we love Oregon more than anyone else (but we do love this state as much as anyone). Our thoughts today, and in the deliberations to come, must spring from our determination to keep Oregon lovable and to make it more livable. …

Quality of life is the sum total of the fairness of our tax structure; the caliber of our homes; the cleanliness of our air and water; and the provision of affirmative assistance to those who cannot assist themselves. True quality is absent if we allow social suffering to abide in an otherwise pristine environment. …

We have written almost the last word for all America in protecting our beaches. …

We have established salmon runs where we knew of none before and assisted nature to increase her bounty elsewhere. Last month we saw in the Elk River of southern Oregon bright, heavy-bodied fish we sent to sea three years ago—now swamping the hatchery of their birth in [a] … monumental achievement.

These are reflections on the determination of Oregonians to win quality in their lives. It means that—after earning a living, we have living that is worthwhile.

But there is a shameless threat to our environment and to the whole quality of life—unfettered despoiling of the land. Sagebrush subdivisions, coastal "condomania," and the ravenous rampage of suburbia in the Willamette Valley: all threatening to mock Oregon's status as the environmental model for the nation.

We are dismayed that we have not stopped misuse of our land—our most valuable finite natural resource.

Umbrage at blatant disrespect for sound planning is not only [felt] at Salem. Less than a month ago, the Jefferson County commissioners appealed to me for a moratorium on subdivisions because the speculators had … [outrun the] local capacity for rational control.

We are in dire need of state land-use policy, new subdivision laws, and new standards for planning and zoning by cities and counties. The interests of Oregon for today, and in the future, must be protected from grasping wastrels of the land. We must [also] respect another truism: that unlimited and unregulated growth leads inexorably to a lowered quality of life.

Thomas L. McCall (1913–1983), newsman, politician (progressive Republican). Raised on a ranch in eastern Oregon, Tom McCall graduated from the University of Oregon with a degree in journalism. He worked both as a reporter and a television newscaster. However, he spent time as a youth in Massachusetts, acquiring a pronounced New England accent that made him an odd fit to be an Oregon newscaster; he spent time in Massachusetts because his grandfather had been governor there. His interest in environmental problems emerged in a dramatic television series he did on pollution in Oregon waterways.

In the mid-1960s, McCall was elected as secretary of state, which was soon followed by two terms as governor of Oregon—from 1967 to 1975. He became a crusader for environmental causes (except on timber issues). He worked to cleanup Oregon rivers, to protect its beaches, to enact a pioneering deposit bill on bottles, and to establish the first statewide land-use bill. He was also noted for making provocative, and newsworthy, statements.

Speaking of the implications for health of runaway subdivisions and of the findings of his health agency that arrangements for handling sewage were not adequate for one-fourth of them, he proclaimed that this constitutes "a serious public health problem."

"Irreversible environmental damage is being done," he concluded.

On a number of occasions, he spoke of industry that should not come to Oregon:

> Oregon has not been an over-eager lap dog to the economic master. Oregon has been wary of smokestacks and suspicious of rattle and bang.
>
> Oregon has not camped, cup in hand, at anyone's affluent doorstep. Oregon has wanted industry only when that industry was willing to want what Oregon is.[*]

Note: Today McCall is remembered as the governor who led Oregon into the environmental era. In the mid-1970s, he traveled the country telling what he called "the Oregon Story" (i.e., the story of Oregon's environmental achievements under him).

Other Oregonians did important things to protect Oregon's natural resources, such as **Judge Alfred T. Goodwin**. When he was on the supreme court of Oregon (1960 1969), he wrote the definitive decision that settled the question of the public's right to cross the dry sands on the coast to reach the ocean. Thereafter, there was no question about the public's right to reach the beaches.

---

[*]   McCall, *Pacific Northwest*, 322.

Extracts from Goodwin's decision in the definitive Oregon beach case:

The only issue in this case … is the power of the state to limit the record owner's use and enjoyment of the dry-sand area (by whatever boundaries the area may be described).

The trial court found that the public had acquired, over the years, an easement for recreational purposes to go upon and enjoy the dry-sand area, and that this easement was appurtenant to the wet-sand portion of the beach, which is admittedly owned by the state as a "state recreation area."

Because we hold that the trial court correctly found in favor of the state on the rights of the public in the dry-sand area, it follows that the state has an equitable right to protect the public in the enjoyment of those rights by causing the removal of fences and other obstacles.

In order to explain our reasons for affirming the trial court's decree, it is necessary to set out in some detail the facts which lead to our conclusion.

The dry-sand area in Oregon has been enjoyed by the general public as a recreational adjunct of the wet-sand, or foreshore area, since the beginning of the state's political history. The first European settlers on these shores found the aboriginal inhabitants using the foreshore for clam-digging and the dry sand area for their cooking fires. The first newcomers continued these customs after statehood.

Thus, from the time of the earliest settlement to the present day, the general public has used the dry-sand area for picnics, gathering wood, building warming fires, and generally as a headquarters from which to supervise children or to range out over the foreshore as the tides advance and recede. In the Cannon Beach vicinity, state and local officers have policed the dry sand, and municipal sanitary crews have attempted to keep the area reasonably free from man-made litter.

Perhaps one explanation for the evolution of the custom of the public to use the dry-sand area for recreational purposes is that the area could not be used conveniently by its owners for any other purpose. The dry-sand area is unstable in its seaward boundaries, unsafe during winter storms, and for the most part unfit for the construction of permanent structures.

While the vegetation line remains relatively fixed, the western edge of the dry-sand area is subject to dramatic moves eastward or westward in response to erosion and accretion. For example, evidence in the trial below indicated that, between April 1966 and August 1967, the seaward edge of the dry-sand area involved in the litigation moved westward 180 feet. At other points along the shore, the evidence showed, the seaward edge of the dry-sand area could move an equal distance to the east in a similar period of time. …

Recently, however, the scarcity of ocean-front building sites has attracted substantial private investments in resort facilities. Resort owners, like these defendants, now desire to reserve for their paying clients the recreational advantages that accrue to the dry-sand portions of their deeded property. Consequently, in 1967, public debate and political activity resulted in legislative attempts to resolve conflicts between public and private interests in the dry-sand area. …[*]

Judge Goodwin then describes ORS 390.610, which declared state sovereignty over the seashore and beaches in Oregon and confirmed easements established by the public in using them.

The state concedes that such legislation cannot divest a person of his

---

[*] State Ex Rel. Thornton v. Hay, 462 P.2d 671 (1969).

rights in land … and that the defendant's record title, which includes the dry-sand area, extends seaward to the ordinary or mean high-tide line. …

In Oregon, as in most common-law jurisdictions, an easement can be created in favor of one person, in the land of another, by uninterrupted use and enjoyment of the land in a particular manner for the statutory period—so long as the use is open, adverse, under claim of right, but without authority of law or consent of the owner. …

In Oregon, the prescriptive period in ten years. … The public use of the disputed land in the case at bar is admitted to be continuous for more than sixty years. There is no suggestion in the record that anyone's permission was sought or given; rather, the public used the land under claim of right.

Therefore, if the public can acquire an easement by prescription, the requirements for such an acquisition here have been met in connection with the specific tract of land involved in this case. …

Because many elements of prescription are present in this case, the state has relied upon that doctrine in support of the decree below. We believe, however, that there is a better legal basis for affirming the decree.

The most cogent basis for the decision in this case is the English doctrine of custom. Strictly construed, prescription applies only to the specific tract of land before the court, and doubtful prescription cases could fill the courts for years with tract-by-tract litigation.

An established custom, on the other hand, can be proven with reference to a larger region. Ocean-front lands from the northern to the southern border of the state ought to be treated uniformly.

The other reason which commends the doctrine of custom over that of prescription, as the principal basis for the decision in this case, is the unique nature of the lands in question. This case deals solely with the dry-sand area along the Pacific shore, and this land has been used by the public as public recreation land according to unbroken custom running back in time as long as the land has been inhabited. ...

Sir William Blackstone set out the requisites of a particular custom. Paraphrasing Blackstone, the first requirement of a custom, to be recognized as law, is that it must be ancient. It must have been used so long "that the memory of man runneth not to the contrary." [Cooley notes in his edition of Blackstone that] "... long and general" usage is sufficient.

In any event, the record in the case at bar satisfies the requirement of antiquity. So long as there has been an institutionalized system of land tenure in Oregon, the public has freely exercised the right to use the dry-sand area up and down the Oregon coast for the recreational purposes noted earlier in this opinion.

The second requirement is that the right be exercised without interruption. A customary right need not be exercised continuously, but it must be exercised without an interruption caused by anyone possessing [and asserting] a paramount right. In the case at bar, there was evidence that the public's use and enjoyment of the dry-sand area had never been interrupted by private landowners.

Blackstone's third requirement, that the customary use be peaceable and free from dispute, is satisfied by the evidence which related to the second requirement.

The fourth requirement, that of reasonableness, is satisfied by the evidence that the public has always made use of the land in a manner appropriate to the land and to the usages of the community. There is evidence in the record that when inappropriate uses have been detected, municipal police officers have intervened to preserve order.

The fifth requirement, certainly, is satisfied by the visible boundaries of the dry-sand area and by the character of the land, which limits the use thereof to the recreational uses connected with the foreshore.

The sixth requirement is that a custom must be obligatory; that is, in the case at bar, not left to the option of each landowner whether or not he will recognize the public's right to go upon the dry sand area for recreational purposes. The record shows the dry-sand area in question has been used, as of right, uniformly with similarly situated lands elsewhere, and that the public's use has never been questioned by an upland owner—so long as the public remained on the dry sand and refrained from trespassing upon the lands above the vegetation line.

Finally, a custom must not be repugnant, or inconsistent, with other customs or with other law. The custom under consideration violates no law, and is not repugnant.

Two arguments have been arrayed against the doctrine of custom as a basis for decision in Oregon. The first argument is that custom is unprecedented in this state, and has only scant adherence elsewhere in the United States. The second argument is that, because of the relative brevity of our political history, it is inappropriate to rely upon an English doctrine that requires greater antiquity than a newly-settled land can muster. Neither of these arguments is persuasive.

The custom of the people of Oregon to use the dry-sand area of the beaches for public recreational purposes meets every one of Blackstone's requisites. While it is not necessary to rely upon precedent from other states, we are not the first state to recognize custom as a source of law. …

On the score of the brevity of our political history, it is true that the Anglo-American legal system on this continent is relatively new. Its newness has made it possible for government to provide many of our institutions by written law rather than by customary law. This truism does not, however, militate against the validity of a custom when the custom does in fact exist. If

Alfred T. Goodwin (1923-), journalist, lawyer, judge. Writing for the Eugene newspaper while in law school at the University of Oregon, he then became a lawyer practicing there. After five years of practice, he began a career in Oregon state courts as a judge—first on the circuit court, then on the Oregon Supreme Court (1960-1969). In 1969 he was appointed as a federal district judge. Elevated in 1971 to the Ninth Circuit, he became chief judge in 1988 and assumed senior status in 1991.

antiquity were the sole test of a custom, Oregonians could satisfy that requirement by recalling that the European settlers were not the first people to use the dry-sand area as public land.

Finally, in support of custom, the record shows that the custom of the inhabitants of Oregon, and of visitors in the state, to use the dry sand as a public recreation area is so notorious that notice of the custom on the part of persons buying land along the shore must be presumed.

In the case at bar, the landowners conceded their actual knowledge of the public's long-standing use of the dry-sand area, and argued that the elements of consent present in the relationship between the landowners and the public precluded the application of the law of prescription. As noted, we are not resting this decision on prescription, and we leave open the effect upon prescription of the type of consent that may have been present in this case. Such elements of consent are, however, wholly consistent with the recognition of public rights derived from consent.

Because so much of our law is the product of legislation, we sometimes lose sight of the importance of custom as a source of law in our society. It seems particularly appropriate in the case at bar to look to ancient and accepted custom in this state as the source of a rule of law. The rule in this case, based upon custom, is salutary in confirming a public right, and at the same time it takes from no man anything which he has had a legitimate reason to regard as exclusively his.

Note: This decision in December of 1969 brought an end to controversy in the late 1960s over control of the dry-sands beaches in Oregon. It has withstood subsequent court challenges.

A number of years after Robert Straub worked to keep highways off Nestucca Spit (when he was state treasurer) and Judge Goodwin settled the question of control over the dry sands, Straub finally became governor—where he continued to do much to push the environmental agenda (see page 152 for Straub's profile).

From Straub's 1975 inaugural message as governor:

> I fully expect Oregon to continue to lead this nation in pioneering enlightened ways to limit man's excesses in his environment.
>
> Oregon's new Land Conservation and Development Commission [LCDC] is turning a new furrow in unplowed ground. In striding toward our goals of statewide land use planning, we will make some mistakes. There will be controversial decisions.
>
> Our goals are reachable, and I urge that we work for full citizen involvement and strong legislative support for LCDC. And I strongly urge the Legislature to approve my recommendations for a sharp increase in the LCDC budget …
>
> The energy shortage will be with us for the rest of our lives. We are obliged—for our own sake and for [the sake of] future generations—to develop new and effective ways to ease the critical imbalance of energy supply and demand. …
>
> Changes are needed in our Willamette Greenway Plan to bring us back to the original intent of the program: to preserve this magnificent resource now and in the future. In the next few weeks, I will forward to you my recommendations on proposed changes in the plan [to strengthen it].

From his 1977 message to the legislature:

> We will also profit from the completion of our comprehensive land-use planning process. My goal is to have the entire state of Oregon

planned and zoned by 1980. To help achieve that goal—at the local level, where it belongs—I am ... [turning] more than two-thirds of the proposed budget ... [for] the Land Conservation and Development Commission [over] to local jurisdictions. Those grant funds—for planning aid to cities and counties—would be increased by more than 100 percent. ...

Successful implementation of Senate Bill 100 is a goal which we must reach to maintain our quality of life in Oregon.

Speaking of the convictions that guide his approach on this matter, Governor Straub said they are:

> First, the conservation and development of our land. Last November, our commitment to sound, sensible land use planning received over-whelming approval. The message was clear—the people of Oregon want us to get the job done. I believe it can be done under the existing law.
>
> Some fine-tuning is needed—but the key principles of SB100 must not be eroded or destroyed: the right of citizens to appeal; the requirement that planning be done at the local level (closest to the people); and citizen involvement in the planning process. ...
>
> Let me tell you of my vision ... and the things I want for my children and my children's children. I want them to be able to share ... [our] enjoyment of backpacking in Oregon's magnificent wilderness areas. I want them to be able to float Oregon's wild rivers and experience their beauty (as we have done). I want them to enjoy Oregon's unique communities which have protected and preserved their special heritage in both their buildings and their environment. I want them to breathe clean air, have clean water, and a clean land.

From his final message in 1979:

It is a time of challenge, a time of opportunity, a time for conviction … a time for moderation. The growth that has often seemed to threaten the beauty and livability of this state must be managed or it will surely manage us.

In the areas of energy and industrial growth, it is hard to deal with people who refuse to moderate, no matter what the cost to others, no matter what the reality of the situation.

Our times can little afford such rigidity. The brilliant English essayist C. P. Snow wrote: "The sooner intellectuals … realize that industrialization is the one hope of the poor, the sooner we shall get hold of a social purpose again."

We must have industry, and we must have the energy to power it—so much depends on that. The very quality of life depends on that.

We have tried in Oregon to develop industrially without violating our sacred trust to preserve this land for those who follow after us. We must continue our efforts to preserve the land—for it is the land, finally, [that] … will shape our future … and give scope and meaning to our dreams.

It is how we live today in relation to our land and its rivers and forests … that will determine our future … and the futures of our children and their children after them.

As the needs for growth and economic development conflict with our natural resources, we will find issues increasingly harder to understand … decisions [that will be] more difficult to make … and a broad consensus perhaps [will be] impossible to come by.

Because of that, it is more imperative now than ever before that we find ways to remain flexible in our thinking … [be] honest in our appraisal of needs … and [be] resilient in the ways we meet the problems confronting us.

We must learn to seek a middle ground between those with a

no-growth attitude … and those with a "live now—pay later" attitude. We must find what the ancient Greeks called "the Golden Mean," the position of moderation between two extremes. That is the sacred trust our citizens place in us.

These words of the great English parliamentarian, Edmund Burke, have always had a special meaning to me. He wrote: "Your representative owes you not [only] his industry, but his judgment; and he betrays you, instead of serving you, if he sacrifices it to your opinion."

I believe that, and I hope I have been faithful to that call.

Note: Even environmentally minded politicians saw the need to be seen as balanced in the way they blended these concerns with practical economics.

Remarks in 1987 by Governor Neil Goldschmidt on Straub's accomplishments:

In recommending that the Nestucca Spit State Park be renamed the Bob Straub State Park, he said the following:

For most of his adult life Bob Straub has worked and fought to preserve Oregon's natural beauty, and to share with his fellow Oregonians the pleasures of outdoor recreation that he, and his wife … have enjoyed so much. …

At a time when few people in elective office dared to stand up for conservation and wise use of our natural resources, Bob was out in front.

He went on to list Straub's accomplishments in this realm:

- leadership in creating water recreation facilities in Lane County
- cleaning up water pollution, particularly in the Willamette River
- keeping highways off the ocean beaches
- conserving and reclaiming rangeland
- guaranteeing full public access to the dry sands of the ocean beaches
- and originating the idea for the Willamette River Greenway.

Note: The state park was then renamed after him.

Sometimes agencies such as the Forest Service hire freelance writers to write the reports they issue. In 1975 their research station in Portland (i.e., the Pacific Northwest Forest and Range Experiment Station) hired **Ivan Doig** to do a major fifty-year overview of their work. That overview was issued in a report in 1977, from which these excerpts are taken. Much of what Doig put forth applies to Oregon forests (as well as to those in other states) and is worth remembering.

From *Early Forestry Research: A History of the Pacific Northwest Forest and Range Experiment Station: 1925–1975*:

> When the Tillamook fire destroyed a vast swath of old-growth timber in northwestern Oregon in August 1933, Leo Isaac and fellow researcher George Meagher followed up with a study of regeneration in burned-over areas. Their findings, which pointed out erosion hazards in the steep Pacific Coast area, made front-page headlines in

the Portland newspapers. The Isaac-Meagher report was perhaps the most widely noticed of the many publications which came from the Station in these years. (p. 13)

Points of conflict between researchers also began to show up during the Depression era. In March 1934, researcher Axel J. B. Brandstrom presented findings on a system called "economic selective logging." The Brandstrom formula called for cutting the highest value trees and leaving the rest to grow into a future timber crop—a sharp break with the prevalent practice of clearcutting entire areas. Brandstrom's idea set off a dispute within the Station that went to the highest echelons of the Forest Service.

In 1936, Brandstrom and Burt P. Kirkland, a well-known Northwest forester, then serving in the Washington, D.C. office of the Forest Service, prepared a report titled "Selective Timber Management in the Douglas-Fir Region."

> [Thornton] Munger and [Leo] Issac objected to many points in the manuscript, particularly what they saw as wholesale conversion to partial cutting in the old-growth Douglas-fir forests. This, they argued, would lead to timber stands of uneven age, which would favor shade-tolerant species of less commercial value than Douglas-fir.
>
> Kirkland and Brandstrom held the view that selective logging was efficient and economical … .
>
> This was an early round in the complex battle over clearcutting. …
>
> The disputed report was published with a foreword by Chief Forester Ferdinand A. Silcox [FDR's appointee] which called the Brandstrom-Kirkland proposals "thought provoking, original, and constructive." Selective cutting did become the

Ivan Doig (1939–2015), freelancer, western novelist. Doig was born in Montana and resided mostly in Seattle. He wrote sixteen novels and won various prizes, including a lifetime Distinguished Achievement Award from the Western Literature Association. Before writing novels, he did freelance work, including a number of major reports for the Forest Service—this among them.

regional policy for several years, until the pendulum of economics swung in favor of clearcutting once again. (p. 13)

However, Thornton Munger revealed that at an early time, commercial pressure did play a role in the amount of clearcutting the Forest Service did. In response to a question in an oral interview after retiring, he admitted that:

> With the [prices for] stumpage so low and the margin of profit so slight in those days, the loggers thought they couldn't afford to go into a stand unless they were going to cut nearly all of it.
>
> So the Forest Service was under pressure to cut as heavily as possible. For that economic reason, we had to sacrifice some silvicultural advantages in those days.[*]

(See oral interview by Amelia R. Fry on page 92; for a profile of Munger, see page 92.)

> By the early 1950s, the figures [on logging volumes] looked bleak; about 300,000 acres were being clearcut each year in the Pacific Northwest, but only about 75,000 acres were being planted. A considerable portion of the logged-over area would restock itself naturally. Other areas would not, and there were scars from the past that were not growing back. (Doig, 24)

> An alternative to clearcutting was studied at the Cascade Head and Hemlock Experimental Forest; it was found that a system called "shelterwood," which left enough trees to shade the site, could be used to reforest the carefully logged areas of Douglas fir, western hemlock, Sitka spruce, and red alder. (Doig, 29)

---

[*]   Munger, interview by Fry, 70.

Over these years, various Forest Service chiefs also issued strong statements, some of which Doig cites:

In 1943 Forest Service Chief Lyle F. Watts said flatly:

The most urgent need is public regulation to stop destructive cutting.

And in 1970, Forest Service Chief Edward P. Cliff said:

Our programs are out of balance to meet public needs for the environmental 1970s, and we are receiving mounting criticisms from all sides. Our direction must be and is being changed. (Doig, 17, 39)

Comment: Environmentalists did not always appreciate that they had allies in the research stations, but the researchers had their own complaints that their voices were not always heard or heeded among those in the operating divisions.

The work of another person who was not from Oregon had a profound effect upon it. He was from Yakima, Washington, but had a cabin in the Wallowas and married more than one woman he'd met in Oregon. This was **William O. Douglas**, the longest serving judge on the US Supreme Court. He also filed dissents in more cases than almost any other justice.

His most memorable one is in the extract that follows, which liberalized the rules governing access to court procedures (i.e., the rules of standing). It grew out of the case of the *Sierra Club v. Morton*, in which Douglas wanted to go even further. I induced the Sierra Club to bring this famous case.

Following is text of dissent by Justice William O. Douglas in the case of *Sierra Club v. Morton*, 405 U.S. 727 (1972). This case removed the requirement that a plaintiff have a financial stake in the matter at issue. Douglas wanted to broaden the grounds of standing even more by giving standing to objects of nature, such as trees.

> The critical question of "standing" would be simplified, and also put neatly in focus, if we fashioned a federal rule that allowed environmental issues to be litigated before federal agencies or federal courts in the name of the inanimate object about to be despoiled, defaced, or invaded by roads and bull-dozers, and where injury is the subject of public outrage.
>
> Contemporary public concern for protecting nature's equilibrium should lead to the conferral of standing upon environmental objects to sue for their own preservation. This suit would therefore be more properly labeled *Mineral King v. Morton*.
>
> Inanimate objects are sometime partied in litigation. A ship has a legal personality—a fiction found useful for maritime purposes. … The ordinary corporation is a "person" for purposes of the adjudicatory processes—whether it represents proprietary, spiritual, aesthetic, or charitable causes.
>
> So it should be as respects valleys, alpine meadows, rivers, lakes, estuaries, beaches, ridges, groves of trees, swampland, or even air that feels the destructive pressures of modern technology and modern life. The river, for example, is the living symbol of all life it sustains or nourishes—fish, aquatic insects, water ouzels, otter, fisher, deer, elk, bear, and all other animals, including man, who are dependent on it or who enjoy it for its sight, its sound, or its life.
>
> The river as plaintiff speaks for the ecological unit of life that is part of it. Those people who have a meaningful relation to that body

WILLIAM O. DOUGLAS

William O. Douglas (1898–1980), lawyer, law professor, official, judge. Douglas grew up in Yakima, Washington, and was introduced to the outdoors in the nearby Cascades. Following graduation from Whitman College, he went to Columbia Law School. After practicing briefly with a New York City firm, he began teaching at the Columbia Law School, later being hired by the Yale Law School—where he made a national reputation.

In 1934 he joined the staff of the federal Securities and Exchange Commission (SEC), where he became part of the New Deal "Brain Trust" and later chairman of the SEC. In 1939 President Roosevelt appointed him to the supreme court, where he served for thirty-six years—the longest service of anyone on the court. He set records, too, for filing dissents, dissenting in 40 percent of the cases that came to him. Sierra Club v. Morton is one of his most remembered ones.

He was widely recognized as an environmentalist and an outdoorsman, maintaining a cabin in the Cascades, west of Yakima. He influenced the

of water—whether it be a fisherman, a canoeist, a zoologist, or a logger—must be able to speak for the values which the river represents and which are threatened with destruction.

I do not know Mineral King. I have never seen it nor traveled it, though I have seen articles describing its proposed "development." The Sierra Club in its complaint alleges that "one of the principal purposes of the Sierra Club is to protect and conserve the … [natural] resources of the Sierra Nevada Mountains." The District Court held that this uncontested allegation made the Sierra Club "sufficiently aggrieved" to have "standing" to sue on behalf of Mineral King.

Mineral King is doubtless like other wonders of the Sierra Nevada such as Tuolumne Meadows and the John Muir Trail. Those who hike it, fish it, hunt it, camp in it, frequent it, or visit it merely to sit in solitude and wonderment are legitimate spokesmen for it—whether they may be few or many. Those who have that intimate relation with the inanimate object about to be injured, polluted, or otherwise despoiled are its legitimate spokesmen.

The Solicitor General takes a wholly different approach. He considers the problem in terms of "government by the Judiciary." With all respect, the problem is to make certain that the inanimate objects, which are the very core of America's beauty, have spokesmen before they are destroyed.

It is, of course, true that most of them are under the control of a federal agency or a state agency. The standards given those agencies are usually expressed in terms of the "public interest." Yet "public interest" has so many different shades of meaning as to be quite meaningless on the environmental front. Congress accordingly has adopted ecological standards in the National Environmental Policy Act of 1969, and guidelines for agency action have been provided by the Council on Environmental Quality.

Yet the pressures on agencies for favorable action one way or the other are enormous. The suggestion that Congress can stop action, which is undesirable, is true in theory; yet even Congress is too remote to give meaningful direction, and its machinery is too ponderous to use very often.

The federal agencies of which I speak are not venal or corrupt. But they are notoriously under the control of powerful interests who manipulate them through advisory committees, or friendly working relations, or who have that natural affinity with the agency which in time develops between the regulator and the regulated. …

The Forest Service—one of the federal agencies behind the scheme to despoil Mineral King—has been notorious for its alignment with lumber companies, although its mandate from Congress directs it to consider the various aspects of multiple use in its supervision of the national forests.

The voice of the inanimate object, therefore, should not be stilled. That does not mean that the judiciary takes over the managerial functions from the federal agency. It merely means that, before these priceless bits of Americana (such as a valley, an alpine meadow, a river, or a lake) are forever lost, or are so transformed as to be reduced to the eventual rubble of our urban environment, the voice of the existing beneficiaries of these environmental wonders should be heard.

Perhaps they will not win. Perhaps the bulldozers of "progress" will plow under all the aesthetic wonders of this beautiful land. That

court to save Kentucky's Red River Gorge, catalyzed efforts that saved the C & O Canal as a national park unit, led walks along the Olympic Beach strip to help save it, and most importantly, wrote this landmark dissent. He was later elected to the Ecology Hall of Fame.

Over his career, Douglas maintained connections with Oregon. He married his first wife in La Grande, met his last wife in Portland, and early on spent summers in a cabin in the Wallowas near Lostine. In his books, he praised its landscapes, and he pleaded with friends in the West (including the author) to do more to save endangered places in Oregon.

is not the present question. The sole question is, who has standing to be heard?

Those who hike the Appalachian Trail into Sunfish Pond, New Jersey, and camp or sleep there, or run the Allagash in Maine, or climb the Guadalupe in West Texas, or who canoe and portage in the Quetico Superior in Minnesota, certainly should have standing to defend those natural wonders before courts or agencies—though they live 3,000 miles away.

Those who merely are caught up in environmental news or propaganda and flock to defend these waters or areas may be treated differently. That is why these environmental issues should be tendered by the inanimate object itself.

Then there will be assurances that all of the forms of life which it represents will stand before the court—the pileated woodpecker as well as the coyote and bear, the lemmings as [well as] the trout in the streams. Those inarticulate members of the ecological group cannot speak. But those people who have so frequented the place as to know its values and wonders will be able to speak for the entire ecological community.

Ecology reflects the land ethic; ... [as] Aldo Leopold wrote in *a Sand County Almanac*: "the land ethic simply enlarges the boundaries of the community to include soils, waters, plants, and animals, or collectively: the land."

That, as I see it, is the issue of 'standing' in the present case and controversy.

Note: In the aftermath of this decision, the rules of standing were relaxed, and cases were then successfully filed in the name of an endangered bird species (see *Palila v. DLNR*, 1979, by their friend, the Sierra Club).

From his *Of Men and Mountains* (1950):

My young experiences in the high Cascades have placed the heavy mark of the mountains on me. And so the excitement that alpine meadows and high peaks created in me comes flooding back to make each adult trip an adventure. (p. xi)

These tangled masses of thickets, ridges, cliffs, and peaks are a vast wilderness area. Here man can find deep solitude, and under conditions of grandeur that are startling he can come to know both himself and God. (p. ix)

From his *My Wilderness* (1960):

It was July when I first climbed Hart Mountain. …

Higher up [above the plateau], I came across startling wildflower [displays] … . In open places, on the lower shoulder of the mountain, I found fields of the delicate rose-colored Clarkia: the flower that Lewis and Clark first discovered on the Clearwater in Idaho and which bears the name of Captain William Clark. David Douglas rediscovered this Clarkia and sent it to England.

I had not gone far before I came across a hillside of the green-banded Mariposa lily—with three lavender and lilac petals whose yellow base is also dotted with dark purple and violet spots. Scattered lavishly among these lilies were the waxen blooms of the delicate bitterroot. The soft, bright colors of the flowers and their delicacy were in vivid contrast to the heavy dullness and coarseness of the sage.

At about 6,500 feet, I found hundreds of acres of lupine in bloom—mostly blue but some white and some mixed. It stood at times almost knee-high … .

As I climbed higher, I came across patches of soft pink alpine phlox, clinging tenaciously to sandy outcroppings—as if it had pledged its life to prevent the coarse topsoil from being blown away.

Note: One of the issues in Oregon on which Justice Douglas asked for the Sierra Club's help in the early 1960s dealt with threats to the Minam River valley (just west of Lostine), into which roads were about to be built so that logging could commence. They asked the author to investigate, and he wrote the text of a mailer they put out. The opposition it engendered helped stop road building, with Senator Hatfield intervening a dozen years later to put the Minam in wilderness (McCloskey 2013, 69–70).

In a book Douglas wrote in 1970, *Points of Rebellion*, he tells of his concerns about what might have happened to this place:

> In 1961–1962 the Forest Service made plans to build a road up the beautiful Minam River in Oregon—one of the few roadless valleys in the State. It is choice wilderness—delicate in structure, sparse in timber, and filled with game.
>
> We who knew the Minam pleaded against the road. The excuse was cutting timber—a poor excuse because of the thin stand. The real reason was road building on which the lumber company would make a million dollars. The road would be permanent, bringing automobiles in by the thousands and making a shambles of the Minam.
>
> We spoke to Senator Wayne Morse about the problem, and he called over Orville Freeman, the Secretary of Agriculture—the agency that supervises the Forest Service. Morse pounded the table and demanded a public hearing. One was reluctantly given. Dozens

of people appeared on the designated day in La Grande, Oregon (I was one of them), not a blessed one speaking in favor of the plan. Public opposition was so great that the plan was suffocated.

Why should not the public be heard whenever an agency decides to take action that will or may despoil the environment?

Sometimes members of the business community are caught up in enthusiasm for nature and outdoor activity. **Garnett "Ding" Cannon** was one of those—he was a mainstay of the Trails Club of Oregon and a regular mountain climber. He also played a key role in catalyzing pressures that brought protection by the city of Portland to Forest Park. In the business world, he was the president of the Standard Insurance Company.

In an interview with the *Oregonian* in 1968, he said:

> It's the desire to get back to elemental things, the grandeur of the outdoors, the solitude and quiet of the wilderness … and the desire to test yourself and push on. You never know what you can do until you try. This time I almost didn't make it … [but] I feel I have been resurrected.*

Note: He was describing how some in his party almost lost their lives in an outing to Goat Rocks, and some did.

---

* Cannon, *Oregonian* interview.

Garnett "Ding" Cannon (1906–1988), businessman, climber, conservationist. From 1956 to 1971, Cannon served as president of the Standard Insurance Company; that firm was originally known as the Oregon Mutual Life Insurance Company. Long associated with the Trails Club of Oregon, Cannon served as its president and then president of the Federation of Western Outdoor Clubs. He was a devoted mountain climber. The Trails Club was first known as the Downtown Businessmen's Hiking Club.

In the period between 1944 and 1946, Cannon took the lead in organizing support for the idea of establishing Forest Park as a city nature park. He first pushed the idea in the City Club and then organized a movement of some fifty outdoor groups to promote the idea, which the city approved in 1947.

Robert W. Packwood (1932-), lawyer, politician (moderate Republican). After graduating from Willamette University, he went to law school at NYU and began practicing in Portland. He immediately plunged into political organizing, which got him elected to the legislature in 1962, where he served until 1968. In 1968 he was elected, by a thin margin, to the US Senate—ousting longtime incumbent Wayne Morse. Reelected four times, he rose to power in the senate, chairing both the Commerce Committee and later the Finance Committee.

He pursued an independent and moderate course, showing some willingness to support environmental causes: opposing the Supersonic Transport (SST) and favoring returnable bottles and solar power. Environmentalists are especially grateful to him for leading the effort to preserve Hells Canyon as a National Recreation Area (closing the river to more dams) and helping materially with the designation of the Columbia Gorge as a National Scenic Area. At times, he was willing to part company with the timber industry. He resigned in 1995 over charges of inappropriate behavior with women in his office.

Wayne Morse was succeeded as a US Senator from Oregon by **Robert W. Packwood**, who sometimes supported environmental positions, but not always. Serving for a long time, he rose to chair both the Commerce Committee and the Finance Committee and became quite influential.

Environmentalists were grateful for his leadership in getting Hells Canyon, and the Snake River in it, closed to any more dams (through having it designated as a National Recreation Area) and help in getting a National Scenic Area established in the Columbia Gorge.

Extract from a statement by Senator Robert Packwood in 1972 at hearings on legislation to buy out pumice mining claims at Rock Mesa in the Three Sisters Wilderness:

At some stage in our careers, we have to quit going around and damming up every river we can find to produce electricity for a half billion people we think will come, and we have to quit cutting down every forest we can find, and we have to preserve a few spots where you can actually go and not hear a chain saw, … or a four-wheel drive jeep clamor[ing] to go through the wilderness.

We are going to have all that if we permit this mining to start in the Three Sisters Wilderness.

He sought approval of the legislation to preserve "the unique beauty of this wilderness in and of itself."

Outcome: Finally, in 1982 Congress brought this long-festering issue to an end, buying out the few mining claims that were thought to be valid (which was only a fraction of them). The author had started the contest in 1963 by filing a formal appeal under the Code of Federal Regulations (McCloskey 2013, 68).

Another businessman who cared about the balance between development and nature was **John Gray**, who developed elegant destination resorts noted for the way they respected their environments.

Quote from Gray (1973):

> If you attend to your stewardship well, your care will be shown in the color of your balance sheet, as well as in the color and shape of the land around us.[*]

A climber who spent time in Oregon while teaching at Washington State University was **Howard McCord**. He wrote these words about the Steens Mountain (1979):

> We are going to the Steens. They are the best place to see the moon in this world. The huge east ridge falls into nothing forever. It's all basalt, and fundamentally boring [from the perspective of climbers], but it is distant, and what P.T. [a character in this work] is after is psychic quiet—which he can't find in the Jarbidge [a range in northern Nevada] because of his own doing. And a range like the Wallowas is simply too

---

[*]   John Gray, "Land Use."

John Gray (1919–2012), businessman, philanthropist. A native Oregonian, with a degree from Oregon State University and an MBA from Harvard, he was noted for his love of the outdoors and sensitivity to nature. Through his donations, he helped restore natural habitat in Portland. After making his fortune as the owner of the Omark firm, he then made his reputation developing elegant destination resorts: at Salishan on the coast, at Sunriver south of Bend, and at Skamania in the Columbia River Gorge. He was also a long-time trustee of Reed College.

Howard McCord (1932–), professor, poet, essayist. Making his living as a professor, he also writes poems, essays, and novels. In the 1960s he taught at Washington State University, where he was given a grant to explore the back roads of the West. He also had been a rock climber, making ascents across the West.

beautiful—and has attracted too many spirits over the millennia. The Steens are lunar, pure ... .*

Oregon has proved to be fertile ground for producing activists who have gone on to become leaders of national environmental organizations (e.g., Sierra Club, Greenpeace, Nature Conservancy). Of these, **Michael McCloskey**, the author, went to the highest levels and stayed there for the longest time.

He served as CEO for the national Sierra Club for seventeen years (actually on two occasions). Then he became its chairman until retiring. He served as a top staff member there for thirty years. He headed the organization during the time it played a pivotal role in the enactment of most of the nation's framework environmental laws. He is from Eugene.

Here is much of the speech he made to the City Club in Portland on March 21, 1980:

Have Environmentalists Really Done All Those Things?

Recently, a new phenomenon has emerged: the disinterested critic of the environmental movement [one who has no vested interest to defend]. ...

At an earlier time—when we were less secure—many of us felt it was poor strategy to be diverted into replying to such criticism. But now I expect that we draw such diverse and contradictory criticism because we are established as part of the mainstream of American values. The criticism comes as often as not from those who are operating outside of that value system.

The most amazing things are said about us. Just a few weeks ago, one of my appearances was picketed by a pamphleteer from the John

---

* McCord, *Arcs of Lowitz*.

Birch Society who was passing out a flyer accusing the Sierra Club of being a front for the oil companies; I didn't know the Birch Society was all that concerned about them. …

Pointing out that critics have placed environmentalists all across the political spectrum, McCloskey then said:

> Those who are so disturbed by what we do really do seem to have trouble figuring out what we do. But, obviously, some have to be wrong because we can't be all of these things at once.
>
> Environmentalists … are often accused of being extremists. Some of our adversaries in industry use the phrase "environmental extremists"—almost the way southerners did the phrase "damn Yankees." The best comment I ever saw on that characterization was in a cartoon in *High Country News*. It showed a miner jumping up and down and screaming: "you environmentalists have got to stop being so extreme," with a meek environmentalist taking this tongue-lashing. Few environmentalists would want to try to match our adversaries' use of invective.
>
> The environmental movement could not possibly have achieved all it has if it were an extreme movement. The environmental movement has been more successful than any other movement in the period since World War II in securing the enactment of a major body of reform legislation. No fringe movement does that. And quite significantly, almost none of that legislation has been repealed nor repudiated. It is passing the test of enduring public acceptability.
>
> Environmentalists are also disparaged as being, variously, a bunch of long-haired hippies; merely a middle class movement; or, as … elitists from the upper echelons of society. Now once again, our critics have not gotten their act together: we can't be all three.

In truth, we probably have folks in our movement from all three strata, and from labor also. Recently in visiting our group in Birmingham, Alabama, I found that they are drawn heavily from blue-collar workers.

However, our demographic surveys show that the environmental movement is heavily middle class in composition. But what is wrong with that? Most of America is middle class. The whole volunteer movement in America (of which we are part) is middle class in character. Almost by definition, an organization cannot be part of the volunteer movement and be anything but middle class (the lower classes don't have the time or discretionary income, and the upper classes tend to lack the interest).

However, it is one thing to ask about the composition of the movement, and it is quite another thing to ask about public sentiment. Repeated surveys throughout the 1970s have shown majority support for strong environmental programs. A recent survey for Resources for the Future showed 63 percent of the public counting themselves as sympathetic to the movement, with 54 percent of the public favoring environmental protection regardless of the cost [an extremely strong stance]. … Other surveys generally show over half to two-thirds of the public favoring strong programs. …

The general trend in the polls also shows that there are majorities sympathetic to the movement in all income and educational classes. Surprisingly enough, the RFF poll even shows slightly more blacks than whites sympathetic to the movement. This is a profound change from the early 1970s. …

In truth, environmentalism has become a central value in thinking of most Americans. It is not a class phenomenon any more than any other set of American values. Rich and poor alike all need clean air.

Some would like us to believe that support for the environmental movement is fading or that a backlash is underway. I have been hearing grim warnings from industry about an imminent backlash ever since 1972. However, it is now interesting to reflect on the fact that far more environmental legislation has been passed since 1972 than before then (roughly twice as many important laws and measures have been enacted since 1972).

Now it is true that environmental problems rarely show up any more on lists of things that most concern the public. The reason is that these tend to be lists of problems which the public feels are *not* being addressed. The public knows that problems of the environment are being addressed through hundreds of programs …

In short, there is no evidence in the progression of polls over the 1970s for the suggestion that there is any basic change in public support for protecting the environment.

Now some people are annoyed because they feel that environmentalists are always negative—that we are always against things. They wish we were more positive.

Well, we do take positive stands for all sorts of good policies. We are *for* many programs. We are for mass transit, for solar power, for insulation, for recycling, for reclaiming waste water, for conserving energy and water, for reforestation and true sustained yield, for integrated pest management, for utilizing nutrient wastes in irrigation, for reclamation of derelict lands, for renovation of railroads, for rehabilitating urban housing, for infilling policies, for clean air and water, for more open space

MICHAEL McCLOSKEY

and parks, for wilderness and wildlife refuges, and for better public health programs.

Unfortunately, most of these positive projects compete with proposals that would counter them, and in dealing with our competition, we are often tagged as being negative. While it may seem to be a more a matter of semantics, this negative side of the coin does seem to draw more publicity.

Moreover, we have not opposed most of the development projects to date. Most subdivisions have been built without objection from us, and the same can be said for the freeways, and the dams, and power plants, and logging plans. Ninety percent or more of the developments to date have proceeded without any protest from us or other environmentalists. Usually, it is only when natural values become scarce and development becomes extremely widespread, that resistance begins to break out.

But the resistance is to the imbalance in the equation. When few wild rivers are left, proposals for further dams will be increasingly unwelcome. When less than five percent of the virgin redwoods are left, they become a scarce natural value.

But stiffening resistance to losing the last residue of a natural resource should not be misread as opposition to the basic use of natural resources as such. Environmentalists are not really "aginners"; we are simply against those who are going too far. We are just trying to keep some balance in the picture.

Now if it is true that we don't, for instance oppose all [new] power plants, some want to know why we don't actually come out and support the construction of such projects. They want to know: when did you actually endorse a development project?

Well, we don't actually endorse projects because we are not in a position to assess the total value of such projects. We are only experts on environmental questions. We are not experts on questions of utility reliability and rates, for instance. We are not set up to serve as a little utility commission—judging the general worth of a project. Because of these limitations, our environmental competence can only find logical expression in either suggestions for improvement, opposition, or [the] absence of opposition.

Some of our critics complain that we are never satisfied—that we are always seeking more. In reality, it is our critics in industry who are always seeking more: the timber industry always wants more stumpage, the mining industry always wants more acreage to explore, the oil industry more drilling concessions, subdivision developers more tracts to build upon, etc. It is their pressures that are unremitting.

In a large sense, it is environmentalists who are seeking stability in relationships and land allocations. There is a finite limit to the amount of accessible and developable land around most cities; you cannot go on forever building subdivisions around urban areas. Environmentalists want society to strike a balance between land allocated to development and open space—and between land allocated to managed resources such as timber and minerals and land allocated to wilderness [or nature]. Too often, society fails to even make the effort, and in succumbing to the pressures of industry, the tide runs the other way. In that event, environmentalists may seem to be always asking for more—but basically it is for more balance.

Our aims are finite too: e.g., we want air that meets objective standards of quality, etc. … Quite often our perceptions of public need will evolve and change over time, and as a result we may ask for things we didn't see at an earlier time. But usually these sharpened perceptions are triggered by even greater pressure on the environment by development. For instance, as open space disappears around

Michael McCloskey (1934–), activist, environmental advocate, manager of a nonprofit organization. McCloskey was born and raised in Eugene, Oregon, the son of an English professor at the University of Oregon, and he took to hiking and climbing as an outgrowth of his time in scouting. After taking degrees from Harvard and the University of Oregon Law School, he decided he wanted to speak for the environment, instead of practicing law.

In 1961 he began a forty-year career working for the national Sierra Club, working his way up over time to be their CEO and chairman. He headed the organization during the time it was instrumental in the enactment of many of the nation's framework environmental laws. He spoke all over the country and wrote prolifically. His work has been recognized with many awards, including the John Muir Award. Since retiring to Portland, he has written a number of books dealing with environmental themes.

cities, sites will be sought for regional parks that would not have looked all that good at an earlier time.

Now some like to call us "preservationists" rather than conservationists or environmentalists. They charge we are only interested in wilderness and not in sound management of resources. Of course, we are interested in *both*. We led the way in securing enactment of a multiple use mandate in federal law for the Bureau of Land Management and have been involved in a number of reforms of Forest Service management laws. We are a principal force behind the effort to keep an "even flow" approach to sustained yield intact in the national forests to maintain stability in employment in forest dependent communities. We have repeatedly decried over-cutting on industrial forest lands, which is leading to declining employment in the saw-timber industry. …

Other critics deride us by asserting that we are "purists" who are seeking an idyllic kind of wilderness that simply doesn't exist anymore. This charge really misses the mark.

In point of fact, we have been critical of federal agencies for being too pure in what they demand for entry into the wilderness system. We have pointed out that the Wilderness Act does not demand absolute pristineness—only that the area appear substantially natural. We have not agreed with earlier efforts by the Forest Service and the Park Service to tear down shelters, ban foot bridges, and remove signs.

There is no need to go to such extremes when the Wilderness Act itself permits exceptions for the continued filing of mining claims until 1984 and indefinite grazing. We understand that wilderness areas are affected by what happens outside them, and indeed have pioneered efforts to prevent degradation of air quality in air-sheds [in] … wilderness areas and parks. …

Critics associated with the housing industry also seem to believe we are opposed to all new housing. In his book—*The Environmental Protection Hustle*, Bernard Frieden seems to feel that we are the upper class intent on keeping the middle class from finding new homes in the suburbs. However, William Tucker is inclined to think … that we are those members of the middle class who have already arrived in the suburbs and who want to keep others out. Others charge that we are conspiring to keep out low-cost housing for the poor. None of these critics—whose assertions run off in contradictory directions— really have very substantial evidence for their charges.

To set the record straight, the Sierra Club supports programs to provide affordable housing in an environmentally responsible way. In most cities, we believe this will be comprised of medium-density, multi-family housing which will not require large tracts in suburban locations. Instead, bypassed tracts of lesser size in already urbanized areas can be used via in-filling. Moreover, we have opposed red-lining and support active programs to rehabilitate older housing. …

Furthermore, most of our members do not even live in suburban tract housing; most of them live closer to city centers. Their interest in open space has nothing to do with preserving vacant lots behind their own backyards. They are genuinely concerned with the environmental costs of sprawl and the destruction of good farmland. …

Discussing the economic impact of pollution control investments, McCloskey goes on to say:

And one can really question too whether this [slight] price rise [attributable to environmental regulations] should even be viewed as inflationary. This increment does not represent an erosion of purchasing power. With pollution control, the public is getting more for its money—better water and air, better health, more productive crops, and longer lasting buildings and homes. In 1977, the economic benefits from air pollution controls were estimated [by the EPA] to more than exceed their costs. …

In conclusion, I don't want to seem to suggest that environmentalists are infallible or that we never make mistakes. Sometimes we do. Particularly in the early stages of specific conflicts, it is hard to get accurate data, and some of our challenges may miss the mark.

But I believe the time has come to respond to those who would perpetuate basic misunderstandings about the environmental movement and its purposes. The need has never been greater for clearer understanding of the context in which public issues are debated.

William G. Robbins (1935-), professor, historian. Born and raised in the East, he earned his graduate degree at the University of Oregon and taught for thirty years at Oregon State University. He wrote over a dozen books, with four on the history of Oregon. In that context, his two most important ones are *Landscapes of Promise: The Oregon Story, 1800-1940* and *Landscapes of Conflict: The Oregon Story, 1940-2000*. The latter recounts conflicts over dams and logging.

The history of the impact of Oregon's developing economy on its environment is recounted in the writings of **William G. Robbins**, an environmental historian. In the first volume of his history, he deals with the period between 1800 and 1940. Here are a few of his observations from his *Landscapes of Promise: The Oregon Story, 1800-1940*:

He perceived that there was "an almost transcendental belief that it is right and proper to engage in the unlimited manipulation of nature to promote the welfare of humankind."

Sensing that the people who were in charge were guided by "an overweening confidence" in what they were doing," he described the "wildly optimistic schemes—such as building dams on every free-flowing river, [with their promoters] only occasionally acknowledging negative social and environmental consequences."

In dealing with the rangeland of eastern Oregon, he concluded that "the intensive grazing of too many cattle and sheep on limited acreages dramatically changed the original grassland communities. Exotic invading grasses replaced the native perennials that once dominated the area."

CHAPTER EIGHT

Oregon as Environmentalism Becomes the Norm

One mountain climber who also became a poet is **Gary Snyder**, who spent his formative years in Oregon, often climbing Mt. Hood. He became one of the most noted poets associated with environmentalism.

This is from "Arktos,"* a poem of his about bears:

> Sighing, bursting: steam—sulfur—lava,
> Rolling and bubbling up, falls out,
> Back in on itself.
> > curling and licking,
> > > getting hard.

---

* Snyder, "Arktos."

Lichens, oak groves, float in up like cloud shadows
Soft, soft,
Loving Plant hands.

Tendrils slip through til they meet
    it pulls taut
Green and quick—sap call swells the hills

      changing cloud mountain
      changing cloud gate

Rainbow glimmering with swallows, looping cranes.
    icefields and snowfields ring
    as she comes
    gliding down the rainbow bridge

Joy of the Mountains
"The Great She bear"

These quotes set forth his views on nature and living with it:

> We are defending our own space, and we are trying to protect the commons. More than the logic of self-interest inspires this: a true and selfless love of the land is the source of the undaunted spirit of my neighbors.
>
> Bioregional awareness teaches us in specific ways. It is not enough to just "love nature" or want to "be in harmony with Gaia." Our relation to the natural world takes place in a place, and it must be grounded in information and experience.
>
> Wilderness is not just the "preservation" of the world, it is the world … Nature is ultimately in no way endangered; wilderness is.
>
> We are all indigenous to this planet; this [is a] garden we are

Gary Snyder (1930–), mountain climber, poet, professor. Snyder went to high school and college (Reed) in Portland and took to mountain climbing. Joining the Mazamas, he climbed Mt. Hood over forty times. During the summers then, he worked as a fire lookout and in the woods. During the 1950s, he became identified with the Beat movement and began to publish poetry. In due course, his poetry won awards: a Pulitzer Prize (1974) and a Bollinger Prize for poetry (1997). He also taught at the University of California at Davis, maintaining a residence in the Sierra foothills. He became associated with the deep ecology movement.

being called upon by nature and history to re-inhabit in good spirit. To restore the land, one must live and work in a place.

The place will welcome whomever approaches it with respect and attention. To work in a place is to bond to a place: people who work together in a place become a community; in time, grows a culture. To restore the wild is to restore culture.

George Venn (1943-), professor, poet, writer. As a professor of English at Eastern Oregon College, he has been described as one of "the most respected poets in the state." It has been said that his poems have broken new ground by "suggesting that the landscape might serve as the focal point for a distinctive regional literature." The Stewart Holbrook Award for "outstanding contributions to Oregon's literary life" has been bestowed upon him.

Another poet is **George Venn**, who taught at the college level (at Eastern Oregon College) and wrote often about scenes in nature. He is regarded as one "of the most respected poets in the state."

He wrote this poem about Eagle Cap in the Wallowas:

The mountain in Mirror Lake does not waver
in the wind. This means Wallowa calm has come.

Even tons of stone have settled down for a few
million years of sleep. From mistletoe and fir,

shade lulls your eyes. From deep water,
your new face rises slow. Some old grief sinks away.[*]

Robin Cody is a writer who is also seen as a "river man." In his book *Voyage of a Summer Sun*, he recounts his eighty-two-day trip down the Columbia River: from the source to the mouth. In the book, in addition to describing the scenery, he comments on what has been done to nature.

The river still supports a fishery of Pacific salmon and steelhead, but

---

[*] Venn, "Eagle Cap."

the wild ones—the natives, with their irreplaceable genetic diversity—are reeling toward extinction as they are replaced by hatchery substitutes. And along the upper shores lurks the malignancy of the nation's largest radioactive waste dump. (p. 241)

At the turn of this century, an estimated 16 million salmon and steelhead annually came up the Columbia River to spawn. Now about 3 million do, and 90 percent of those are hatchery fish. (p. 248)

We caught too many fish, way too fast. And as more and more people filled the land, fish habitat got hammered. Early lumber mills took their first timber near the water. Log rafts scoured out spawning grounds and jammed the narrows. Logging roads pushed deeper into the forest, where clear-cuts removed shade and fouled the gravelly shallows where salmon spawned. Cattle grazed at riverside and broke down the banks.

Irrigators impounded small streams and returned the water laden with silt, pesticides, and herbicides. Dredge mining tore up streambeds and added metallic poisons to the toxic runoff from cities and roads. And then came the dams, compounding the impact of overharvest, habitat loss, and pollution. The wonder of it all is there are any wild, oceangoing fish left in the river at all. (p. 269)

I looked up from the widening Columbia to more rock-stacked copper cliffs and basalt columns capped with forest green. Horsetail Falls, Multnomah Falls, Wahkeena Falls, and smaller white laces tumbled off the precipices, and gold lichen and maidenhair fern grew in the canyon slits, where the sun never shines. (p. 277)

He spoke of:

Robin Cody (1943–), "river-man," writer, administrator. Robin Cody was born in St. Helens, Oregon, raised in Estacada, and now lives in Portland. He was educated at Yale University. For a while, he served as dean of admissions at Reed College, and then he worked as a writer for the Bonneville Power Administration. He also wrote for the *Oregonian*. He has written a number of highly acclaimed books, including the story of his eighty-two-day trip down the Columbia River: *Voyage of a Summer Sun* (1995 and 2012).

People dependent upon government subsid[ies] for using nature up. The U.S. Forest Service sells logs from National Forests at prices below the cost of replacing them. The Bureau of Reclamation waters land at little cost to farmers. The Army Corps of Engineers subsidizes river shipping, and the Bureau of Land Management gives out mineral and grazing rights as if it were still 1890. … Now we can do with nature what we will … The taming of the West has come less at the hands of rugged individualists than the continuing legislative clout of Western senators. … (p. 288)

Among the horrors that had come to light by the time I paddled past was that [of the] Trojan [Nuclear Reactor's] emergency cooling system [which] had been defective from the start. The Nuclear Regulatory Commission time and time again slapped PGE with fines for safety violations. The plant, only fourteen years old, was falling apart. Parts cracked, crumbled, broke. Safety related down-time meant the plant was no longer reliable, and it had never been cheap. Trojan was rated as the worst-performing reactor of its type in the country. Not only that, but its electricity wasn't [even] in local demand. … With repair costs still rising, PGE decided it would be "uneconomic" to keep Trojan running. The plant was shut down for good in January, 1993. (p. 294)

Sustained yield is the answer, but we got ahead of it. In the last three decades, we marched through old-growth timber faster and faster. Ever more efficient computerized mills used fewer sawyers and closed mill towns, even while more timber than ever came out of the woods—much of it now even to be milled here but to be exported to Japan. (p. 294)

One of the experts who provided a deep insight into all that was wrong with the management of Northwest old-growth forests was **Chris Maser**, a trained ecologist who had studied these forests while working for the Bureau of Land Management. His book *Redesigned Forest* (1988) furnished an intellectual framework for making sense of what the "timber wars" were really all about.

> Nature designed Pacific Northwest forests to be unique in the world, with twenty-five species of conifers, the longest-lived and the largest of their genera anywhere; we are designing a forest that is largely a single-species [operating] on a short rotation.
>
> Nature designed a forest to be a flexible, timeless continuum of species; we are trying to design a forest to be a rigid, time-constrained monoculture.
>
> Nature designed a forest of interrelated processes; we are trying to design a forest based on isolated products.
>
> Nature designed a forest with diversity; we are trying to design a … [uniform and simple] forest.
>
> Nature designed a forest of long-term trends; we are trying to design a forest of short-term absolutes.
>
> Nature designed a forest over a landscape; we are trying to design a forest on each … [acre].
>
> Everything we humans have been doing to the forest is an attempt to push nature to a higher sustained yield. We fail to recognize, however, that we must have a sustainable forest before we can have a sustainable yield (harvest). In other words, we cannot have a sustainable yield until we have a sustainable forest.

A few years before this, in 1984, he wrote reports with Jim Trappe, including *The Seen and Unseen World of the Fallen Tree*,

Chris Maser (1938–), ecologist, researcher, writer. Born in Corvallis, Oregon, Maser earned degrees in vertebrate zoology and in ecology (MS) at Oregon State University. While working for the Bureau of Land Management (BLM), he spent six years studying old-growth forests in Western Oregon. Because he insisted on bringing news of his findings to the public, he was forced out at the BLM, having worked for them for over a dozen years. He then went on to work for the EPA and thereafter forged a career as a researcher, writer, and lecturer. He has written thirty-nine books and hundreds of scientific articles. Those books focusing on Northwest old growth are *Redesigned Forest* (1988) and *Forest Primeval* (1989). Maser played a significant role in providing a critique of the way the old-growth forests in the Northwest were being managed by the BLM and the Forest Service. He woke people up to the values of old growth as habitat.

which pointed out that fallen trees were full of insects that were part of the food chain that built the complexity of the old-growth forest. He described their role in recycling nutrients and in storing moisture. In a popular version (*There's More to Forests Than Trees*), he observed:

> By converting old growth to young stands, we're re-designing forests. We can't duplicate what nature has been doing for centuries.
>
> The forest is a living organism. As part of that organism, the fallen tree is only superficially dead. It supports the larger being.
>
> Old growth is an investment in the next stand.

While **Judge William Dwyer** was not from Oregon, his decisions had a profound effect upon the state and its forests. As a hiker in Washington State, he undoubtedly also walked in Oregon's forests. His decisions are clearly written and free of jargon.

In his decision that set the stage for the Northwest Forest Plan, he wrote the following on the condition of the northern spotted owl:

> As its habitat has declined, the owl has virtually disappeared from some areas, and its numbers are decreasing in others.
>
> A great conifer forest originally covered the western parts of Washington, Oregon, and Northern California—from the Cascade and Coast mountains to the sea. Perhaps ten percent of it remains. The spaces protected as parks or wilderness areas are not enough for the survival of the northern spotted owl. …
>
> The most significant implication from our new knowledge regarding old-growth forest ecology is that logging these forests destroys not just trees, but a complex, distinctive, and unique ecosystem. (Audubon v. Evans, 12–13)

Speaking of the violations of statutory obligations by the Forest Service, he said:

In the fall of 1990, the Forest Service admitted that the ROD [Record of Decision] was inadequate after all [in] that it would fail to preserve the northern spotted owl. In seeking a stay of proceedings in this court in 1989, the Forest Service announced its intent to adopt temporary guidelines within thirty days. It did not do that within thirty days, or ever.

When directed by Congress to have a revised ROD in place by September 30, 1990, the Forest Service did not even attempt to comply. The FWS [Fish and Wildlife Service], in the meantime, acted contrary to law in refusing to list the spotted owl as endangered or threatened. After it finally listed the species as "threatened" (following Judge Zilly's order), the FWS again violated the ESA [Endangered Species Act] by failing to designate critical habitat as required. Another order had to be issued setting a deadline for the FWS to comply with the law.

The associate chief of the Forest Service testified that the agency experts began in early 1990 the work to have a revised plan in place by September 30 of that year (as Congress had mandated in sec. 318). But the Secretaries of Agriculture and Interior decided to drop the effort. The public was not told of this decision to ignore what the law required. …

The most recent violation of NFMA [the National Forest Management Act] exemplifies a deliberate and systematic refusal by the Forest Service to comply with the laws protecting wildlife. This is not the doing of the scientists, foresters, rangers, and others at working levels of these agencies. It reflects

William Dwyer (1929-2002), trial lawyer, judge. Dwyer served as a trial lawyer in Seattle for thirty-four years and then as a federal district judge for fifteen. He was an outdoorsman and climber. In 1987 he was appointed to be a federal district judge by President Ronald Reagan, despite being a Democrat. He was the federal district court judge who heard the key case that set the stage for the Northwest Forest Plan. Among the many cases in the early 1990s involving the fate of the northern spotted owl, this was the most consequential one—the one that led to the greatest change on the ground. It was also noted for the clarity of its language. It is cited as Seattle Audubon Society v. Evans, 771 F. Supp. 1081 (W.D. Wash. 1991).

decisions made by higher authorities [i.e., political appointees] in the executive branch of government. (Audubon v. Evans, 14–17)

The problem here has not been any shortcoming in the laws, but simply a refusal of administrative agencies to comply with them. ... This invokes a public interest of the highest order: the interest in having government officials act in accordance with the law. ... The Forest Service here has not taken the necessary steps to make a decision in the first place, yet it [now] seeks to take action with major environmental impact [viz., to go forward with logging another 66,000 acres]. ...

To bypass the environmental laws, either briefly or permanently, would not fend off changes [of] transforming the timber industry. The argument that the mightiest economy on earth cannot afford to preserve old growth forests for a short time, while it reaches an overdue decision on how to manage them, is not convincing today. It would be even less so a year or a century from now.

For the reasons stated, the public interest and the balance of equities require the issuance of an injunction directing the Forest Service to comply with the requirements of NFMA by March 5, 1992, and preventing it from selling additional logging rights in spotted owl habitat until it complies with the law. (Audubon v. Evans, 27–28)

For a discussion of the fall-down in the level of cutting in the wake of this decision, see the author's *Conserving Oregon's Environment*.*

The person whose expertise was used to frame the Northwest Forest Plan

---

* McCloskey, *Conserving Oregon's Environment*, 200.

was **Jack Ward Thomas**, who spent decades as a Forest Service researcher in La Grande, Oregon, working on the problems of forest health in the Blue Mountains. His work in putting the plan together catapulted him into the position of chief of the Forest Service.

From an interview in 2001 with Harold K. Steen:

> The [new] mission [for the Forest Service that] emerged [from the spotted owl controversy] is the enhancement and protection of biodiversity and sustainability. This ... [was] exactly what the ... committee of scientists ... [had] identified as the [needed] mission.
>
> If we don't get questions over our mission straightened around, we will continue to flounder.

In his memoir, he identified over-cutting as at the heart of the problem.

In a speech he gave in 1995 (on June 26) to the Outdoor Writers Association, he proclaimed:

> These [public lands are] ... our lands, and [are]... all the lands most of us will ever own ... . Such a birthright stands alone— in all the earth. ... This heritage is too precious ... to be traded away ... .

He urged them to speak out in defense of public lands.

Jack Ward Thomas (1934-2016), wildlife biologist, researcher, official, professor. Jack Ward Thomas lived in La Grande, Oregon, for some twenty years as he ran the Forest Service research station there doing research on wildlife. He loved going into the wilderness in the nearby Wallowas. He had graduate degrees in wildlife management and land planning. That background drew him into pivotal roles in devising a plan to protect the northern spotted owl through the Northwest Forest Plan, which drastically reduced logging levels.

It was the controversy over the spotted owl that brought him to the attention of President Bill Clinton and in 1993 catapulted him into the position of chief of the Forest Service.

An Oregonian who has spent his career making the case for large, old trees and trying to root forestry in more well-grounded science is **Jerry Franklin**. As a research ecologist, he spent years associated with the HJ Andrews Experimental Forest, while teaching at various universities.

Jerry Franklin (1936–), research ecologist, professor. Franklin was born in Oregon and did graduate work in forest management and botany. He was stationed in Corvallis, Oregon, from 1959 to 1973, working on research for the Forest Service as a plant ecologist and until 1986 directing a research project in Blue River at the HJ Andrews Experimental Forest. He has also taught in the Forestry Department at Oregon State. Since 1986 he has shifted his primary teaching responsibilities to the University of Washington.

His research has focused on old growth and how forest ecosystems recover from disturbances. He has been critical of standard clear-cutting practices and has encouraged leaving more large trees in areas being logged, as well as dead trees and woody debris. He has pioneered notions of forestry better rooted in findings of science. His work has been recognized with many awards. He also served on the committee of scientists that devised the Northwest Forest Plan.

In an interview he gave to the editors of American Forests in 2013, he elaborated on a theme that has long been implicit in his research findings:

We really don't have forest management policies that call for … maintaining populations of big, old trees. … We don't have a policy that says we recognize that the big, old trees are a structural element of our forests that we want to retain (and restore where we've lost it) because it's important to the completeness of these ecosystems.

In response to a request to clarify what he meant, he said:

Where we've got them [i.e., large, old trees], we keep them.

Where we don't have them, … we manage [a portion of the remaining intermediate-aged stands] … in a way that's going to lead to the development of large, old trees.

You really need all stages of successional development of forests in our federal forest landscapes. … But big, old trees aren't just oddities and objects of interest. We need to have populations of big, old trees present in much of our forest landscape in order to provide the kinds of habitat that we need for a lot of our wildlife.

Afternoon Sky, Harney Desert by Childe Hassam (1908)
Provided courtesy of the Portland Art Museum

Harney Desert by C. E. S. Wood (1908)
Provided courtesy of the Portland Art Museum

Cascade Head by Charles McKim (1916)
Provided courtesy of the Portland Art Museum

Tongue Point by Cleveland Rockwell (1905)
Provided courtesy of the Oregon Historical Society

Oregon Coast by Cleveland Rockwell (1907)
Provided courtesy of the Oregon Historical Society

Whipping the Trask by Cleveland Rockwell (1884)
Provided courtesy of the Oregon Historical Society

Provided courtesy of the Oregon Historical Society

Provided courtesy of the Oregon Historical Society

CHAPTER NINE

Oregon in Contemporary Times

US Senator Mark Hatfield did not associate himself with the changes that came with the Northwest Forest Plan. He was viewed as the timber industry's most powerful ally in Congress, but at the same time, he sought to maintain viable relations with environmentalists, often adding wild rivers in Oregon to the national system and shepherding middle-of-the-road wilderness bills through Congress. As elections approached, he usually tried to improve his environmental record.

Extracts from his foreword to *Treasures of the Oregon Country* by Maynard C. Drawson (1973):

> Oregon is a land of enchantment, with unknown treasures to be found around every corner. …
>
> Even a native of the state is constantly discovering [its] … rich heritage which abounds from coast to mountains, through valleys

Mark Hatfield (1922–2011), professor, politician (independent Republican). Hatfield grew up near Salem, Oregon, and attended college there. After service in the navy in WWII, he earned a master's degree in political science at Stanford University, which equipped him then to teach political science at Willamette University.

He quickly began an ascent through political offices in Oregon: seats in the legislature, then secretary of state, followed by two terms as governor of Oregon. At that point, he won a seat as a US Senator (an open seat). He kept winning reelection, becoming Oregon's longest serving senator ever (serving longer than even Charles McNary). Ultimately, he became chairman of the influential Senate Appropriations Committee.

While he was viewed as a moderate Republican, he quite regularly looked after the interests of the timber industry—estranging himself from environmentalists in the process. Nonetheless, he shepherded a number of packages of wilderness bills for Oregon through Congress—though,

and in the highlands and deserts. It would be difficult, indeed, to find an area more diverse and exciting. ...

From the rugged coast (ranked by many as the most beautiful seashore anywhere) to the lush green forests of the coast and Cascade Mountain ranges, ... the land beckons the explorer...

Oregonians, being particularly proud of their state with its breath-taking scenery, ... have rightfully become defensive about it. Steps are being taken constantly ... to help maintain the all-important harmony between man and nature, which will assure that Oregon is preserved for generations to come.

Remarks of Sen. Mark Hatfield on how the Opal Creek Wilderness got saved, made in 2004 in a speech to the Friends of Opal Creek.

This has been ... a national treasure that had to be protected. And it was worthy of your support, worthy of your perseverance, and all these factors have made it a reality. ...

I would to also say that my impression [of it] very much coincided with [that of] of Mr. Seideman, who wrote that ... "logging in Opal Creek would be [like] defiling a church."

As we all know, Opal Creek represents one of western Oregon's last remaining intact, low-elevation areas of old growth ... [forests]. But it is much more than that. It is a powerful symbol to so many of you. It is an inspiration. It is a place of ... spiritual renewal, and exploration. To walk among the century old hemlock[s] and cedar[s] inspires ... awe, and instills ... perspective on life itself. ...

I want to also say we had reached ... ground zero ... [in] the great timber debates that raged in the

Northwest in the 1980s. I think that … the history of [those debates] … [includes] … debates [at Opal Creek] between Tom Hirons and George Atiyeh. …

I have [now] learned patience. It does not come naturally to me. But I've learned another thing, and that is that patience goes only so far. And 1996 was [the] time to act.

He had been holding off action in Congress until a consensus emerged among the contenders, but it never emerged.

Some have … asked … why did you wait to do it [until] the last year of your Senate career? I wanted to see it done. I indicated that in 1984 and 1989, and so consequently I knew this was the time to act before I had to leave the … [senate].

He then explained that the house majority leader would not allow it to be brought up in the appropriations bill and steps were being taken to delete it from the pending bill in a meeting of the conferees. He then explained:

I then said: "May I speak to the motion?" I said: "If that motion passes, I can assure you that I will [then] bring the entire bill down."

Hatfield then headed the Senate Appropriations Committee and could do that.

And they knew I had announced my retirement. They knew I had nothing to lose. And so there was a silence. … But as we sat there, and they saw that I was serious … Finally, Newt Gingrich … said: "I think that we have your message, and it stays." … [And at that point] we had [saved] Opal Creek.

most of them hued to the middle of the road.

However, he did please environmentalists by getting Congress to confer federal wild river status on many rivers in Oregon, even small ones. And he did oppose a few proposed federal dams, such as the proposed Cascadia Dam on the South Santiam River. He also secured important funding for the urban wildlife program developed by staff of the Portland Audubon Society. His record is hard to classify in conventional terms. It consists of some liberal, some conservative, and some libertarian positions. He cherished his independence; some even viewed him as a maverick.

Remarks relating to Senator Hatfield's work to reduce the arms race and nuclear testing:

> When I entered Hiroshima [as an American naval officer], the charred bodies were still being pulled out of the rubble. The horror that I experienced burned a lasting impression in my conscience.
>
> To this day, it serves as a philosophical anchor—my beacon of clarity in [the] … political arena; [I] turn a deaf ear … [to] those who … speak the exotic language of megatons, kill-probability ratios, and other terms that desensitize us to the true nature of nuclear war. …
>
> There is no ethical dimension to the arms race—to our abuse of our natural and human resources, to our waste of scientific genius, to the bankrupting of the Federal Treasury to pay for weapons of mass destruction.

Note: Senator Hatfield was a long-time leader in Congress in pushing for arms control and a ban on nuclear testing. He deserves to share in the credit for the progress that has been made to date in this regard.

Dr. John Kitzhaber served as governor of Oregon at a later time than

Hatfield, but he was elected as governor more times than anyone else (four times). He was known for championing the welfare of the salmon and supporting removal of problematic dams on the lower Snake River. He also worked to strengthen the state's Forest Practices Act. He left office before completing his fourth term because of questions raised about the influence of his fiancée on his official duties.

Passages from his State of the State Address of 1997:

> For sure, ... [the essence of Oregon is like] ... standing on a beach watching the sunset. For others, it is [like] standing on a mountain, watching the sun rise. ...
>
> It has something to do with the place itself—its natural beauty, its abundance of natural resource, its variety of landscape.
>
> It has something to do with us—our reverence for the land and open spaces that makes us skeptical of growth, even as we welcome prosperity. Whatever it is, whatever its components, Oregon has some quality that we cannot define, but that we can all recognize. It's why we're here. It's why we chose to come. It's why we chose to stay.

Passages from a foreword to *The Rogue: Portrait of a River* (2007):

> Rivers have always held a special place in my heart. ... As I grew older, my father and I took ... to the banks of the great rivers of western Oregon—rivers with

Dr. John Kitzhaber (1947–), physician, politician (Democrat). Kitzhaber was raised in Oregon. Taking a degree at Dartmouth and an MD from Oregon Health & Science University, he began as an emergency room doctor in Roseburg, Oregon.

From there, he was elected to serve in the state legislature and then went on to serve three terms as a state senator—becoming senate president in his last term. In that position, he is credited with leading the way toward the enactment of the Oregon Health Plan, as well as modest improvements in Oregon's Forest Practices Act. In 1994 he was elected governor of Oregon and, on and off, was elected three more times. He served longer in this position that anyone else. He resigned early in his fourth term when questions were raised about the propriety of the involvement of his fiancée in the affairs of his office.

He defended the Oregon land-use planning process, fending off efforts to weaken it. He championed the needs of the endangered salmon—calling for removal of dams that impeded their runs. He initiated a plan to promote better land management practices to advance the welfare of salmon through urging landowners to collaborate with salmon activists, but it is still unclear whether that effort made much of a difference.

names like the Santiam, the Umpqua, and the Rogue. It was along these rivers that I first met the salmon in its native habitat and developed my lifelong fascination with it and its life cycle.

It was here that I first watched the Chinook fight their way upstream against the current—fighting impossible falls, hurtling their silver bodies skyward with the spray breaking the light into rainbows.

If I had to pick a metaphor for the Rogue River—something that captures its essence, the intangible dimensions of this special place—it would be the salmon, which is, more than anything else, dedicated to the future—to nurturing, sustaining, and giving to that which will follow.

Jane Claire Dirks-Edmunds was a scientist who wrote like a poet. A long-time professor of biology at Linfield College, she spent decades studying the microorganisms on the forest floor. She did path-breaking work in recording the immense number of them and studying the effect of ecological change. She made major contributions to understanding the complexity and organic richness of old-growth forests.

In her book *Not Just Trees* (1999), she describes what she saw there. On first arriving, she reveled in the beauty of the setting.

All about us, deeply-grooved Douglas-firs, four to six feet in diameter and bare of branches for at least 100 feet, towered skyward like columns in a vast temple. Details of the trees' wide-spreading crowns were lost in the dark green canopy high above. Hemlocks, smoother of bark, stately and straight of trunk, reached up at least 150 feet into the lower branches of the firs. A short distance in front of us, an equally large smooth-barked noble fir added its branches to the canopy of green.

Recently-fallen logs formed convenient paths through scattered patches of sword fern, salal, and Oregon grape, while older logs, moss-covered and disintegrating, supported rows of young hemlocks or clusters of huckleberry and salal. (p. 6)

At trailside in the deeper woods, green Lilliputian sentinels stood guard above the moss carpet, each one soon-to-open, [the] heart shaped main leaf of lily-of-the valley, sheathing a spike of tiny white flowers. Sprays of false Solomon's seal over-hung the lilies-of-the-valley, and Clintonia blossoms dotted the ground like dime-sized, white stars where the carpet of moss was thin.

Here and there, graceful panicles of purple bleeding heart nodded among their delicately dissected leaves, but the lovely white trilliums, which had been plentiful a few weeks earlier, had all but disappeared. Only a few, now pink with age, remained.

Every clump of sword fern had in its center a ring of fiddle necks, fuzzy unfurled fronds only a few inches tall, like brownish-green gnomes standing at prayer with bowed heads.

The conifers, too, showed new growth. Boughs of hemlock were etched in palest green, and in openings young Douglas-firs bore soft green paint brushes at the tips of their branches.

Near some of the larger trees, dainty white blossoms peeked out from beneath the three-lobed leaves of wood sorrel, and all along the way candy-striped, spring beauty flowers sprinkled the forest floor. (p. 14)

She tried to estimate the number of micro-organisms in the forest floor.

In [the] ... duff she found: "... more than a billion and a half little creatures in the top four inches of an area slightly

Jane Claire Dirks-Edmunds (1912–2003), biologist, ecologist, professor. She moved to western Oregon as a child (to the Roseburg area) and then earned her bachelor's degree at Linfield College and later a PhD at the University of Illinois. For most of her career, she taught at Linfield. Her studies took her to the Sonoran Desert and to Guatemala.

She was deeply influenced by her mentor at Linfield, Professor James Macnab. He took her to his research site on Saddleback Mountain near the Lincoln County-Polk County line. Over the next thirty-five years, they returned there again and again to examine ecological changes as its management evolved. Together, they did pioneering ecological studies on all the organisms on the forest floor. She described them in a book that she finally published in 1999 entitled *Not Just Trees: The Legacy of a Douglas-fir Forest.*

larger than two football fields." … "Tread lightly. The ground is full of life." (p. 287)

Giant fir trees were the skyscrapers in our forest. Recent research has revealed that the canopies of such trees, which tower 250 to 300 feet (twenty to thirty stories) above the ground, overflow with a bounty of nitrogen-fixing lichens and myriad other kinds of life.

Also marvel of marvels, hidden beneath the surface of the forest floor, a great web of fungal filaments—mycorrhizae—entwine the roots of the trees, constantly supplying them with essential nutrients from the soil.

The huge trees temper the weather, moderating wind force and extremes of temperature. Their needle-laden branches intercept winter snows and summer showers, keeping the ground beneath them relatively dry. When curtains of fog roll in from the ocean, those same towering crowns offer a place for moisture to condense and drip to the absorbent cushion of [the] sponge-like forest floor. (p. 290–91)

At the top of this, [in a] hidden world, is a sponge-like mat of dead twigs, fir and hemlock needles, decaying leaves and bits of wood. Mosses cover the forest floor in all but the most dense thickets of young trees. Tree limbs and logs of many sizes, in all stages of decay, lie on the moss, or make up a layer of litter beneath the moss.

The mat protects the forest floor inhabitant in many ways. It keeps them from drowning or being washed away by winter's rains. It also blankets them from the cold. By releasing moisture slowly, it acts as an air-conditioning system in summer, regulating humidity and preventing sudden temperature changes.

Below the new litter, or duff, is the humus layer, relatively shallow, but dark and rich and composed of bits of organic material.

Beneath these layers is the soil itself which has been changed, through eons of time, from the underlying primordial rock into material which sustain the many kinds of life found in the forest city. (p. 292)

Then, emerging from the trees on the far side of the river, I stopped, shocked with disbelief. Where I had expected to see a thriving young forest [the research site had been lightly logged in 1940], a great swath of clearcut stretched before me. Mere days before, hemlocks, firs, and cedars had soared skyward in that place. … Now, only occasional battered stumps, shards of shrubs, and a few splintered saplings relieved the barrenness scraped free of everything organic. Every trace of the spongy forest floor with its untold abundance of life was gone.

So, this is … clear-cutting, I thought. (p. 295)

Note: Late in her career, she was active in trying to save surviving ancient forests through establishment of the Northwest Forest Plan.

As a US Senator, **Ron Wyden** has struggled to find a way to satisfy environmentalists in Oregon on forest issues and still appear to be balanced. He also struggles to meet the demands of environmentalists on trade issues while catering to major industries in the state that trade abroad.

But at times, he has been a leader, as he was in combatting the polluting

Ron Wyden (1949–), lawyer, politician (Democrat). After earning a degree from Stanford, he took his law degree from the University of Oregon. He began his career teaching gerontology and founded the Gray Panthers of Oregon. At the young age of thirty-one, he won a Congressional seat representing Portland—which he held for fourteen years. In 1996 he was elected to the US Senate—a seat that he has held since.

He struggles with forest issues, finding it difficult to satisfy both environmentalists and those trying to keep the timber industry going. He has not been able to find a viable path on O & C Lands in southwestern Oregon, nor on providing real protection to old growth elsewhere.

While he has supported many positions backed by environmentalists and is regarded as a liberal, he seeks the support of the high-technology industry. Thus, he has supported most trade agreements, such as NAFTA, which was opposed both by environmentalists and labor. His voting record has bounced around. Nonetheless, in 2016 he scored 100% on the League of Environmental Voters scorecard. He is most intensely involved with issues of civil liberties and peace, and takes independent positions on matters of health care and tax policy.

effects of benzene in gasoline brought into the state. And in recent years, he has had a perfect environmental voting record (from an environmentalist's standpoint). And he has been a progressive leader on other issues.

Press release from Senator Wyden on the need to reduce high levels of benzene in gasoline in Oregon (November 1, 2006):

Oregon and the Northwest could be hurt, not helped, by a proposed new federal rule regarding the amount of the cancer-causing benzene that can be in gasoline … unless the rule is changed to protect Oregonians and others in the Northwest.

According to the Oregon Department of Environmental Quality (DEQ) … gasoline in Oregon and the Northwest contains almost twice as much cancer-causing benzene as the national average, and three times as much as California gasoline (which is strictly regulated).

Ironically, federal regulators allow the high levels of benzene in gasoline in Oregon and the Northwest because when the US EPA started to regulate air, they focused on the dirtiest, most populated areas. Thus, because the air was (and is still is) cleaner here, the federal government did not regulate fuel in Oregon and the Northwest, and its residents are put more at risk by the allowance of unlimited amounts of benzene in fuel.

The proposed US EPA rule could turn the Northwest into an environmental sacrifice zone, endangering our residents by the very air they breathe. We need a nationwide minimum standard that says you can have this much benzene and that's it. It should not vary from region to region. …

Oregon gets 90 percent of its gasoline from refineries in Washington State, with more than 80 percent of that gasoline coming from oil from the North Slope of Alaska. The Alaskan oil may have 10 times the benzene as oil from other parts of the country (according to US EPA).

Note: The proposal by the Bush Administration for the EPA was dropped after Senator Wyden threatened to hold up confirmation of their nominee for General Counsel of EPA. However, they only promised to phase out varying levels of benzene over many years.

Ted Kulongoski has had a remarkable career in state government, serving in all three branches and being elected twice as governor of Oregon. Environmentalists gave him high marks while he was in office, and he spoke in moving terms about the state's environmental role.

He led the way in getting the state to commit to renewable fuel resources and in blocking destination resorts in the Metolius Basin. Yet he seems to have made little memorable impression, which is unfortunate.

Extracts from the inaugural speech of Governor Theodore (Ted) Kulongoski on January 8, 2007:

> Oregon is the state that beckons us to search out and find where the sunrise begins and the river ends—part nature, part spirit, part memory, [and] part dream…

TED KULONGOSKI

... A generation ago, Oregon led the nation by preserving our coastline and beaches, and by our stewardship of public land. Today we must lead on global warming—and the development of biofuels and other alternative sources. Past is prologue. On energy independence, where Oregon goes, America will learn to follow.

As for a sustainable economy, I will say simply this: put aside legalisms and complexities for a moment, and remember why we care about the environment in the first place. Protecting open spaces, our forests, our rivers and wetlands defines us as Oregonians. It is who we are!

Sustainability is another opportunity—an opportunity to stay true to ourselves, and to pass to future generations the same environmental treasure that our forebears—both native and pioneers—passed [on] to us.

From his State of the State Address to the legislature on January 12, 2009:

There is a green revolution stirring in America, and Oregon is the beating heart of that revolution. But it won't be for long if we call a timeout on our move toward investing in renewable energy and green technology.

We have already laid down clear markers of leadership in building America's new energy future:

- the largest number of photovoltaic solar cells in North America will be manufactured in Oregon;
- the most ambitious renewable energy portfolio was codified in Oregon;

- the highest per capita use of hybrid vehicles is here in Oregon;
- and the longest—and most storied—tradition of protecting our natural heritage remains in Oregon.

The state is taking the lead in cutting greenhouse gases: everything from buying electric cars to investing in wave energy.

But meaningful reductions will require changes in the way we produce and use energy.

If we're going to significantly cut greenhouse gases, we are going to have to think bigger than capping emissions and trading credits.

We are also going to have to innovate, educate, and invest!

This means more research and development into energy efficiency and conservation: creating a larger science infrastructure that will attract and train scientists and engineers, and making sure Oregon businesses have the opportunity to generate a critical mass of brainpower, financial power, and marketing power.

When it comes to fighting climate change, recently I have been hearing a chorus of naysayers singing a three-part harmony of: too costly, too burdensome, and too soon.

But this is out of tune—and out of touch—with Oregon's future.

The time has come to put away the old songbook about a healthy environment being an impediment to a steady, strong, and sustainable economy. It wasn't true 30 years ago, and it is not true now. …

Theodore Kulongoski (1940–), lawyer, public official (Democrat). Ted Kulongoski moved to Oregon after he earned his bachelor's and law degrees, commencing a practice in Eugene as a labor lawyer. A few years later, he began an amazingly diverse career in public service in the state: serving a few years in both houses of the legislature and then serving as state insurance commissioner. In 1992 he was elected as the state's attorney general and a few years later was elected to the state's supreme court.

When John Kitzhaber stepped aside after two terms as governor, Kulongoski resigned as a justice and ran for governor, winning two terms (between 2003 and 2011). He won his second term by a comfortable margin. He is one of the few public officials in Oregon to have served in all three branches. He had a good environmental record but did not have a high profile.

The Portland Audubon Society has pioneered the understanding that many wild birds find suitable habitat in the urban area. Many migrating birds are attracted by the diverse vegetation growing in the urban area; few places support so many species of trees as Portland. Landscaped yards provide bushes of particular interest to birds, as well as to butterflies. For some birds, good nesting and roosting sites can be found in the urban area. In this sense, many aspects of the wild can be found in the city.

Mike Houck has developed this idea and features it in the book he has edited, *Wild in the City*, along with incorporating essays of well-known writers who offer additional insights.* He is a naturalist, who, since 1980, has been professionally associated with the Portland Audubon Society. In this book, he also identifies remnants of wild lands that survive in the Portland urban area.

Extracts from Mike Houck et al. in *Wild in the City*:

> [Mt. Tabor Park] is … a hotspot for resident and migrant birds, and an unofficial checklist contains upwards of 150 species (including an impressive list of rare migrants—"one-day wonders"—that have shown up over the years). Because it contains such a diversity of habitats—parkland dotted with tall firs and big-leaf maples, thickets and hedge-rows, and a remnant coniferous forest near the summit—Mt. Tabor is a good birding spot year round. But is especially spectacular between late March and mid-June, when this green atoll becomes a magnet for the migrating songbirds that are pouring through Portland. During that period, a short stroll around the butte can easily turn up thirty to forty species. (essay by Bob Wilson, 138)

---

* *Wild in the City*, ed. by Houck and Cody.

Each fall, Vaux's swifts gather at the Chapman Elementary School chimney and for a month or so, put on an unbelievable aerial sunset show. Vaux's swifts (*Chaetura vauxi*) arrive in Portland from their southern wintering grounds in late April and nest throughout the area.

In late August, they start gathering at Chapman … in Northwest Portland's Wallace Park to roost in the school's large chimney. Ever greater numbers of swifts gather over the next month and each night treat delighted onlookers to aerial vortices and antics with a climactic downward "pouring" of birds into the chimney—an avian tornado—as the sky darkens. (essay by Jennifer Devlin, 113)

Lying at the heart of the beautifully manicured Reed College campus, the Reed College Canyon remains an island of untamed nature in the center of an urban area. … The canyon has been the focus of an ambitious habitat restoration project for the past decade. This work has restored the canyon to its "natural" state while improving opportunities for visitors to appreciate its beauty.

Watershed planning efforts over the years repeatedly identified Crystal Springs (especially its headwaters) as a high priority for restoration in order to benefit steelhead, cutthroat trout, and coho salmon spawning and rearing habitat. The Oregon Department of Fish and Wildlife … gave the creek the second highest score for supporting fish populations of all tributaries sampled in Portland.

Reed College began restoration of its lake and canyon in 1999. It has [now] achieved a number of [its] objectives, including the observed diversity of wildlife [there] … The Reed Canyon is a local treasure—a carefully managed wilderness in the heart of the city. (essay by Zachariah Perry and Bob Salinger, 268–69)

Regarding Forest Park:

The sights and sounds of a deep forest habitat define the experience, although the steady hum of the city [can occasionally be heard]. The song of the wren permeates the forest year-round, and the wild cackles of the pileated woodpecker and northern flicker are a less common delight.

Recent research has confirmed that the park holds a thriving population of northern pygmy owls, who are just one of the dozens of native birds actively nesting in Forest Park. In recent years, bald eagles have returned to nest in the northern section of the park. Two of the larger watershed in the park, Balch and Miller creeks, feature vibrant populations of native cutthroat trout and coastal giant salamanders. (essay by Stephen Hatfield, 128)

Despite this great change [i.e., habitat destruction], Oregon [white] oaks and the plant and animal communities associated with them survive in small places.

Recently it was discovered that some oak woodlands in our urban landscape contain intact remnant populations of locally rare and regionally significant plant communities [such as at the Camassia Nature Preserve in West Linn]. Over two hundred species of amphibians, reptiles, mammals, and birds are known to use [these trees] within [their] range in Western Oregon …

Big, old, and isolated Oregon white oaks may have great value for biodiversity by providing stepping-stone connections between fragmented habitats. With the onset of climate change, the habitat connections between these legacy trees may provide an important way to help some wildlife migrate to new, more suitable places to live. (essay by Mark G. Wilson, 67)

In the late 1960s, Oaks Pioneer Park was well on its way to conversion to industrial development … . As early as 1963, the Audubon Society of Portland, the Sierra Club, and the Nature Conservancy … [pushed to have the] Oaks Pioneer Park … be established as [the] Wapato Marsh Wildlife Refuge.

In 1988, the Portland City Council adopted the Oaks Bottom Wildlife Management Plan, which was … [produced] by the Portland park staff [among others, thus saving the area]. (Houck, 76)

Describing a ride along the Holgate Channel, author and editor Mike Houck muses:

> You are now [on a dirt trail near the Springwater Trail] walking across rubble deposited from the construction of the Interstate 405 freeway in the late 1960s … . Fortunately for us, civic leader John Gray and another … negotiated with [the] Drake Construction Company, which had plans to develop the north fill into an industrial park, and persuaded the company to sell it to them. The land was held until the city was able to purchase it (at cost). [After rehabilitation] … this unsightly fill [became] … a wildlife-friendly meadow and wetland. (78)

Government Island is a bit like the land that time forgot. It is a place where coyotes stalk the beaches at dawn and black-tailed deer swim between the islands at sunset. Beavers fell cottonwoods as big round as VW bugs and drop them in a futile effort to dam the mighty Columbia.

Prehistoric-looking great blue herons, with crooked necks and heavy wing beats, flap in and out of their rookery, bringing food to their croaking, beak-clacking, three-quarter grown young. Recently fledged peregrine falcons "cack" from nearby trees, demanding food from their parents. A convocation of

Mike Houck (1947–), zoologist, urban naturalist. Houck is a native Portlander. He earned a bachelor's degree in zoology and a master's degree in biology. Since 1980, he has been associated with the Portland Audubon Society as an urban naturalist. In 1999 he founded the Urban Greenspaces Institute, which he directs out of Portland State University, where he is an adjunct professor. In 2003–2004 he had a Loeb Fellowship at the Harvard School of Design and has won numerous awards.

He has put together two editions of *Wild in the City* (2000 and 2011), both of which he edited. Many of those who have written individual sections of the book are associated with the Portland Audubon Society.

nearly a dozen bald eagles, some full adults with their telltale white heads and tails ... feast on a Canada goose on the beach, only to find themselves doing battle with a bold raccoon whose hunger has overcome his common sense.

The fact that the island remains in a natural state at all is amazing. It was originally given the name of Diamond Island by Lewis and Clark, who camped there on November 3, 1805 and hunted ducks, swans, and geese by moonlight from a canoe. The U.S. government laid claim to it in 1850 for "military purposes" ... [such as raising] cattle for livestock ... .

More recently it could easily have morphed into a community of high-end condominiums and boat marinas. Worse yet, at one point, it was targeted to serve as the third runway for Portland International Airport (which purchased the island in 1969)—a feature that would have stretched across the narrow channels separating the island from the mainland, turning much of the island into deforested tarmac. However, the very thing that most threatened the island is ultimately what served to save it.

Public opposition, and financial constraints, caused the Port of Portland to abandon the runway project, and noise and safety regulations, associated with the nearby airport, precluded most forms of development. Instead, the Port used Government Island as a mitigation site to compensate for ... [environmental] impacts from [expansion of] the airport just across the channel, thus ushering in an era of restoration.

In March 1990, the Port of Portland signed a ninety-nine year lease with Oregon State Parks to manage Government Island as part of the State Park System. (essay by Mary Coolidge and Bob Salinger 313–14)

Paul Hawken is a nationally acclaimed sustainability "guru." His epiphany began with the garden supply company he started and went on from there. In 2009, in a commencement speech he gave to a graduating class at the University of Portland, he proclaimed:

> Here is the deal: Forget that this task of planet-saving is not possible in the time required. Don't be put off by people who know what is not possible. Do what needs to be done, and check to see if was impossible only after you are done.
>
> When asked if I am pessimistic or optimistic, my answer is always the same. If you look at the science about what is happening on earth and aren't pessimistic, you don't understand the data. But if you meet the people who are working to restore the earth … and you aren't optimistic, you haven't got a pulse.
>
> What I see everywhere in the world are ordinary people willing to confront despair, power, and incalculable odds in order to restore some semblance of grace, justice, and beauty to the world. …
>
> Humanity is coalescing. It is reconstituting the world, and the action is taking place in schoolrooms, farms, jungles, villages, campuses, companies, refugee camps, deserts, fisheries, and slums. …
>
> … For the first time in history [referring to those who pushed for the abolition of slavery in the 19th century], a group of people organized themselves to help people they would never know [and] from whom they would never receive direct or indirect benefit. And today millions of people do this every day.
>
> It is called the world of non-profits: civil society, schools, social entrepreneurship, non-governmental organizations, and companies who place social and environmental justice at the top of their strategic goals. The scope and scale of this effort is unparalleled in history.
>
> The living world is not "out there" somewhere, but in your heart.

Paul Hawken (1946-), businessman, author, sustainability activist. Hawken studied at UC Berkeley and San Francisco State, is an activist in various causes, and began his career in business. A garden supply business that he helped start enjoyed success; following that, he began to experiment with applying principles of sustainability in other businesses. In this country, he has been a leader in promoting the approach of the Natural Step. As his grasp of these principles deepened, he began writing books about sustainability—seven to date. Some of them have done well. He now speaks widely and appears on television, attracting acclaim.

What we do know about life? In the words of biologist Janine Benyus, life creates the conditions that are conducive to life. I can think of no better motto for a future economy. …

We are the only species on the planet without full employment. Brilliant! We have an economy that tells us that it is cheaper to destroy earth in real time rather [to] renew, restore, and sustain it. You can print money to bail out a bank, but you can't print life to bail out a planet.

At present we are stealing the future, selling it in the present, and calling it the gross domestic product. We can just as easily have an economy that is based on healing the future instead of stealing it. We can either create assets for the future or take the assets of the future.

One is called restoration and the other exploitation. And whenever we exploit the earth, we exploit people and cause untold suffering. Working for the earth is not a way to get rich. It is a way to be rich. …

Ralph Waldo Emerson once asked what we would do if the stars only came out once every thousand years. No one would sleep that night, of course. The world would create new religions overnight. We would be ecstatic, delirious, made rapturous by the glory of God. Instead, the stars come out every night, and we watch television.

This extraordinary time—when we are globally aware of each other and the multiple dangers that threaten civilization—has never happened, not in a thousand years, not in ten thousand years. Each of us is as complex and beautiful as the stars in the universe. We have done great things, and we have gone way off course in terms of honoring creation.

You are graduating to the most amazing, stupefying challenge ever [bequeathed] … to any generation. The generations before you failed. They didn't stay up all night. They got distracted and lost sight of the fact that life is a miracle every moment of your existence. Nature beckons you to be on her side. You couldn't ask for a better boss.

The most unrealistic person in the world is the cynic, not the dreamer. Hope only makes sense when it doesn't make sense [at all] to be hopeful. This is your century. Take it and run as if your life depends on it.

Another person whose writings have drawn acclaim is **David James Duncan**, who was born along the Columbia River, east of Portland. He is now viewed as a major nature writer.

This all began with his book *The River Why* (1983), which the Sierra Club published when no one else would. It is now viewed as a classic. That book featured a fictional river along the northern Oregon coast and tells the story of those who fished it and the destruction that began to envelop those waters.

Extract from *The River Why*:

The night grew more and more extraordinary, yet more and more familiar: I felt as though I were returning to some forgotten, ancient home. The river shimmered and glowed and shattered the moon. …

The moist sky with its few faint stars seemed to glow like a boundless river, and the … [coastal river] with its glittering bands of moonshine seemed like a ribbon of the Milkey-Wayed sky … (p. 380)

Duncan's fictional river was a combination of five rivers on the northern Oregon coast, rivers like the Nestucca.

The timber company … thinks that sawing down 200-foot tall spruces and replacing them with two-foot … [fir saplings] is no different from farming beans ... . They even call the towering spires they wipe from the earth's face forever a "crop"—as if they planted the virgin forest! (p. 97)

From a 2007 interview in *Grist*:

In responding to a question about good books that he had read, Duncan mentioned Paul Hawken's book *Blessed Unrest*. He said:

Paul's book is about the largest social movement in human history, which is rising up right now, in opposition to the powers of the WTO [World Trade Organization], the neocons, the World Bank, and the "free-market fundamentalists."

The resistance has taken the form of hundreds of thousands of NGOs dedicated to conservation, human rights, indigenous rights, life, and health before profit. Many books describe the world in ways that break our hearts.

Paul's book invokes a heartbreak from which light is pouring. He's a great storyteller—poetic or hard-minded as the case requires. The book moves, from a litany of "free-market" abuses and WTO crimes against the earth and humanity, to the countless life-saving actions of literally millions of altruists now enveloping the earth and uniting in response. It gave me chills. Read it and rejoice.

He concludes:

Nature's power rises up from below, inexorable as karma. As [poet] Jim Dodge says, "Nature bats last."

Keep trying. Keep serving. Worrying is praying for what you don't want. Keep trying to feel grateful for what is beautiful, even as you're trying to change what is deadly.

David James Duncan (1952-), writer. Duncan was raised near the Columbia River east of Portland and wrote his first book, *The River Why* (1983), about fishing in Oregon's coastal waters and the destruction of nature. When other publishers rejected it, the Sierra Club published it. It is now viewed as a classic of its kind, and Duncan is viewed as a major nature writer in the tradition of Thoreau.

The integrity of rivers and coasts is a major concern of law professor **Mary C. Wood**, a great granddaughter of Charles Erskine Scott Wood. She has recently written a provocative book: *Nature's Trust*, which has stimulated public interest law suits to test the concept.

In 2011, at Oregon State University, she set forth her ideas of how to protect nature through a public trust doctrine as part of a lecture series:

> The United States has the most elaborate and convoluted set of environmental laws in the world. Though directed at different problems, nearly all environmental statutes have one thing in common: they rely on agencies to carry out their mandates.
>
> You see, all of nature has been partitioned among various bureaucracies—many hundreds in all, spanning the federal, state, and local levels. These agencies are supposed to protect natural resources for present and future generations.
>
> But nearly all laws have a permit provision by which agencies can approve damage to nature. The permit provisions were never intended to swallow the statutes, but they have. The bulk of the agencies' work today is issuing permits, or blanket approvals, for pollution and destruction of natural resources. In surveys across multitudes of agencies, you see that only about 1 percent of the permits are denied.
>
> Congress and state legislatures gave these agencies tremendous discretion: because they are expert bodies, and they are assumed to exercise their judgment in an objective manner—for the good of the public and in accordance with the statutes' goals. But this agency

MARY C. WOOD

Mary C. Wood (1962–), lawyer, professor, author. She is the great granddaughter of Charles Erskine Scott Wood and was born at a site along the Columbia River bearing her family's name. She earned her law degree at Stanford University. After a clerkship with the Ninth Circuit of the Court of Appeals, she practiced for a few years in the Northwest.

For most of her career, she has been teaching at the University of Oregon School of Law, directing its Environmental and Natural Resources program (which she founded). She teaches courses in property law, natural resources law, public lands law, wildlife law, federal Indian law, and public trust law. The quality of her teaching has been recognized with a flock of awards. She has written a number of textbooks and now is speaking widely on her newest book, *Nature's Trust*.

discretion has been corrupted, and its role in the modern demise of nature cannot be overstated. ...

It is telling that the most accelerated damage to [the] earth's resources has occurred during the modern era of environmental laws—that is since the 1970s. Overall, according to various assessments, the earth's natural ecosystems have declined by 33 percent during the last thirty years.

Would we be worse off without environmental laws? Almost certainly yes, but that's not the relevant question. The only relevant question is whether environmental law is doing its job to keep us in compliance with nature's laws. ...

You see, though there are some exceptions, the agencies are perpetrators of legalized destruction. They use the permit provisions (that are contained in every statute) to authorize colossal damage. For example, two-thirds of the greenhouse-gas pollution in this country is emitted pursuant to government-issued permits.

The pollution of rivers, the killing of species, and the destruction of wetlands and coastal zones are all carried out pursuant to permits or blanket regulation under environmental statutes. ...

The environmental law system legalizes colossal damage, and institutionalizes a marriage of power and wealth behind the veil of bureaucratic formality and scientific objectivity.

After four decades of this, humanity has no more time to waste in confronting the corruptive influence [of these practices] on agencies, [which includes] the politicization of science [in the exercise] ... of agency discretion. ... [These practices are permitting too much] damage to the environment; [we also need to confront] the failure of public process, and the shriveled role of the judicial branch in reviewing agency decisions. ...

I have devised a ... change that I call Nature's Trust. It rests on a bedrock principle that we already have in our legal system known as the public-trust doctrine. The public-trust doctrine was adopted by courts in the earliest days of our nation for the purpose of holding government accountable in protecting ecology, but it has been all but lost in the administrative jungle that has choked the field of environmental law over the last three decades. ...

The principle says that government holds our priceless natural assets in trust for present and future generations of citizens. A trust is [a] property construct whereby one manages assets for the benefit of another. ... Under the public-trust construct, natural assets, that are crucial to society's well-being, are the property of the people ... and they are managed by government according to strict fiduciary principles.

The lodestar public-trust opinion in this country is *Illinois Central Railroad Co. v. Illinois*. In that case, the Illinois legislature had given away the shoreline of Lake Michigan to a private railroad corporation—no doubt a result of political corruption. The U.S. Supreme Court said the legislature did not have the power to do that.

It held that the shoreline of Lake Michigan was held in public trust by the State of Illinois; and as a trustee of this priceless asset, government must protect it for the public and could not give it away to a private entity. The lakebed, it said, was a "subject of public concern for the whole people of the state," and therefore could not be alienated.

The essence of this doctrine requires management of natural resources for public benefit rather than for private exploit[ation] or political advantage. Simply stated, government trustees may not allocate rights to destroy what the people rightly own for themselves and for their posterity. Just as the trust would not allow the Illinois legislature to privatize the shoreline of Lake Michigan, the trust would not allow agencies to privatize all of [the ecosystems] by issuing hundreds of thousands of permits to pollute.

Trust principles also impose a strict duty of loyalty to the public beneficiaries. When agency officials act in self-interest, to benefit a politically powerful corporate interest over the public, or to advance their own bureaucratic ambition, they violate this basic fiduciary duty of loyalty. …

[This trust duty] … describes the citizens as beneficiaries holding a clear public property interest in natural resources … It views polluting corporations as marauders of the trust, rather than as … political "stakeholders" [who can use their power to] control the political sphere. And it presents nature as a priceless endowment comprised of tangible, quantifiable, assets holding value for future generations rather than a vague "environment" possessed of rather intangible and indeterminate value.

Others, such as **Barry Lopez**, try to protect nature by fostering an appreciative response to the language of his writings. He now makes Oregon his home and is regarded as America's "premier nature writer."

Quotes from Barry Lopez from an interview in *Wild Oregon* (Fall 1984):

[If] you turn people like [reductionists] … loose in science and let them testify in courts of law, … you [will] have chaos. And in some ways, that is part of the difficulty of bringing environmental issues into courts of law.

You get people who say: "Well, I can quantify all this. I can quantify beauty and stand up and make an argument for it in court." Well, of course, you can't—unless you debase it, or twist it, or turn it into something that it's not.

Passages from an account of a trip up French Pete Creek on August 14,

2014. French Pete Creek was the site of a famous and long-lived environmental contest (the forest won).

Hundreds of small deer's-head orchids are blooming, lavender and fuchsia in a jungle of green hues on the forest floor; thimbleberry thickets, tussocks of sword ferns in their fiddlehead stage, salal and Oregon grape, woodland strawberries, vanilla leaf, nodding stems of Solomon's seal, tufts of bear grass. ...

Gentle rain, light winds, errant shafts of sunlight piercing the forest canopy where fires crown, and the crash and roar of the bounding creek, all coming at once, so occupy the ear and eye that my bare hands, with their sensitivity to temperature, to the texture of tree bark and the strike of rain, bring me information for which there is hardly room.

I sense wild ginger and bleeding heart are close by—but can't spot them.

The white blossoms of trillium (a kind of lily), ... by now darkened to shades of magenta, are melting like colored tissue in the rain. We're still weeks from hawthorn blossoms, blue huckleberry fruit, pale pink trumpets blaring in the rhododendron thickets, nuts bedded in spiny bracts on the chinkapins, native blackberries ripening along with yellow-orange salmonberries. ...

Sheets of mist, slipping sideways on bursts of wind, roil ten thousand infant leaves on vine maples against a chiaroscuro sky—an Impressionist furze and yet one more shade of green, this one a pale one, leaning to yellow. When sunlight strikes them, the sheen of their wetness makes them seem lit from within.

In the understory are still other greens: jade and celery, apple

Barry Lopez (1945–), nature writer. He was born in the East and educated in the Midwest, but he has made his home in Oregon on the McKenzie River. Both his works of fiction and nonfiction usually have nature as a theme. His book *Arctic Dreams: Imagination and Desire in a Northern Landscape* (1986) won a National Book Award. He has also won the Literary Lion Award from the New York Public Library.

and shamrock, the celadons and malachites. In the canopy above, bottle and deep-blue-greens, the greens of emeralds.[*]

Another acclaimed writer about nature (a native Oregonian) is writer and poet **Kim Stafford**. He is the son of noted poet William Stafford. He teaches at Lewis & Clark College in Portland.

From his book *Having Everything Right: Essays of Place* (1986):

Kim Stafford (1949–), poet, writer, teacher. Kim Stafford has been teaching writing at Lewis & Clark College since 1979 and has published over a dozen books. He earned his PhD at the University of Oregon. He is the son of the noted poet William Stafford. Nature has been a setting for many of the poems of both writers.

From the rim of Joseph Canyon [in northern Wallowa County], … [I] started down. A snow squall ended in sunlight, where elk bedded across a meadow [were] ignoring me, and I followed their trails … down through the pines that flavored the wind I sipped, rollicking through damp needle-duff with a swinging step all afternoon. … And I plunged down the slope. …

My walk down Joseph Canyon was filled with sensation, with danger, meditation, and discovery—pitch and smoke, rain down my back, a bed of rock at the top of Starvation Ridge. An owl called as I crossed the net of moonlight filtered through trees. … I fed on nettle and fern root, and wood ticks fed on me. …[**] (p. 56)

From a poem of his entitled "Naknuwisha":

Young friend, be part of something old.
Be home here in the great world,
where rain wants to be your coat,

---

[*] Barry Lopez, "The Case for Going Wild," August 14, 2014.

[**] Kim Stafford, "Story That Saved a Life."

where forest wants to be your house,

where frogs say your name and your name,

where wee birds carry your wishes far

and sunlight reaches for your hand.

Be home here.

Be healed.

Be with us all,

young friend.[*]

Others who work to sustain the integrity of nature are scientists, such as **Dr. Dominick DellaSala**, who heads the Geos Institute in Ashland, Oregon. A PhD plant ecologist, he writes papers and books and testifies before public bodies. Not long ago, in 2009, he gave this testimony on the role of old-growth forests in forestalling climate change to a congressional committee that held a hearing on climate change:

> Our nation's forests absorb the equivalent of about 10% of our carbon emissions from fossil fuels (Smith and Heath, Depro 2007). Many studies have shown that old-growth forests accumulate carbon for centuries, and that these forests are not neutral holders of carbon but continue to sequester large amounts of it, even as they age—from 300 to 800 years (Luyssaert et al. 2008).
>
> Studies also have shown that when old trees are cut down and replaced by younger ones, there is a net reduction in carbon stores (Law et al., 2004, Depro et al., 2007). Much of this stored carbon is released to the atmosphere:
>
> • through loss of carbon in soils,

---

[*]   Kim Stafford, "Naknuwisha."

- decomposition and burning of slash left on site by loggers, and

- shipping and processing of wood products (Harmon et al., 1900, 2001). The relatively short shelf life of most wood products exacerbates these losses.

The losses are neither trivial nor compensated by fast growing, young trees; it could take hundreds of years until the new forests store as much carbon as did the original old forest (Harmon 2001).

Losses of stored carbon are particularly severe on industrial forest lands, where timber harvest rotations are much shorter (40–100 years), than [the time] it takes for carbon stored in the original old forest to be replenished (Harmon 2001, Luyssaert et al., 2008).

In Oregon, coastal old-growth forests store more carbon per acre than any other forest on Earth (Smithwick et al. 2002), [as well as being] … rich in unique fish and wildlife species.

However, the BLM [Bureau of Land Management] has finalized plans to increase logging of old forests in western Oregon (Western Oregon Plan Revisions, WOPR) by more than 400% in the coming decade, largely through clearcutting. According to BLM's own analysis, in comparison to letting these old forests grow, logging would release approximately 180 million tons of carbon that is currently stored in these forests. This is equivalent to driving one million cars for a period of 132 years.

The WOPR, in particular, is tantamount to liquidating one of our nation's most significant carbon stores while putting the viability of several endangered species at risk and compromising ecosystem services like clean water and air. New statutory direction is needed for BLM to optimize carbon storage and fish and wildlife habitat.

Dr. Dominick A. DellaSala (ca. 1956–), plant ecologist. DellaSala earned his PhD from the University of Michigan. He currently heads the Geos Institute in Ashland, Oregon, which he founded it in 2006. Before that, he worked for the World Wildlife Foundation. He has written over 200 technical papers on forest ecology and managing endangered species. Frequently quoted in the media, his recent book on the rainforests of the world received an award in 2012 from *Choice* magazine. He serves as an adjunct professor at Southern Oregon College.

In general, changing forestry and other land management practices on federal land represents one of the most powerful, and, quite frankly, least costly tools that the nation has in fighting climate change. Increasing carbon storage on and decreasing GHG emissions from federal lands is feasible across extensive areas and can be effectively implemented.

To combat climate change on public lands, a fundamental shift from current forestry practices is needed that:

(1) retains existing stores of carbon in mature and old forests as "carbon banks;" and

(2) … helps plantations and other intensively managed public forests optimize carbon stores by re-growing to older conditions (Harmon 2001).

Another important Oregon author who has written about life along the Oregon coast is **Brian Doyle**, whose book *Mink River* (2010) depicts life in Tillamook County. The Mink River is a fictional river, but may be based on the Nestucca River. Here is his effort to capture the essence of that river:

> I begin as a sheen on leaves high in the hills, a wet idea, a motion, a dream, a … [mystery], and then I am a ripple, and I gather the small waters to me, … the rills of the hills, and … run to her, muscling through wood and stone, cutting through everything, singing and shouting, … roiling and rippling, and there she is: waiting and whispering, her salty arms always opening and always open … (p. 151)

And he gives a marvelous evocation of the Oregon coast in the summer:

Brian Doyle (1956–2017), author, poet, editor. Brian Doyle edited the alumni magazine for the University of Portland, *Portland Magazine*. Under his leadership, it was usually rated as one of the best in the country. He also wrote over two dozen books, including novels, poems, and essays.

On a clear day, the Oregon coast is the most beautiful place on earth—clear and crisp and clean, a rich green in the land and a bright blue in the sky, the air fat and bracing, the ocean spreading like a grin. Brown pelicans rise and fall in their chorus lines in the wells of the waves, cormorant arrow, and an eagle, kingly [and] queenly, floats south—high above the water line. (p. 183–84)

Andy Kerr not only writes about the plight of nature in Oregon, he lobbies to protect it. He is probably the most successful and tenacious forest activist in Oregon. He probably has the best insights on how the environmental movement in Oregon can progress.

Extracts from an op-ed he wrote on January 6, 2015, for the Medford *Mail Tribune* on remaining efforts to log old-growth in Oregon:

Since 1995, Forest Service policy generally prohibits the logging of trees over 21 inches in diameter at breast height. In addition, since 2001, large roadless areas are generally off-limits to logging. There are no comparable protections on Bureau of Land Management (the so-called "O & C") lands in Western Oregon.

… The Forest Service has moved toward stewardship contracts, where timber revenues are retained by the agency and used for non-commercial forest and watershed restoration activities and developing more ecological restoration projects.

In contrast, the BLM still envisions a return to the bad old days when the O & C counties were rolling in federal timber receipts. Such was only possible when over two square miles per week of Oregon old-growth forests were being clearcut.

Milling capacity on the east side is [now] more closely aligned with ecological restoration needs. Since 1995—the year the protections for the west-side northern spotted owl and the east-side's big trees went into full effect—the number of wood products mills and jobs in Oregon have halved. Yet today, milling capacity (the appetite for logs) is one-quarter larger than it was in 1995. Far fewer mills and mill jobs, but the remaining mills are much larger and more efficient.

There are eight mills—centered in Douglas and Lane counties—that require very large logs from very large and old trees. Seven of these dinosaur mills actually modernized their equipment to more efficiently use large logs (like modern whaling stations that use every bit of the whale). Their business model requires large logs, now found only on federal lands and for which the social license to log has expired and won't be renewed. The nearly 40 other west-side Oregon sawmills have moved beyond old growth.

More significant than forest type or geography are the differences between the Forest Service and the BLM. The Forest Service now generally views logs as a byproduct of scientifically sound ecological restoration. The BLM still generally views logs as the paramount purpose of O & C lands. The Western Oregon federal public forestlands managed by the BLM … [should instead be] managed by the Forest Service.

Sen. Ron Wyden advanced O & C legislation in the Senate that would have protected more forests and also increased log supplies. There is a lot in his bill that I did not like, but I supported it.

In contrast, Reps. Greg Walden and Peter DeFazio passed a bill through the House of Representatives that would have effectively privatized 1.5 million acres of O & C lands to be logged like adjacent private timberlands.

Wyden's bill died because Senate leaders didn't have time to deal with a bill that they knew Walden would kill in the House.

Andy Kerr (1956–), environmental activist, consultant. After growing up in Creswell, Oregon, Kerr attended Oregon State University for a while but then dropped out. For two decades, he worked for the Oregon Natural Resource Council (now Oregon Wild)—helping to establish scores of wilderness areas in Oregon. He also led the fight to scale back logging of old-growth forests in Oregon. The *Oregonian* once said he "was the most despised environmentalist in timber country." Now he prepares policy papers and lobbies in the nation's capital.

I don't know of any credible conservation organization that says never another federal log. I do know of O & C counties and west-side mills that still want to clearcut old-growth forests and refuse to scale their demands to those which are ecologically, economically, and socially acceptable.

Another activist who works on the front lines and who has been doing it for years is **Cameron La Follette**. After earning a law degree, she chose instead to lead campaigns to protect nature where she felt the need was greatest. For quite some time, that has been along the Oregon coast. But early on, she prepared very important policy papers that identified the amount of remaining old growth and its value.

In 1979 Cameron La Follette gathered data around the state from national forest offices, preparing what turned out to be the first inventory of remaining old growth in the state's national forests. She titled it *Saving All the Pieces: Old Growth Forests in Oregon* (published by Oregon Student Public Interest Research Group). These are extracts from the introduction and conclusions:

> The majority of wilderness areas, where old growth might be provided, are in the subalpine zone or above [the] tree line. Few contain low elevation old growth. Therefore, most of the remaining old growth is in the already roaded portions of the national forests which have been opened for timber harvest.
>
> An evaluation dealing with priceless natural resources must take into account the irreversible and irretrievable nature of many possible decisions, and trade-offs that are made in implementing them.
>
> Without the inventory, no sound basis exists for ultimately determining whether any measures adequately protect the resource. For this reason, the question this paper addresses is not how much

old growth there should be or whether it should be [reserved at all]. … Rather this study examines whether the inventory is well enough done … to make a good evaluation.

Inventories of old growth in Oregon … are completely unstandardized at the moment; no two depict the same thing.

Old growth areas are frequently isolated from surrounding areas by poor timber sale layout or land use planning. This results in "islands" of old growth that lack communication with other "islands."

Allocation of land to [reflect] a certain resource emphasis does not happen without a rationale showing the benefits of doing so. Research of the sort [that] Jerry Franklin … and others have spearheaded provides an overview of the ecological importance of old growth … .

Multiple use is still … a somewhat fuzzy term. The Forest Service has frequently interpreted it to mean that all, or many … [of them], should be crowded into a given acre. … Multiple use does, however, include maintaining the productivity of the land. To reach this end, old growth must be retained, as old growth itself is multiple use.

Three [national forests, the Willamette, Mt. Hood, and the Umpqua,] are the major reservoirs of old growth left in Oregon, but they also have [the] highest resource conflicts. Liquidation of the remaining stocks is occurring rapidly, which increases the isolation of remaining stands. Without old growth [preservation] plans, this will continue unchecked.

Extracts from a 1981 proposal for a pilot plan for forest diversity:

Survival of an ecosystem approach in wildlife management on the public lands may signal a broader trend in perceiving the lands as an ecosystem—a series of interwoven threads, each of which is connected to all the others. … There are many components to the concept of landscape diversity. The idea of diversity evolved as a remedy to clarify the vagueness of the term "multiple use."

Extracts from her recent communications to the legislature on behalf of the Oregon Coast Alliance:

We write in strong opposition to SB 25, a bill to exempt eight counties in eastern Oregon from the land use laws if they have not shown population growth.

This bill, if passed, will set a terrible precedent for maintaining the integrity of Oregon's unique land-use laws. Though the majority of coastal counties where ... [the Alliance] works have shown modest growth in some years, ... at any time [they may] temporarily cease to have population growth—[owing] ... to economic factors.

They, too, would certainly want to apply for legislation similar to this bill ... [so that it could] ... be crafted for them. This would be a disaster. The coast is subject to nearly continuous natural hazards (coastal erosion, winter gales, increasing wave heights [during storms], very high tides, etc.) ... Strong land-use planning—to protect communities, [public] health and safety, and the transportation network—is critical. Land-use planning is also the prime tool that protects riparian habitat essential to providing clear, cold water necessary for the healthy salmon runs, so critical to coastal economies.

The only through highway on the coast is Highway 101. In many areas [it is threatened] with landslides and erosion, and [is] clogged with excessive development.

Highway 101 is the only lifeline for all communities, and it is essential to have an overall planning system that takes coastal transportation into account.

Sanitation infrastructure on the coast [whether urban or rural] is already in a shaky state, due to porous soils, unstable landforms, and insufficient funding for upgrades. In addition, many coastal areas suffer from old and leaking private septic systems, which then pollute groundwater, lakes, and streams. …

[The] Oregon Coast Alliance urges the committee not to pass SB 25. It is not conducive to a healthy, productive, and livable Oregon. (February 23, 2015)

We request the Committee's support for SB 830, with the amendments proposed by Senator Bates. This is a crucial bill to restore livability and salmon habitat to two major river systems on the south coast (among others in the state): the Rogue and its tributaries (including the Illinois); and the Umpqua.

She went on to say that with needed amendments, it "will create a regulatory framework to protect our rivers" and would include these elements:

1. A cap of 850 permits total … per year for suction dredge mining. The Department of Environmental Quality [would] … be the main permitting agency, with the Department of State Lands in an advisory … capacity. This streamlines the permitting process, making it less confusing for miners, the public, and the agencies themselves. It … limits permits to a reasonable number so that river systems and their fragile habitats are not destroyed.

2. Prohibiting mining in [the habitat of] sensitive species, including essential salmonid … lamprey, bull trout, and mollusk habitat.

La Follette added that the health of the riverine habitat and the species that depend on it turns on the overall health of the rivers themselves.

3. Granting DEQ authority to set fees for suction dredging

that … cover the cost of an effective program to analyze [cases], issue [permits], and enforce the program (including monitoring and [analyzing subsequent] … needs). This lifts the burden from taxpayers and sets it squarely on the shoulders of the miners, whose activities trigger the need for the program.

4. … Individual permits [should be required] for [mining in] … water-quality impaired streams—[mining that impacts] sediment, temperature, [triggers release of] toxic metals or [affects] other conditions that suction dredging exacerbates; … [permits should also be required for mining affecting] biologically sensitive waters and [in a zone] 100 yards alongside them.

These restrictions make sense, given the known sensitivity of riparian areas and their great importance both to rivers and to species that inhabit them, including salmonids, [which] … rely on riparian zones for cool water refugia.

5. Limiting mining in areas that would undermine Oregon's investment in salmon habitat restoration.

This last point is a tremendously important one. Oregon has spent millions of taxpayer dollars on salmon habitat restoration over the last decade. So much money has been spent in rural areas of the state that we are seeing the emergence of a restoration economy in rural areas, especially in the coastal zone. …

All of this investment is severely endangered by the large number of suction dredge miners congregating on the most productive salmon rivers, which also have some of the highest [investments] … in [this] … restoration economy—[these include] … the Rogue, Illinois, and Umpqua watersheds. The cumulative impacts of these dredges cause major harm to [these] … rivers. (April 15, 2015)

Extracts from a letter to a Wisconsin newspaper in Sheboygan County on May 5, 2015, regarding a disputed golf course there proposed by the Kohler Company, which had tried to build a destructive one in Oregon:

[The] Kohler Company appears to have a [tendency to place] … golf courses in unspoiled and cherished areas, as Oregonians came to learn. [The] Kohler Company seems to be currently pursuing the same strategy in its home state.

[In 2011] the company … failed in an Oregon attempt to combine 625 acres of the treasured Floras Lake State Natural Area, with land owned by Curry County, to create a massive, 1,263 acre golf course on Oregon's remote and beautiful south coast.

[The] Oregon Coast Alliance was one of the leaders in bringing about the defeat of this project, along with the impassioned residents of the little town of Port Orford and rural Curry County.

"When it was all said and done," Mr. Kohler said, "the environmentalists stirred up people, and they just decided they didn't want … development of any kind. … The environmentalists were just too determined. We'd be messing with them for five to seven years before we'd have anything."

Mr. Kohler's description was largely, but not wholly, accurate. It was "environmentalists," among others, who defeated the proposal. More importantly, it was the residents of Port Orford and rural Curry County who let it be known—loud and clear—that they would defend Floras State Natural Area and the quiet rural life they treasured. They succeeded.

Cameron La Follette (ca. 1957–), career organizer, poet. She is related to the La Follette family of Wisconsin. She earned a degree in journalism and advanced degrees in law and psychology. Much of her working career has been in Oregon, where she has devoted herself simultaneously to both environmental advocacy and poetry. Early on, she distinguished herself in tracking down the amount of old growth left in the forests of Oregon and in identifying its values, working for OSPIRG (Oregon Student Public Interest Research Group) and with the Oregon Wilderness Coalition. In this research, she visited all of the offices of the national forests in Oregon and even some of the offices for ranger districts. Later, she played a leading role in saving the old growth in Crabtree Valley east of Albany, Oregon. Over time, she worked for a succession of Oregon environmental groups: OSPIRG, 1000 Friends of Oregon, the Oregon Shores Conservation Coalition, and the Oregon Coast Alliance, the last of which she is now executive officer.

While campaigning for the coast, she has also written poetry. Here is an example, a poem entitled "Wide Sea, Deep Sea."

> Let us go down to the swan-white sea,
> Weave a net of silvery shore grasses,
> And down through spindrift follow it softly;
> Deep-sea fish flicker by trailing with light,
> And each one speaks, sparkling as it passes; …
> Strange fish rise up from caves glimmering deep,
> Show their pulsing faces where waves run swift,
> And flowering dark-blue seas wash in sleep.
> Let us fill our hands with deep-sea green,
> Amethyst and blue jewels and flecks of gold,
> And paint the eyes of ghost-fish we have not seen;
> On the waves the old men of the sea wander and roam,
> Tossing their dark green hair; and the mist grows bold,
> And we beg to be fish leaping the foam.

Extracts from a new book which she has co-authored with Chris Maser entitled *Sustainability and the Rights of Nature* (2017):

> Many will dismiss the central thesis of this book out of hand … Some

will argue that a Rights of Nature [thesis] is "anti-people," and cares nothing for human lives and needs. Nothing could be farther from the truth. "There are no jobs on a dead planet … ." We argue that no economic system can flourish—and human life cannot flourish—if Nature does not flourish first. This simple truth has been ignored for a long time, as the consequences of human overreach has been unclear. Now, however, they are becoming starkly obvious.

"Sustainability" in our vision simply means the ability of a natural system to maintain critical functions. By analogy, if you commence cutting the strands of a net, it will retain capacity to act as a net only so long as enough of the strands remain interconnected. But the net's overall effectiveness is reduced with the severing of each strand. When enough of the apparently useless strands have been slashed, the net will develop such large holes that its ability to function as it was designed to will end.[*]

Those whose experience in nature moves them to write poetry have varied backgrounds. **John Des Camp Jr.** works in the field of investment banking, but his hiking in the backcountry has inspired him to write poetry, much of it in the form of the haiku. Here are a few of his pieces in this form:

November

Autumn's harsh trumpet
White wings under silver skies
Swan slips through the thin clouds.

---

[*] La Follete and Maser, *Sustainability*, xxvi.

John Des Camp Jr. (ca. 1941–), attorney, investment banker, poet. Educated at Seattle University and Lewis & Clark Law School, he now works in the Portland area as an advisor in the field of investment banking, specializing in securing the financing to rehabilitate older business buildings. As a backcountry hiker, he also writes and publishes poetry, specializing in haikus reflecting his immersion in nature.

Fog

Thin December fog
Caught soft in naked branches
Lemon winter sun.

Kate Brown is the second woman to serve as governor of Oregon, and she has embraced environmental positions and advanced them. She was also the first woman to serve as majority leader in the state senate. After advancing to the governorship on the resignation of Dr. John Kitzhaber, she has been elected to the balance of his fourth term. She has tried to stay close to the positions advocated by environmental groups.

Passages from an address by Governor Kate Brown to the Oregon League of Conservation Voters, May 1, 2015:

> [But our] legacy of environmental victories is currently under threat. All of that good work could be lost and forgotten, unless we do something meaningful—and soon—about global warming.
>
> This is THE issue of our time.
>
> Oregon's unique and special way of life is being stalked by climate change. Unchecked, it will have devastating effects on all that we, as Oregonians, hold dear. And future generations will rightly judge the morality and leadership of this generation (our generation) by the fact of climate change, but how we [have] responded to it.
>
> The evidence is compelling: record low snowpack, the warmest winter since 1895, and seven Oregon counties in states of drought emergency before the end of April. …
>
> Along with drought, we have its nefarious companion: wildfire, not only for this upcoming season, but summers yet to come. As our

forests change, wildfire is going to be an ever-increasing challenge for Oregonians.

So, what do we do—faced with the inevitability of climate change?

We need to take action, both to reduce greenhouse gas emissions and to prepare for the consequences of warmer temperature. We need to play for both the long-term and the short-term. This is not a challenge that is going to be overcome by the flip of a switch or a vote in the legislature.

For the short-term, we must invest in solutions that will enable our communities to cope with drought, wildfire, and other consequences of a warming climate.

Over the longer term, as our … Cascade snowpack shrinks, we … need to change how we manage our water resources. …

At the same time that we are grappling with drought and wildfire, we also are facing pressure on the quality of our rivers and streams. Last year, public recreational use of the lower Willamette was shut down for 16 days with an algal bloom (due at least in part, to low water levels and warm temperatures).

We have increased the percentage of Oregon waterways with good water quality [or better] from 27%, in 1990, to 50% in 2013. However, there is still much work to do to assure that our children have access to clean water. …

… [Recently] the legislature was able to pass … the Clean Fuels bill. This legislation represents a collaborative effort between Oregon, Washington, California, and British Columbia, which combined make up one-fifth of the world's economy.

Kate Brown (1960-), lawyer, politician (Democrat). After Kate Brown earned a bachelor's from the University of Colorado and her law degree in 1985 from Lewis and Clark College, she started a juvenile law practice in Portland. Her political career commenced with two terms in the state House of Representatives, followed by nearly a decade of service in the state senate. In 2004 she was chosen to be the senate majority leader—the first woman to serve in that capacity.

In 2008 she ran successfully for the position of secretary of state of Oregon and then served for six years in that capacity. When John Kitzhaber resigned early in his fourth term (because of controversy over the role of his fiancée), she became governor. (Under Oregon's constitution, the secretary of state is next line to fill a vacancy in that position). In 2016 she was elected to the rest of Kitzhaber's term.

In her political career, most of the time she has been careful to keep her positions in line with those of environmental organizations. Most recently, she led the campaign on the State Land Board to prevent the sale of the Elliott State Forest and to keep protection for endangered species.

We all value clean air. And not only does the new law mean cleaner air for Oregonians, this structure is an important step toward reducing transportation-related carbon emissions by ten percent over the next decade.

Yes, we can make a difference. But there is still much left to do to reduce emissions.

It is one thing to have an elected official stay close to the positions of environmental groups; it is another to have an elected official actually be a card-carrying member of such a group. **Senator Jeff Merkley** is such a person, and he has had a very successful career as a politician. In one year, he was the only US Senator to be rated as always voting with the positions of the League of Conservation Voters. He recently easily won reelection.

Merkley made the following statement in introducing a bill to keep fossil fuels from being leased for development by the federal government (November 4, 2015):

Climate change is already impacting our world through greater forest fires and droughts, with serious effects on our farming, fishing, and forest economies. The main cause is carbon pollution, and the impacts will only get worse in the coming decades if we keep burning fossil fuels unchecked.

One key part of the solution is lying literally beneath our feet. A major contribution to this challenge would be stopping new fossil fuel leases on our public lands that lock in oil, gas, and coal extraction for decades into the

Jeff Merkley (1956–), non-profit manager, politician (progressive Democrat). Merkley was born in Oregon, and earned a bachelor's degree at Stanford and a master's degree at Princeton. He began his career in Portland working for Habitat for Humanity and then began pursuing a career in politics, starting with the state House of Representatives, where he represented a district in East Portland. After a number of terms, he was chosen as speaker of the house, where he led the way in getting many reforms enacted.

In 2008 he ran for the US Senate, winning by three percentage points. In 2014 he easily won reelection. Early in his senate career, he was the only senator that year to win a 100 percent rating from the League of Conservation Voters, and he won that top rating again in 2016. His positions closely track those of many environmental organizations.

future. Our public lands should be managed for the public good, not for private profit. …

Our society is still dependent on fossil fuels, but affordable and reliable technology exists to gradually transition to clean energy and clean transportation. Making that transition happen smoothly should be a central priority of the federal government. …

Together, we must accelerate the transition from a fossil fuel economy to a clean energy economy.

In doing so, we will create huge numbers of good paying jobs.

But we need to make sure that we don't leave any of our workers behind. They've spent their lives providing the energy that has fueled tremendous growth in our economy—often at the expense of their health and wellbeing. This must not be a green versus blue transition, but a green and a blue movement—working together, side by side.

For many decades, **Jack Churchill** worked in policy positions in federal agencies, hoping that in retirement he could write a definitive treatise on water policy. But instead he found himself writing poetry about nature, as he enjoyed summer life at his cabin at Agness near the confluence of the Rogue and Illinois Rivers.

Here are two of his poems:

John R. Churchill (1926–), political economist, policy advisor, educator. Born in Portland and educated at Reed and Harvard, he spent decades working on policy in various federal agencies: the Departments of Agriculture and the Interior (in the BLM and the EPA). He also served as an adjunct professor at Portland State University. Since leaving government, he has often shaped public policy as a citizen activist.

Looking Up[*]

(Note that the Tom Fry to which he
refers is a small stream near his cabin.)

Into the Tom Fry I find my way;
wandering in [a] changing world.
Today was one of those times
when god's grace came to me.

Alder canopies swaying high over head;
sunlight filters through mottled skies;
whispering leaves flutter so gently;
weaving images of kaleidoscopic delight.

Waters flowing down the creek,
casting shadowy waves on [a] rocky floor,
as sunlight sparkles, igniting rapids
in brilliant flashes of dazzling light.

Wind whispering nurturing caresses;
floating wisps of spring's gentle fragrance;
water spirits dancing tunes in my ears;
[a] squirrel calling sharply for her mate.

This spot I love and know so well.
I sink into [the] forest floor;
[I] feel the earth spin;
my spirit floats into the sky."

---

[*]   Churchill, *Poems from the Tom Fry*, 26.

Advent of Demise: We Opened the Savage Rapids Dam

No truer words were uttered
about a river
(not intended)
when Jean-Jacques Rousseau proclaimed:
"man is born free
but is everywhere in chains."

Harnessing rivers,
an affliction of mankind,
a way to get them into the GNP;
a manifest in engineering ego.

Unharnessing a river,
un-christen a dam;
a truly unique event
in [the] annals of [a] river fate.

Let this day be remembered,
as a milepost
in conservation history:
where rivers gain standing,
where precedent moves momentum. …

Today … two thousand and nine,
freeing [a] river of man's chains,
is [a] manifesto for many.

We cut the ribbon;
opened the dam,
returned our Rogue,
to flow in freedom evermore.[*]

---

[*] Churchill, *Tom Fry*, 76–77.

Ursula Le Guin (1929–), author of novels in the fantasy genre. Ursula Le Guin grew up in Berkeley, the daughter of noted anthropologist Alfred Kroeber. Her mother wrote about the last member of the Yahi tribe. Earning degrees at Radcliff (BA) and Columbia (MA), she then spent some years in France studying, where she met her husband, Charles Le Guin. In due course, she moved to Portland when he began teaching French at Portland State.

After a trying start, she began publishing her works of fantasy and science fiction. They often had environmental themes, as well as themes involving anarchism. But one of her works was not in the science fiction genre at all: a book featuring images of the Steens Mountain and its region, with poetry. Her visits there provided background for the letter featured here.

Her great outpouring of work has drawn widespread recognition. In 2014 she was given a medal from the National Book Foundation for her "Distinguished Contribution to American Letters." A few years earlier (2000), the Library of Congress honored her as a "Living Legend" in the category of Writers and Artists.

A woman writer, with a distinguished record in the genre of science fiction/fantasy has also been deeply involved in celebrating special places in eastern Oregon, such as the Steens Mountain. This is **Ursula Le Guin**, who plunged herself into the defense of the Malheur National Wildlife Refuge when it was taken over by protesters. Here are passages from a widely circulated letter she wrote in January 2016 about the occupation of the Malheur National Wildlife Refuge:

[The headline and article] "Effort to free federal lands" [in the *Oregonian* on January 17, 2016,] is inaccurate and irresponsible. The article that follows is a mere mouthpiece for the scofflaws illegally occupying public buildings and land, repeating their lies and distortions of history and law.

Ammon Bundy and his bullyboys aren't trying to free federal lands, but to hold them hostage. I can't go to the Malheur refuge now—though as a citizen of the United States, I own it and [should feel free to use] … it.

That's what public land is: land that belongs to the public—me, you, and every law-abiding American. The people it doesn't belong to, and who don't belong there, are those who grabbed it by force of arms … .

Speaking of the federal government, she said:

They should make it clear—by words first, then by deliberate actions—that ranting about the Constitution does not get you a permit to break the law, [to] fail to pay your grazing fees, [to] cut a rancher's fences, [to] steal government cars, [to] misuse public property, and [to] keep a lot of good American citizens under a stupid, brutal reign of terror for … days [on end].

How much longer? Enough is enough.

Outcome: By spring in 2016, federal authorities finally closed in on the party headed by Ammon Bundy while traveling to a rally in a neighboring county. Most of them were arrested and tried, but ultimately, a few were acquitted of the heavy charge of conspiracy (which is difficult to prove). The rest have since been found guilty of destroying government property and trespassing. For forty-one days, they had occupied the headquarters of the Malheur National Wildlife Refuge.

URSULA LE GUIN

From the early 1990s, federal judges in Portland have been regularly overseeing management of salmon in the Northwest, and not happily. They have been responding to lawsuits brought by fishing interests and environmentalists who have been aroused by the decline of the native strains of salmon. In particular, they have focused on the obstacles posed by the dams on the lower Snake River to downstream migrants.

Over time, these judges in Portland questioned the adequacy of the biological opinions of the National Marine Fisheries Service on programs for the recovery of various stocks of salmon in the Columbia River system.

These salmon stocks had been classified as endangered under the Endangered Species Act.

The sparring in court over this topic began in the early 1990s and continues to this day. In 2007 Judge Garr King in Portland ruled that data from the government of Oregon could not be used to determine endangerment of a salmon species under the federal Endangered Species Act, and in that same year, Judge Michael Hogan in Eugene ruled that hatchery fish could not be used to determine the viability of a species of native salmon.

Extracts from Judge Michael Simon's opinion in the latest case are presented below: *National Wildlife Federation et al. v. National Marine Fisheries Service et al.* There is a long list of other parties and interveners.

The latest opinion was written by Judge Simon and issued on May 4, 2016. Judge Simon began by quoting the opinions of judges who had been handling this line of cases.

In a decision in 1993, Judge Malcolm Marsh wrote:

[The] NMFS [National Marine Fisheries Service] has clearly made an effort to create a rational, reasoned process for determining how the action agencies are doing in their efforts to save the listed salmon species.

But the process is seriously, [even] "significantly," flawed because it is too heavily geared toward the status quo that has allowed all forms of river activity to proceed in a deficit situation—that is, [in] relatively small steps, minor improvements and adjustments—when the situation literally cries out for a major overhaul.

Instead of looking for what can be done to protect the species from jeopardy, NMFS and the action agencies have narrowly

---

Judges quoted in the cases involving salmon:

Malcolm F. Marsh (1928-), lawyer, judge. Marsh is from McMinnville and Salem, Oregon. He was appointed by President Ronald Reagan in 1987. His family had been prominent in Oregon politics.

James A. Redden (1929-), lawyer, office holder, judge. While practicing law in Medford, Oregon, he was appointed to the federal bench by President Jimmy Carter in 1980. Before that, he had served as the treasurer of Oregon and its attorney general.

Michael H. Simon (1956-), lawyer, judge. He was born in the East and came to Portland to head the litigation practice in the office of Perkins Coie. Before that, he had worked in the Antitrust Division of the Department of Justice. In 2010 President Obama appointed him to the federal bench.

focused their attention on what the establishment is capable of handling with minimal disruption. (850 F. Supp. 886)

Judge James Redden heard a series of cases and consistently found shortcomings in the government's work. He rejected the biological opinions prepared in 2000, 2004, 2008, and 2010. He used these words in his judgment in 2010:

In remanding the 2000 BiOp [Biological Opinion], I instructed NOAA Fisheries [NMFS] to ensure that a similarly ambitious but flawed mitigation plan ... [would not be proposed].

Instead of following this court's instructions, NOAA Fisheries abandoned ... [the approach in its previous BiOps] and altered its analytical framework to avoid the need for any reasonable and prudent alternatives [RPA]. As the parties are well aware, *the resulting BiOp was a cynical and transparent attempt to avoid responsibility for the decline of listed Columbia and Snake River salmon and steelhead* [italics used by Judge Redden].

NOAA Fisheries wasted several precious years interpreting and reinterpreting the Endangered Species Act's regulations. Also during that remand period, NOAA Fisheries abruptly attempted to abandon summer spill [release of more water from dams], despite the 2000 BiOp's conclusion that it was necessary to avoid jeopardy [of an endangered species].

Even now, NOAA Fisheries resists ISAB's [Independent Scientific Advisory Board] recommendation to continue recent spill operations. Given federal defendant's history of abruptly changing course, abandoning previous BiOps, and failing to follow through with their commitments to hydropower modifications proven to increase survival (such as spill), this court will retain jurisdiction over this matter to ensure that federal defendants develop and implement the mitigation measures required to avoid jeopardy. ...

As I have previously found, there is ample evidence in the record that indicates that the operation of the ... [federal dams on the Columbia River] causes substantial harm to listed salmonids ... NOAA Fisheries acknowledges that the existence and operation of the dams accounts for most of the mortality of juveniles migrating through the ... [system of federal dams]. As in the past, I find that irreparable harm will result to listed species as a result of the operation of ... [these dams]. (839 F. Supp. 2d 1130)

In his 2016 decision, Judge Michael Simon found (p. 14–15):

The best available information indicates that climate change will have a significant negative effect on the listed populations of endangered or threatened species. Climate change implications that are likely to have harmful effects on certain of the listed species include:

- warmer stream temperatures;
- warmer ocean temperatures;
- contracting ocean habitat;
- contracting inland habitat;
- degradation of estuary habitat;
- reduced spring and summer stream flows, with increased peak river flows;
- large-scale ecological changes, such as increasing insect infestations and fires affecting forests lands;
- increased rain, with decreased snow;
- diminishing snow packs; and
- increased susceptibility to fish pathogens and parasitic organisms ... [when] fish become thermally stressed.

It strains credulity to assert that information regarding habitat and fish populations remains the same in 2014 as it did in the 1990s.

In remanding the draft BiOp in 2008, Judge Redden said:

> Mitigation measures may be relied upon only where they involve "specific and binding plans" and a "clear, definite commitment of resources to implement those measures." …
>
> Mitigation measures supporting a biological opinion's no jeopardy conclusion must be reasonably specific, certain to occur, and [be] capable of implementation; they must be subject to deadlines or otherwise [be] enforceable obligations; and most important, they must address the threats to the species in a way that satisfies the jeopardy and adverse modification standards. (839 F. Supp. 2d at 1125)

Judge Simon found that NMFS had not adequately explained many of its conclusions, nor connected its findings so as to show how they support the program choices it made. Also, it often failed to use the best available science and sometimes did not set forth reasonably prudent alternatives. And some of its efforts relied on documents that were many years old and suffered from the deficiency of being stale and out of date.

Regarding the proposed 2014 BiOp, he said:

> This analysis does not apply the best available science, overlooks important aspects of the problem, and fails properly to analyze the effects of climate change, including its additive harm, how it may reduce the effectiveness of the RPA actions, particularly habitat actions that are not expected to achieve full benefits for "decades," and how it increases the chances of a catastrophic event. (839 F. Supp. 2d 1130 (2016), 91)

At one point he even said, "This is not a rational conclusion based on the facts found." At another, he found, "NOAA Fisheries merely recited or ignored all the new information and did not apply any of it." At another point, he said, "The effects of climate change may not only reduce effectiveness of habitat mitigation efforts and cause additive harm, but may result in a catastrophic event that can quickly imperil the listed species."

For these reasons, Judge Simon found many of its conclusions to be arbitrary and capricious and not entitled to deference by the court under the presumption of administrative regularity (the doctrine by which courts presume an agency is regularly using logical processes to reach conclusions on which action is predicated).

He went on to say:

> More than 20 years ago, Judge Marsh ... [observed] that the federal Columbia River Power System "cries out for a major overhaul." Judge Redden ... urged the relevant ... action agencies to consider breaching one or more of the four dams on the lower Snake River.
>
> For more than 20 years, however, the federal agencies have ignored these admonishments and have continued to focus essentially on the same approach to saving the listed species—[minimizing changes] ... in hydropower operations, with a predominant focus on habitat restoration.
>
> These efforts have already cost billions of dollars, yet they are failing. Many populations of the listed species continue to be in a perilous state.
>
> The BOR [Bureau of Reclamation] must improve ... operations to stop the destruction of critical habitat.
>
> The 2014 BiOp continues down the same well-worn and legally insufficient path taken during the last 20 years. It impermissibly relies on supposedly precise, numerical survival improvement assumptions

from habitat mitigation efforts that, in fact, have uncertain benefits and are not reasonably certain to occur. It also fails adequately to consider the effects of climate change and relies on a recovery standard that ignores the dangerously low abundance levels of many of the populations of the listed species. …

The Federal Columbia River Power System remains a system that "cries out" for a new approach and for new thinking if wild Pacific salmon and steelhead, which have been in these waters since well before the arrival of *homo sapiens*, are to have any reasonable chance of surviving their encounter with modern man. (839 F. Supp. 2d (2016), 14–15.)

Judge Simon rejected the proposed BiOp and ordered NMFS to prepare a new BiOp and a programmatic environmental impact statement by March 1, 2018, as well as specific impact statements on implementing actions.

There are those who think that **Jane Lubchenco** could have done more on behalf of the salmon when she headed NOAA, which oversees the National Marine Fisheries Service. But she did take steps to end over-fishing off the nation's coasts. As a marine biologist from Oregon, she certainly understood what was at stake.

She is now helping to lead the way in Oregon to get practical things done to deal with the challenge of climate change.

Open letter from top Oregon climate scientists to the governor and legislature, February 1, 2016:

As scientists from Oregon with expertise in many disciplines relevant to the understanding of climate change, its impacts, and its solutions, we are deeply concerned that climate change compromises our quality of life and threatens our state's future. We need your

Jane Lubchenco (1947–), marine ecologist, professor, public official. Jane Lubchenco is one of the nation's most respected biological scientists. In 1975 she earned a PhD in that field at Harvard. Since 1977, she and her husband have been teaching at Oregon State University, specializing in marine ecology.

She is one of the world's most frequently cited ecologists and has won the Blue Planet Prize (2011), as well as a MacArthur "Genius" fellowship. She has been president of the American Association for the Advancement of Sciences (1997–98), and has been elected to the council of the National Academy of Sciences.

President Obama appointed her as the administrator of the National Oceanic and Atmospheric Administration (NOAA), where she served from 2009 to 2013. She made sure that all the regional fishery councils had management plans to bring an end to over-fishing. In her work there and since, she has been emphasizing sustainability and strengthening connections between science and public policy. She has also been emphasizing the need to deal with climate change.

leadership now more than ever to reduce the risks of a dangerously warming climate.

The science is clear that human activity is the dominant cause of warming over the last half century. If global heat-trapping emissions continue to rise, the scope and severity of risks will accelerate.

Already Oregonians are addressing many threats from climate change. For example, we are facing changes in water availability brought on by smaller snowpack and earlier snowmelt; our forests and related industries are threatened from increasing wildfires, insect outbreaks, and tree diseases; and our coastal communities are impacted by rising sea levels and increasing ocean acidity.

We must adapt to the inevitable impacts of a changing climate by investing in communities to make them more prepared for the current impacts and future risks of climate change. At the same time, Oregon must also take appropriate steps to reduce heat-trapping emissions that would cause much more devastating consequences in the decades to come. Oregon is well positioned to tackle this challenge. **Our state already has a legislatively established goal to reduce heat-trapping emissions to 75 percent below 1990 levels by 2050. We ask that you adopt policies to ensure Oregon reaches this emission reduction target**.

Now is the time to take action. The emissions choices we make today—in Oregon and throughout the world—will shape the planet our children inherit. Please help create a cleaner, safer, and healthier future for Oregon. Let this be our legacy.

The lead signer was Dr. Jane Lubchenco, and it was also signed by over two dozen other natural scientists working at universities in Oregon.

Note: In the spring of 2016, Oregon was the first state to eliminate coal from its mix of future energy supplies (by 2030)—a directive embodied in legislation passed by the legislature and signed by Governor Kate Brown.

It was already nearly impossible to construct new coal-fired power plants in the state; under 2009 legislation, base-load power plants face a very low ceiling on how much carbon dioxide they can emit—a ceiling that coal plants cannot meet. Now utilities cannot even *import* energy produced from coal or other hydrocarbons. The global level of greenhouse gasses has now exceeded the level of 400 ppm. Earlier, it had been feared that any concentration over 350 ppm would trigger irreversible trends.

Sources

Boardman, Samuel H. Quoted in *Oregon State Park System, a brief history.* Portland, OR: Oregon Historical Society, 1956.

Boardman, Samuel H. Quoted from sections on the Talbot St. Park, on the Cove-Palisades St. Park, the Silver Creek St. Park, and the Cape Lookout St. Park.

Brant, Irving. Quoted in *Administrative History of the Willamette National Forest, 1945-1970.* Durham, NC: Forest History Society, 2008.

Broughton, W. R. Quoted in J. E. O'Connor. "The Evolving Landscape of the Columbia Gorge." *Oregon Historical Quarterly* 105, no. 3, (2004): 390–421. https://en.wikipedia.org/wiki/Mount_Hood

Brown, Kate. Remarks to the Oregon League of Conservation Voters, May 1, 2015.

Cannon, Garnett ("Ding"). Quoted in Historian's blog. Trails Club of Oregon, January 2017.

Carney, Byron G. "Stream Pollution and Fish Life." Radio broadcast. Izaak Walton League radio program. November 29, 1937. Transcript.

Chamberlain, George. Remarks made on April 23, 1910. Published in *Mining and Scientific Press* 100, (Jan–June 1910): 591–92.

Charlton, David B. Statement at a conference. Published in *Proceedings of the Third Session of a Conference on Pollution of the Lower Columbia River and Its Tributaries.* Department of Health, Education, and Welfare, September 8–9, 1965, 311–13.

"Chief Joseph." Wikimedia Foundation. https://en.wikipedia.org/wiki/Chief_Joseph

Churchill, John R. *Poems from the Tom Fry.* lulu.com, 2017.

Cody, Robin. *Voyage of a Summer Sun: Canoeing the Columbia River.* Corvallis: Oregon State Press, 2012.

Condon, Thomas. "The Rocks of the John Day Valley." *Overland Monthly* 6, no. 5 (May 1871): 393–98.

Dana, Marshall N. "In the High Mountains." July 1962. Proposed editorial held by Oregon Historical Society.

Davis, H. L. *Honey in the Horn.* New York: Harper and Brothers, 1935.

Deady, Matthew. Independence Day "Oration," 1885.

Des Camp, John, Jr. *False Summit.* Portland, OR: Wind Mountain Press, 2017, 133, 166.

DeVoto, Bernard. "Easy Chair." *Harper's Magazine.* January 1955. Reprinted in *DeVoto's West,* edited by Edward K. Muller, 2005, 256–57.

Dirks-Edmunds, Jane Claire. *Not Just Trees: The Legacy of a Douglas-fir Forest.* Pullman: Washington State Press, 1999. Used with the permission of the Washington State Press (wsupress@wsu.edu).

Doig, Ivan. *Early Forestry Research: A History of the Pacific Northwest Forest & Range Experiment Station, 1925*-1975. Portland, OR: Forest Service, US Department of Agriculture, November 1977.

Douglas, William O. *My Wilderness: The Pacific West.* Garden City, NY: Doubleday, 1960. Reprinted in Gordon B. Dodds. *Varieties of Hope.* Corvallis: Oregon State University Press, 1993, 168.

Douglas, William O. *Nature's Justice.* Edited by James M. O'Fallon, 230–31. Corvallis: Oregon State University Press, 2000.

Douglas, William O. *Of Men and Mountains.* New York: Harpers Brothers, 1950.

Doyle, Brian. *Mink River.* Corvallis: Oregon State University Press, 2010, 151, 183–84.

Duncan, David James. "David James Duncan: author and fly fisher, answers questions." In *Grist* newsletter, April 3, 2007.

Duniway, Abigail Scott. *From the West to West: Across the Plains to Oregon.* Chicago: A.C. McClure, 1905, 223.

Dutton, Clarence E. "Crater Lake, Oregon, a Proposed National Reservation." *Science,* February 26, 1886. Quoted in Harlan D. Unrau and Stephen Mark. *Administrative History of Crater Lake National Park.* US Department of the Interior. National Park Service, 1987.

Eber, Ron. "John Muir in Oregon" *John Muir Newsletter* 3, no. 4 (Fall 1999).

Eliot, Reverend Thomas Lamb. Sermon in June 1879. First Unitarian Portland.

Finley, William L. *Oregon Sportsman,* September 1925: 3–6

Finley, William L. *Proceedings of the North American Wildlife Conference called by President Franklin D. Roosevelt.* Conference in February 3–7, 1936. Washington, DC: Government Printing Office, 1936, 61–62, 66–67, 74–75.

Franklin, Jerry. Interview by editors of *American Forests, American Forests,* August 12, 2013.

Gabrielson, Ira N. *Birds of Oregon.* Corvallis: Oregon State University Press, 1940.

Gabrielson, Ira N. *Wildlife Conservation.* New York: Macmillan, 1941.

Garnett Cannon, interview by the *Oregonian,* October 6, 1968.

George Venn. "Eagle Cap." *West of Paradise.* La Grande, OR: Ice River Press, 1999.

Goldschmidt, Neil. "Governor Neil Goldschmidt Comments on Renaming Bob Straub State Park." 1987. *Documents.* Paper 7. http://digitalcommons.wou.edu/straub_papers/7

Gray, John. "Land Use: Profits and Environmental Integrity." Address. National Association of Home Builders. Houston, Texas, January 8, 1973. Quoted by Laura Jane Gifford. "Planning for a Productive Paradise." *Oregon Historical Quarterly* 115, no. 4 (2014).

Grey, Zane. "Vanishing America.," *Izaak Walton League Monthly* 1, no. 2 (September 1922).

Grey, Zane. Quotes from a story reported in the *Oregonian,* July 28, 1935: 5.

Hallock, Blaine. Article. *Oregon Sportsman,* January 1916: 11, 14–15.

Hanley, William. *Feelin' Fine! Bill Hanley's Book,* edited by Anne Shannon Monroe. Garden City, NY: Doubleday, Doran & Company Inc., 1930.

Hatfield, Mark. Foreword to *Treasures of the Oregon Country* by Maynard C. Drawson. Dee Pub. Co., 1973.

Hatfield, Mark. Speech at conference of Opal Creek Association. February 5, 2004.

Hawken, Paul. "You Are Brilliant, and the Earth is Hiring." Commencement address. University of Portland, May 3, 2009. Portland, OR.

Hawkins, William J., III. *The Legacy of the Olmsted Brothers in Portland, Oregon.* Portland, OR: Vinnie Kinsella Publishing Services, 2014, 41, 142.

Hearing on "The Role of Federal Lands in Combating Climate Change," March 3, Before Subcommittee on National Parks, Forests and Public Lands Oversight, 111th Cong. (2009) (testimony of Dominick A. DellaSala, Chief Scientist and Executive Director of Programs of National Center for Conservation Science & Policy).

Hill, Richard. "Ken Kesey and Ecology." *The Pacific Northwest Forum* VII (Winter 1982): 6–12.

Holbrook, Stuart. "Yankee Go Home." *Look,* 1962.

Holbrook, Stuart. *Tall Timber.* New York: Macmillan, 1941, 38, 43, 55, 97, 163.

Holmes, Robert D. *Oregonian,* December 9, 1956.

Hussey, John. *Champoeg: A Place of Transition*. Portland: Oregon Historical Society Press, 1967.

Jackman, E. R., and R. A. Long. *The Oregon Desert*. Caldwell, ID: Caxton Press, 1964. Used with the permission of the Caxton Press.

Jackson, C. S. C. S. Jackson to Gov. George E. Chamberlain, February 23, 1907. Held by Oregon Historical Society.

Kerr, Andy. Op-ed. *Mail Tribune*, January 6, 2015.

Kesey, Ken. *Sometimes a Great Notion*. New York: Penguin Book, 1964, 457, 497.

Kitzhaber, John, M.D. Foreword to *The Rogue: Portrait of a River*, by Roger Dorband. Astoria, OR: Raven Studios, 2007.

Kitzhaber, John, M.D. State of the State Address. 1997.

Kulongoski, Theodore. Remarks at Rally for the Environment. March 23, 2003.

Kulongoski, Theodore. Speech to the legislature. January 8, 2007.

Kulongoski, Theodore. State of the State Address. January 12, 2009.

La Follette, Cameron, and Chris Maser. *Sustainability and the Rights of Nature: An Introduction*. Boca Raton, FL: CRC Press, 2017.

La Follette, Cameron. *An Analysis of the Oregon Inter-Agency Spotted Owl Management Plan*. Forest Research Paper # 6 CHECK. September 1979, 2–3, 27–28.

La Follette, Cameron. Letter to the editor. *Sheboygan Press*, May 5, 2015.

La Follette, Cameron. *Pilot Plan for Forest Diversity*. Forest Research Paper # 9. Bureau of Land Management at Coos Bay, April 1981, iv, 22, 30, 42.

Lampman, Ben Hur. "A Fish Called Euchelon." *Nature Magazine*, 1925. Quoted in *Varieties of Hope*, edited by Gordon Dodds, 196. Corvallis: Oregon State University Press, 1993.

Lancaster, Samuel C. *The Columbia: America's Great Highway through the Cascade Mountains to the Sea*. Portland, OR: J. K. Gill, 1926, 130-31.

Lane, Harry, M. D. "Edible Mushrooms - Here is Information of Value to the Oregon Epicure." *The Sunday Oregonian*, November 8, 1896, 6.

Lane, Harry, M. D. "Promoting the Culture of Mushrooms." *The Morning Oregonian*. February 9, 1897, 5.

Langille, Harold Douglas. *Northern Portion of the Cascade Range Forest Reserve*. U.S. Government Printing Office, 1903.

Le Guin, Ursula. Letter to the editor. *Oregonian*, January 19, 2016.

Lopez, Barry. "The Case for Going Uncivilized." *Outside*, August 4, 2014.

Lopez, Barry. Interview. *Wild Oregon*, 1984, 14–15.

Lubchenco, Jane, et al. Jane Lubchenco et al. to Governor Kate Brown and members of the legislature, February 1, 2016.

Mark Hatfield. Foreword to *Hoover: the Fishing President*, by Hal Elliott Wert. Mechanicsburg, PA: Stackpole Press, 2005.

Markham, Edwin. *California, the Wonderful*. New York: Hearst's International Library, 1914, chap. XIX, sec. 381.

Marsh, Malcolm. National Wildlife Federation et al. v. National Marine Fisheries Service et al., 850 F. Supp. 886 (1993).

Maser, Chris, and James M. Trippe. *The Seen and Unseen World of the Fallen Tree*. General Technical Report. Portland, OR: US Department of Agriculture, Forest Service, 1984. Quoted in Jay Heinrichs. "There's More to Forests than Trees; There's a World of Hidden Wildlife." *National Wildlife* 26, no. 2 (February/March 1988).

Maser, Chris. Preface to *Redesigned Forest*. San Pedro, CA: R. E. Miles, 1988.

Mason, David T. "Forestry: Oregon's Problem." Oregon Bankers' Association. Gearhart, OR, June 12, 1928.

McAllister, Tom. *Our First 50 Years—1902–1952*. Audubon Society of Portland, undated, 1–3.

McAllister, Tom. Interview by Bureau of Environmental Service of the City of Portland, January 22, 2008, 8. Transcript.

McCall, Thomas. Quoted in *The Pacific Northwest: An Interpretive History* by Carlos A. Schwante, University of Nebraska Press, 1989.

McCall, Tom. Final message as governor to the legislature, 1973.

McCall, Tom. *Pollution in Paradise*. Produced by Tom Dargan and Tom McCall. Featuring McCall. Aired November 21, 1962. KGW-TV.

McCall, Tom. Remarks as governor. Oregon-Washington Bottlers Association. Portland: Benson Hotel, February 2, 1970

McCloskey, Michael. "Have Environmentalists Really Done All Those Things?" Speech to City Club of Portland. Benson Hotel, March 21, 1980.

McCloskey, Michael. *Conserving Oregon's Environment*. Portland, OR: Inkwater Press, 2013.

McCord, Howard. *Arcs of Lowitz*. Salt Works Press, 1979.

McKinley, Charles. *Five Years of Planning in the Pacific Northwest*. Portland, OR: Northwest Regional Council, 1939.

McKinley, Charles. *Uncle Sam in the Pacific Northwest*. Berkeley: University of California Press, 1952.

McNary, Charles L. Account of trips to Fircone. *Central Press*, December 9, 1933.

McNary, Charles L. Charles L. McNary to Ben Claggett, February 7, 1935.

Meier, Julius L. Message to the legislature of 1931.

Merkley, Jeff. Statement introducing Keep It in the Ground Act. November 4, 2015.

Merriam, C. Hart. "Mammals of Mt. Mazama, Oregon," *Mazama* 1, no. 2 (1897): 204–17.

Merriam, Lawrence C. *Oregon's Highway Park System (1921–1989): An Administrative History*. Salem, OR: Oregon Parks and Recreation Dept., 1992, 28, 33.

Miller, Joaquin, "Twenty Carats of Fire." *Shadows of Shasta*, Indiana: Jansen, McClurg, 1881. Quoted in *Blue Mountain Eagle,* summer 1907.

Mills, Hazel, and Constance Bordwell. *Frances Fuller Victor: The Witness to America's Westerings*. Waterbury, VT: Peregrine Productions for Oregon Historical Society, 2002, 223.

Mische, Emanuel T., 1913. Quoted in William F. Willingham. *Open Space and Park Development: 1851–1965*. Portland Parks and Recreation, 2010.

Mische, Emanuel T. Letter to the editor. *Oregonian*, 1910.

Morse, Wayne L. 103 Cong. Rec. 1909 (1957).

Munger, Thornton. Interview by Amelia R. Fry of the Bancroft Library. Forest History Society. Berkeley, 1967. Transcript.

National Wildlife Federation et al. v. National Marine Fisheries Service et al., 839 F. Supp. 2d 1130 (2016).

Neal, Steve. *McNary of Oregon*. Portland: Oregon Historical Society, 1985, 91.

Neuberger, Richard L. "Our Natural Resources and Their Conservation." Public Affairs Pamphlet (no. 230), January 1956.

O'Donnell, Terence. *That Balance So Rare: The Oregon Story*. Portland: Oregon Historical Society Press, 1988.

Olcott, Ben W. Message to legislature, 1921, 21, 36. Transcript.

Olcott, Ben W. Scenic Beauty message to legislature, 1921. Transcript.

Olmsted, John Charles. *Outlining a System of Parkways, Boulevards, and Parks for the City of Portland*. Olmsted Brothers, 1903.

Olmsted, John Charles. Report prepared for Sen. Charles McNary, 1930, 9.

Onthank, Karl. Karl Onthank to Stewart Brandborg, Februrary 21, 1966. Box #1 of his archives in the Special Collection of the University of Oregon library.

Packwood, Robert W. Hearing on bill to buy out pumice mining claims at Rock Mesa in the Three Sisters Wilderness. Congress, 1972. Transcript.

Palmer, Joel. *Journal of Travels Over the Oregon Trail in 1845*. Portland: Oregon Historical Society Press, 1997.

Palmer, Joel. *Journal of Travels over the Rocky Mountains to the Mouth of the Columbia River*. Cincinnati, 1847. Reprinted in Thwaites, R.G., in *Early Western Travels, 1748–1846*, 1906.

Pinchot, Gifford. Quoted in Stephen R. Mark. "Seventeen Years to Success: John Muir, William Gladstone Steel, and the Creation of Yosemite and Crater Lake National Parks." Presented at 43rd annual meeting of California History Institute. Stockton, California, May 5, 2017, 4–5.

Pittock, H. L. "First Ascent of Mt. Hood." *Oregonian*, August 2, 1864.

Public Health Section of the City Club of Portland. "Stream Pollution in Oregon." *Supplement to Portland City Club Bulletin* VII, no. 30 (April 22, 1927).

Putnam, George Palmer. *In the Oregon Country*. New York: Knickerbocker Press, 1915, 93–94.

Redden, James. National Wildlife Federation et al. v. National Marine Fisheries Service et al., 839 F. Supp. 2d 1125, 1130 (2010).

Reed, Jack. "America." Quoted in Michael Munk. *Jack* Reed. Marxists Internet Archive. https://www.marxists.org/archive/reed/bio/portland.htm

Reed, Jack. "Twilight." Quoted in Michael Munk. *Jack* Reed. Marxists Internet Archive. https://www.marxists.org/archive/reed/bio/portland.htm

Riley, Frank Branch. *Ambassador of the Pacific Northwest*, Portland, OR: Kilham Stationery & Printing Co., 1956.

Robbins, William G. *Landscapes of Promise: The Oregon Story 1800-1940*. Seattle: University of Washington Press, 1997, 239, 250, 302.

Roosevelt, Theodore R. "People of the Pacific Coast," *Outlook*, September 1911.

Roosevelt, Theodore. "People of the Pacific Coast." *Outlook*, September 1911.

Sawyer, Robert W. "The Whole Story." *American Forests*, March 1953, 10.

Seattle Audubon Society v. Evans, 771 F. Supp. 1081 (W. D. Wash. 1991).

Senate Bill 25. Hearing on SB 25. February 23. Before the Senate Committee on Environment and Natural Resources, Oregon. (2015) (statement of Cameron La Follette).

Senate Bill 830. Hearing on SB 830. April 15. *Before the Senate Committee on Environment and Natural Resources, Oregon.* (2015) (statement of Cameron La Follette).

Sierra Club v. Morton, 405 U.S. 727 (1972).

Snead, Bobbie. *Judge John B. Waldo: Oregon's John Muir*. Maverick Publications, 2006, 32–33, 42, 78, 93–95, 97–99, 100–103.

Snyder, Gary. *Songs of Gaia*. Port Townsend, WA: Copper Canyon Press, 1979.

Sprague, Charles A. Inaugural message as governor, 1939.

Sprague, Charles A., Speech to Keep Oregon Green Association, 1941.

Stafford, Kim. "A Part of Something Old: Writer Kim Stafford's Storied Places." *High Country News*, October 5, 2011.

Stafford, Kim. "Naknuwisha." *Prairie Prescription*. Boise: Limberlost Press, 2011. Used with permission of the author.

Stafford, Kim. "The Story That Saved a Life." *Having Everything Right: Essays of Place*. Seattle, WA: Pharos Editions, 2016. Used with permission of the author.

Stafford, William. "Malheur Before Dawn." *Even in Quiet Places*. Confluence Press, 1996.

Stafford, William. "The Tillamook Burn." *The Way It Is: New & Selected Poems*. Minneapolis: Gray Wolf Press, 1999.

State Ex Rel. Thornton v. Hay, 462 P.2d 671 (1969).

Steel, William Gladstone. Quoted in *Judge John B. Waldo: Oregon's John Muir*, by Bobbie Snead. Bend, OR: Maverick Publications, 2006.

Straub, Robert W. Farewell message as governor, 1979.

Straub, Robert W. Inaugural message as governor, 1975.

Straub, Robert W. Message to the legislature as governor, 1977.

Straub, Robert W. Speech in defense of the Nestucca Spit State Park. Highway Commission meeting, Tillimook, Oregon, November 29, 1967.

Teal, Joseph N. Commonwealth Day address. University of Oregon, Eugene, February 13, 1909.

Thomas, Jack Ward. Interview by Harold K. Steen. Forest History Society. May 12, 2001.

Thomas, Jack Ward. Speech to Outdoor Writers of America, June 26, 1995.

Vancouver, George. *A Voyage of Discovery to the North Pacific Ocean, and Round the World*, 1792, 206.

West, Oswald D. "Early Day Land Frauds," *Oregon Grange Bulletin*, June 20, 1945, 12.

West, Oswald D. "Seashore Conservation" *Oregon Journal*, August 8, 1949.

West, Oswald D. Inaugural message to legislature as governor, 1911.

West, Oswald D. Message as governor, 1913.

West, Oswald D. Message as governor, 1915.

Wild in the City, edited by Michael C. Houck and M. J. Cody. Corvallis: Oregon State University Press, 2011.

Wilkes, George. *History of Oregon: Geographic and Political*. W. H. Colyer, 1845.

Wood, Charles Erskine Scott. "Impressions." *Pacific Monthly*, July–December 1907: 389–91.

Wood, Charles Erskine Scott. *The Poet in the Desert*. Portland, OR: F. W. Baltes Co., 1915.

Wood, Charles Erskine Scott. "The Worst Microbe." *Pacific Monthly*, 1908.

Wood, Mary C. "Nature's Trust" (key note address), 2011. "Ideas Matter" lecture series. Oregon State University.

Wyden, Ron. Press release from his office, November 1, 2006.

Yeon, John. "Problems of Conservation and Development of the Scenic and Recreational Resources of the Columbia Gorge in Washington and Oregon." Pacific Northwest Planning Commission. National Resources Board, January 1937.

Yeon, John. John Yeon to Sen. Mark Hatfield, ca. 1985 (undated).

Note: I have taken the liberty of editing their words to only use parts that are still of interest and to eliminate wording that was unclear or awkward. I have also added proper punctuation. But I have always tried to maintain their intent (as best I imagined it to be). These liberties have all contributed to a book that is much more readable. For those who have doubts, you had best look at the original documents.

CPSIA information can be obtained
at www.ICGtesting.com
Printed in the USA
LVHW061600030119
602636LV00006B/71/P